The Heavenly Contract

The Heavenly Contract

Ideology and
Organization in
Pre-Revolutionary
Puritanism

David Zaret

The University of Chicago Press
Chicago · London

For my parents
Minna and Sol Zaret

DAVID ZARET is associate professor
of sociology at Indiana University.

The University of Chicago Press, Chicago 60637
The University of Chicago Press, Ltd., London

Library of Congress Cataloging in Publication Data

Zaret, David.
   The heavenly contract.

   Includes bibliographical references and index.
     1. Puritans—England—History—17th century.
2. Sociology, Christian—England—History—17th century.
3. Clergy—England—History—17th century.   4. Laity—
England—History—17th century.   5. England—Church
history—17th century.   I. Title.
BX9333.Z37   1984   285'.9'0942   84-16473
ISBN 0-226-97882-6

Contents

Preface

Puritan clerics often referred to the spiritual debts and obligations that true believers dutifully seek to discharge. Intellectual debts are acknowledged not chiefly out of duty but for the sheer pleasure this affords the debtor. In this spirit I want to acknowledge the many debts and obligations I have incurred in the course of writing this book. I have greatly benefited from—and enjoyed!—the guidance of experts, the caveats of specialists, the encouragement and praise of friends, and the ever helpful cajoling and criticisms of colleagues in my own and other universities. But due acknowledgments, though pleasurable, are not easily made, for many colleagues are also friends, and former mentors become colleagues.

First and foremost are intellectual and personal debts to Christopher Hill and Steven Lukes, of Balliol College, Oxford. They supervised the dissertation which formed the point of departure for this book, and provided a challenging and extraordinarily pleasurable experience that continues to reinforce my commitment to merging historical and sociological styles of inquiry. Their wisdom never compromised their kindness toward me as their student; to regard them now as colleagues is to flatter myself.

Equally complex debts are owed to Craig C. Calhoun and Thomas F. Gieryn. At various points over the last several years, they have read and reread more drafts of this book than anyone else, and their suggestions have greatly improved its substance and style. The contribution made by Tom, a colleague and friend at Indiana University, extends well beyond the realm of intellectual commentary: his support and encouragement have been crucial to the completion of this work. Craig's advice has been invaluable to me ever since we were fellow students at St. Antony's College.

Ann Swidler read carefully two drafts of this book and provided detailed and extensive commentary on it. I am grateful to her for this undertaking and for the many improvements in the book which have resulted from it. I have also benefited from the expert advice of Paul Seaver and Keith V. Thomas. Major parts of this book have been read by several colleagues—or former colleagues—from Indiana University, who have provided me with useful comments and criticisms; among them are Larry J. Griffin, Charles C. Ragin, James R. Wood, and Allen D. Grimshaw, who continues to profess astonishment at the thought of Puritans traveling twenty miles to hear sermons. Julie Knost-Goodwin read the entire draft of the book, some parts more than once; her comments and encouragement have been invaluable. I am also grateful to Norman Birnbaum, Guenther Roth, and Theda Skocpol for their support. In particular, Norman has continuously encouraged and supported my work in countless ways, beginning with my undergraduate studies.

This research has relied in part on several archival collections and libraries. I am indebted to the archivists and staffs at the Bodleian Library in Oxford, at the British Library and the Public Record Office in London, and at the Indiana University Library. Peter Burke cheerfully provided much help with the word-processing facilities of the Department of Sociology at Indiana University, as did Greg Travis.

I have also been assisted by an Amherst College Memorial Fellowship in sociology and by a junior faculty sabbatical leave given by the Department of Sociology at Indiana University. Members of that department maintain a remarkably congenial and collegial environment, and it is not inappropriate to conclude these acknowledgements by calling attention to it.

Abbreviations

To save space, references to sixteenth- and seventeenth-century books list the date but not place of publication, which is London unless otherwise noted. Spelling has been modernized except for titles and verse.

AfR	*Archiv für Reformationsgeschichte*
AHR	*Agricultural History Review*
APC	*Acts of the Privy Council of England.*
	Edited by J.R. Dasent. 32 vols. London, 1890–1907.

BoL   Bodleian Library, Oxford
           MSS. Bodleian Bodleian Manuscripts
           MSS. Jones Jones Manuscripts
           MSS. Rawls. Rawlinson Manuscripts
           MSS. Tanner Tanner Manuscripts

BrL   British Library, London
           MSS. Add. Additional Manuscripts
           MSS. Lands. Landsdowne Manuscripts
           MSS. Sloan Sloan Manuscripts

CH   *Church History*

CJ   *Journals of the House of Commons*

CS   *Camden Society*

CSPD   *Calendars of State Papers, domestic*

EETS   *Early English Text Society*

EHR   *English Historical Review*

EcHR   *Economic History Review*

ENT   *Elizabethan Nonconformist Texts.*
           Edited by Albert Peel and Leland H. Carlson. 6 vols.
           London, 1953–70.

Foxe   John Foxe, *Acts and Monuments of the English Martyrs.*
           Edited by S.R. Cattley. 10 vols. New York, 1965.

FS   *The English Revolution: Fast Sermons to Parliament.*
           Edited by Robin Jeffs et al. 34 vols. London, 1970–71.

HMC   Reports of the Historical Manuscripts Commission

JEH   *Journal of Ecclesiastical History*

LL   *The Lisle Letters*
           Edited by Muriel St. Clare Byrne. 6 vols. Chicago, 1981.

L&P   *Letters and Papers, Foreign and Domestic, of the Reign of Henry VIII.*
           Edited by J.S. Brewer, J. Gairdner, R.H. Brodie. 36 vols.
           London, 1862–1932.

NRS   *Northampton Record Society*

P&P   *Past and Present*

PRO   Public Record Office, London
           SPD SP 12 *State Papers*, domestic series, Elizabeth I
           SPD SP 14 *State Papers*, domestic series, James I
           SPD SP 16 *State Papers*, domestic series, Charles I

PS   *The Parker Society for the Publication of the Works of the Fathers and Early Writers of the Reformed English Church.*
           55 vols. Cambridge, 1841–55.

SCH   *Studies in Church History*

VCH   *Victoria County History*
ZL   *The Zurich Letters, 1558–1579.*
         Edited by H. Robinson. Cambridge, 1843.

The Heavenly Contract

1
Introduction

This book studies an old topic from a new perspective. As an inquiry in historical sociology it uses recent developments and perspectives in social history to address analytic issues raised by sociological studies of social movements and beliefs. The topic of this book is Puritanism in pre-Revolutionary England—its organization, its ideology, and the relations between them. To understand organizational and ideological developments in Puritanism, sociological analysis must follow the lead of the now not so "new" social history that, under the banner of "history from below," has brought the activities and mentalities of the lower classes into the forefront of historical research.

My work traces links between two aspects of Puritanism which have been the subjects of separate fields of inquiry. One is the appearance of a distinctively Puritan divinity, covenant theology, a topic explored by specialists in religious history, who stress the importance of biblical precedents and the learned disputations of university-trained clerics. The other is lay involvement in religious changes, a topic studied by historians interested in the social rather than the intellectual history of the Reformation. I show that doctrinal developments of interest to specialists in religious history cannot be understood apart from organizational developments associated with new forms of intellectual independence and initiative in lay religious life.

The relations between clerical reformers and lay groups in the popular Reformation reflected a shifting balance between clergy and laity that increasingly favored popular intellectual initiatives in religion. The appearance of an articulate, intrusive laity posed both manifest and latent threats to clerical prerogatives in religious life, and this inner tension in the Reformation strongly influenced the direction of doctrinal and liturgical changes. These changes produced a distinctively Puritan version of Calvinist divinity, which today is referred to as covenant theology or, for New England, federal theology. The centerpiece of this divinity is the idea of a heavenly contract.

The capacity to conceive of a *Bund, pactum,* or heavenly contract that unites God and humanity may well be universal. References in the Old Testament to God's covenant with Abraham and Israel indicate that this is an old theological concept, for which Hittite war treaties may have been the model.[1] In the late sixteenth and early seventeenth centuries the idea of a heavenly contract became—to use Perry Miller's apt phrase—the marrow of Puritan divinity. Why this happened is puzzling, because the idea of a heavenly contract is chiefly economic in inspiration, and this idea, with its connotations of exchange and reciprocity, coexists uneasily with other ideas that also were central to Puritan divinity, such as the doctrines of free grace and predestination.

The solution I propose for this puzzle is quite different from the one advanced in previous discussions of Puritan covenant theology. Studies of this theology by specialists in religious history have been limited to intellectual history, which explains movements in belief and thought in terms of intellectual precedents. Nearly fifty years ago Perry Miller first suggested that Puritan covenant theology derived from precedents established by the parliamentary opposition to the early Stuart monarchy. Parliamentarians opposed to James and Charles developed the idea of a social compact that subsequently influenced speculation by Puritan clerics on humanity's relation to God; thus "federal theology was the lengthened shadow of a political platform."[2] Religious specialists have built up an extensive literature that generally dismisses Miller's argument. Some identify biblical precedents as the chief source of Puritan speculation on the heavenly contract. "The covenant doctrine was emphasized primarily because it was discovered to be a central biblical concept. It was emphasized in the sixteenth and seventeenth centuries (rather than in some previous era) because the Protestant Reformers studied the whole Scripture intensively."[3] Other specialists, who trace the origins of Puritan covenant

1. For a discussion of this issue see Klaus Baltzer, *The Covenant Formulary in Old Testament, Jewish, and Early Christian Writings* (Philadelphia, 1971).

2. Perry Miller, "The Marrow of Puritan Divinity," *Publications of the Colonial Society of Massachusetts* 32 (1935), p. 258, and *The New England Mind: The Seventeenth Century* (Cambridge, Mass., 1939), pp. 412–13.

3. George Marsden, "Perry Miller's Rehabilitation of the Puritans: A Critique," *CH*

theology to writings by continental reformers, debate among themselves whether the greatest influence on Puritanism derived from Calvin or Beza in Geneva, from Heidelberg theologians influenced by Beza, from Zwingli and Bullinger in Zurich, or from Tyndale's use of Zwingli's ideas in polemical writings and in glosses for his English Bible.[4]

The availability of these intellectual precedents does not, however, indicate why contractarian ideas assumed the importance they did and why they became the means by which Puritan clerics presented to their followers a popular version of the Calvinist economy of grace and salvation. My work suggests instead that organizational *pressures* are no less important than intellectual *precedents* for understanding the origins and development of Puritan covenant theology. An adequate account of the appearance of a distinctively Puritan version of Calvinism therefore must establish connections between the ideological and organizational aspects of Puritanism. I use the phrase "organizational pressures" to refer to the social and institutional setting which led Puritan clerics to use certain precedents in order to create their theological system. More specifically, I show how these clerics adopted and emended biblical references and continental antecedents in response to obstacles and opportunities confronting them in their dual role as ordained ministers in a comprehensive church and as pastoral leaders of a popular social movement.

Lay followers of the Puritan clergy did not accept uncritically the authority of any clerics, including their own. Popular dissent in the Reformation cultivated lay initiative and intellectual independence in religious matters and set in motion an insurgency from the pews that eventually undermined the religious principle of lay subordination to clerics. Broad changes in social structure and culture contributed greatly to the growth of this popular dissent, which provided Puritan clerics with sympathetic

---

39 (1970), p. 99. See also John S. Coolidge, *The Pauline Renaissance in England* (Oxford, 1970), p. 150.

4. For a general survey of the early development of covenant theology by continental reformers see Otto Ritschl, *Dogmengeschichte des Protestantismus* (Göttingen, 1926), pp. 412−58. For discussion of the relationship between continental antecedents and Puritan covenant theology see Everett H. Emerson, "Calvin and Covenant Theology," *CH* 25 (1956), pp. 136−44; Richard L. Greaves, "The Origins and Early Development of English Covenant Thought," *The Historian* 31 (1968), and "John Bunyan and Covenant Thought in the Seventeenth Century," *CH* 36 (1967); E. Brooks Holifield, *The Covenant Sealed: The Development of Puritan Sacramental Theology in Old and New England, 1570−1720* (New Haven, 1974); R.T. Kendall, *Calvin and English Calvinism to 1649* (Oxford, 1979); Michael McGiffert, "William Tyndale's Conception of the Covenant," *JEH* 32 (1981); Jens G. Møller, "The Beginnings of Puritan Covenant Theology," *JEH* 14 (1963); John New, *Anglican and Puritan: The Basis of Their Opposition* (London, 1964), pp. 92−95; Leonard J. Trinterud, "The Origins of Puritanism," *CH* 20 (1951).

lay audiences but also with restive followers and radical critics. Historians such as Patrick Collinson, A.G. Dickens, and Christopher Hill have emphasized the importance of popular dissent in facilitating clerical endeavors to promote religious reform. My study builds on their work by showing how popular dissent continuously pushed Puritan clerics in the direction of radical reforms that generally undermined ministerial authority and specifically threatened to force clerics out of the Church of England.

The doctrinal and liturgical developments that today denote Puritanism were thus molded as much by popular dissent as by the Puritan clerics; these developments reflect efforts by the clerics to resist or contain the radical reforms urged on them by zealous laypersons. Therefore, internal organizational factors are of utmost importance for understanding Puritan covenant theology because different stages in its development emerge from efforts by the clerics to maintain their authority over the popular Reformation. The solution I propose to the puzzle of the heavenly contract thus leads away from intellectual history and learned disputations among clerics to sociology and social history.

In its emphasis on lay contributions to Puritanism my analysis also differs from earlier sociological studies of Puritanism. With the partial exception of Max Weber, noted below, sociologists have uniformly neglected the laity and focused on clerical writings and preoccupations. They devote far less attention to the social and organizational contexts of Puritan ideology than might be expected from practitioners of a discipline that stresses the existential conditioning of ideas. Instead, they interpret Puritan ideology in order to explain why Puritanism appealed to certain groups, flourished in certain polities, and promoted new patterns of worldly behavior.[5] Unfortunately, Puritanism, like its talisman, the Bible, can be read plausibly in different ways, leading to different interpretations. Interpretation should rely on analysis of the organizational and social contexts in which Calvinist beliefs were developed and disseminated in England. For example, I show how these contexts were shaped by the spiritual and secular interests of a lay vanguard within the church; I then attempt to trace connections between these contexts and the content of Puritan thought. Sociological interpretation of beliefs can thus be checked by careful analysis of their social and organizational contexts, but this re-

5. Reinhard Bendix, *Kings or People: Power and the Mandate to Rule* (Berkeley and Los Angeles, 1978); David Little, *Religion, Order, and Law: A Study in Pre-Revolutionary England* (Oxford, 1970); Guy Swanson, *Religion and Regime: A Sociological Account of the Reformation* (Ann Arbor, 1967); Michael Walzer, *The Revolution of the Saints: A Study in the Origins of Radical Politics* (Cambridge, Mass., 1965).

quires precisely the critical style of historical scholarship that is so often absent in sociological writing.[6]

A direct consequence of this lack of historical rigor in previous sociological studies of Puritanism is the implicit assumption that Puritanism equals clerical Puritanism. This neglect of Puritanism's lay component is an old historiographic problem. It arises out of uncritical acceptance of reports by contemporary and later observers whose cultural biases prevented them from regarding lay intellectual initiatives as anything other than a pale reflection of clerical agitation. When confronted in 1571 by an obstreperous lay vanguard, Bishop Cox complained of Puritan clerics "who by the vehemence of their harangues have so maddened the wretched multitude, and driven some of them to that pitch of frenzy, that they now obstinately refuse to enter our churches, either to baptize their children, or to partake of the Lord's Supper, or to hear sermons." Seventeenth-century observers like Thomas Hobbes and Lord Clarendon also argued that Puritan ministers caused dissent and therefore the Civil War. Referring to the 100,000 persons allegedly slain in that war, Hobbes asked rhetorically, "Had it not been much better that those seditious ministers . . . had all been killed before they preached? It had been (I confess) a great massacre; but the killing of 100,000 is a greater."[7]

This historiographic bias reappears in sociological studies that focus on clerical activities and attitudes, presuming Puritanism to be the product of a one-directional influence exercised by clerics over an intellectually inert laity. For the most part this presumption is implicit, especially in studies that address Max Weber's thesis on Puritanism and capitalism. Other studies explicitly make this point. For example, in his examination of the relation between religious doctrine and political regime, Swanson defines Calvinism as a doctrine that asserts "the ordinary member of the church does not have the power to understand Scripture rightly."[8] On this basis neither Puritan clerics nor the Puritan laity can be considered Calvinist. Other studies cite the small number of lay Puritan authors as evidence of the preponderant influence of clerics. Michael Walzer's influential study

6. I have discussed this issue in "Sociological Theory and Historical Scholarship," *American Sociologist* 13 (1978).

7. *ZL*, p. 237; Thomas Hobbes, *Behemoth or the Long Parliament* (London, 1969), p. 95; Lord Clarendon, quoted in R.C. Richardson, *The Debate on the English Revolution* (London, 1977), pp. 31–32.

Later historical studies of Puritanism that explicitly ignore the role of the laity include Charles Davis Cremeans, *The Reception of Calvinist Thought in England* (Urbana, 1949); M.M. Knappen, *Tudor Puritanism* (Chicago, 1966); R.G. Usher, *The Reconstruction of the English Church* (New York, 1910).

8. Swanson, *Religion and Regime*, p. 15.

of "masterless men" in the rise of Puritanism emphasizes the role of clerics and the gentry as "alienated intellectuals." He argues that Puritanism
"was from its beginning a clerical and evangelical movement . . . Puritan
ideology was entirely a clerical creation. Until the 1630s no important lay
authors can be counted among the English Calvinists."[9] But the lack of
important lay authors does not permit us to conclude that the laity had no
influence over doctrinal and liturgical developments in Puritanism. This
misleading conclusion overlooks a crucial aspect of lay initiative in the
Reformation: there were many lay intellectuals, but few of them were
authors.

This neglect of Puritanism's lay dimension by sociologists now seems
archaic in view of recent trends in social history. During the last two decades social historians have described the reciprocal links between elite and
popular cultures in late medieval and early modern Europe. Moreover,
they warn against assuming that in the early modern era only elite culture
was literate while popular culture remained exclusively oral. Specifically
with regard to Puritanism, some have emphasized the intimate involvement of the laity in the pre-Revolutionary era. One historian of Puritanism remarks: "That the Puritan laity, sometimes condescendingly
called 'simple gospellers' by the Puritan clergy, were not a submissive following or captive audience but a vigorous source of initiative should come
as no surprise."[10]

These preliminary observations indicate why Puritan theology might
profitably be examined with reference to lay concerns. I think it is as futile
to interpret Puritan thought without reference to the spiritual and secular
concerns of the Puritan laity as, for example, it would be to interpret
twentieth-century variants of Marxism without reference to their development and dissemination in specific social and organizational contexts.
The latter assertion seems self-evident, the former less so, precisely because it is assumed, without much justification, that in the development of
religious dissent clerics exercised a unilinear influence over the laity. My

9. Walzer, *Revolution of the Saints*, p. 115. A nearly identical statement occurs in Paul S.
Seaver, *The Puritan Lectureships: The Politics of Religious Dissent, 1560–1662* (Stanford,
1970), p. 39. See also Cremeans, *Reception of Calvinist Thought in England*, pp. 121–22.
Nonetheless, it remains to be shown that Henry Finch, Francis Hastings, John Norden,
Francis Rous, and William Vaughan were *unimportant* lay Puritan writers.

10. Patrick Collinson, "Towards a Broader Understanding of the Early Dissenting
Tradition," in C. Robert Cole and Michael E. Moody, eds., *The Dissenting Tradition*
(Athens, Ohio, 1975), p. 17. Other historians who have emphasized lay initiatives in
Puritanism include Christopher Hill, R.C. Richardson, and Margaret Spufford. See be-
low (chapter 2, p. 25) for a more general discussion of trends in the social history of
popular culture.

analysis of the development and content of Puritan covenant theology shows this assumption to be untenable.

My analysis also has important implications both for major sociological theories and for some recent historiographic trends. Debates over religion and the rise of capitalism have occupied a place in the development of sociological analysis similar to that of the French Revolution in historiography or of *E. coli* in biology. What depends on the outcome of these debates are general assessments of the relative importance of cultural and economic factors in social change. Max Weber's *The Protestant Ethic and the Spirit of Capitalism* provided the point of departure for an assessment that resists economic reductionism and upholds the independent importance of cultural factors. By now an extensive and well-known literature has accumulated that features not only debates over Weber's assumptions and methods but efforts to empirically "test" hypotheses that often bear little resemblance to Weber's own work.[11] Despite all this interest in Puritanism, neither of the topics with which I am particularly concerned—covenant theology and lay initiatives—has received much, if any, attention from sociologists. This is surprising, because both topics display several points of obvious relevance to Weber's thesis.

Ultimately it was the laity that promoted, under the influence of Calvinism, a rationalization of economic life. No less relevant to Weber's thesis is the appearance of a covenant theology that took a contractarian idiom from economic life and used it to fashion a popular theology intellectually accessible to ordinary laypersons. Both topics take on even greater relevance to Weber's thesis when one considers that their interconnections hold the answer to an important problem posed but not solved by Weber.

In his analysis of Calvinism's contribution to early capitalist development, Weber recognized that there were many differences between Calvin's writings and the Calvinism of the late sixteenth and seventeenth centuries, which Weber associated with the spirit of capitalism. Foremost among these differences is the problem of *certitudo salutis*, the problem of discovering whether one was in a state of grace or not. This problem provides the link Weber sought between religion and capitalism. According to Weber, Puritan clerics defined certain kinds of behavior as tangible outward evidence of one's inward spiritual status; one such behavior was methodical labor, which also, though inadvertently, facilitated a rationalization of economic conduct. Weber further suggested that it was the

11. Two conspicuous exceptions to this last remark are thoughtful studies by Little, *Religion, Order, and Law*; Gordon Marshall, *Presbyteries and Profits: Calvinism and the Development of Capitalism in Scotland, 1560–1707* (Oxford, 1980).

laity's need for assurance of salvation that led to a modification of orthodox Calvinism that in turn encouraged individuals to seek actively for behavioral evidences of election.[12] Weber does not say much about this modification other than that he thinks it took place. However, Perry Miller and Christopher Hill do offer clues to this development in their observations about how covenant theology modified Calvinism in ways that made it more palatable to the laity.[13] My study explains how and why Puritan clerics used a contractarian idiom borrowed from economic life in order to create this more palatable version of Calvinism. In addition, surprising implications for Weber's thesis on Puritanism and capitalism emerge from this examination of Puritan ideas about a heavenly contract.

One conclusion I have reached is that the relation between Puritanism and economic life is far more reciprocal than Weber thought it was. More than this, the evidence I explore in chapter 6 provides compelling support for some hypotheses that explicitly contradict those held by Weber. I certainly do not think that the conclusions of my study validate a theoretical stance that dismisses cultural factors as epiphenomenal. Indeed, my discussion of the historical preconditions of popular dissent in chapter 2 attaches great importance to cultural factors. Nonetheless, I think that my study will require sociologists to reconsider not only Weber's thesis itself but also the ways in which it has been debated and tested. For readers interested in this issue I provide a final chapter, in which I tease out the larger theoretical implications of this study.

My emphasis on lay initiative and lay intellectual independence will no doubt be controversial for many historians. Although prominent historians of Puritanism have, as noted above, turned their attention to its lay dimension, they have, in my opinion, neglected or underestimated the kinds of conflicts and tensions that occurred between the clerics and the laity. Moreover, they have missed the relevance of these organizational issues for the development of Puritan covenant theology. Aside from the intellectual precedents discussed above, the only explanation offered for this development by Hill and Miller cites practical precedents established by the growing importance of economic contracts in early capitalism.[14]

12. Max Weber, *Economy and Society* (Berkeley and Los Angeles, 1978), p. 1199; H.H. Gerth and C.W. Mills, eds., *From Max Weber* (New York, 1958), pp. 111–12; and Weber, *The Protestant Ethic and the Spirit of Capitalism* (New York, 1958), pp. 109–12, 220.

13. Christopher Hill, *Puritanism and Revolution* (New York, 1964), pp. 246–47, and *Society and Puritanism in Pre-Revolutionary England* (New York, 1967), p. 489; Miller, *The New England Mind*, pp. 394–96. See also Knappen, *Tudor Puritanism*, p. 395; New, *Anglicans and Puritans*, p. 128; John von Rohr, "Covenant and Assurance in Early English Puritanism," *CH* 34 (1965).

14. Christopher Hill, "Covenant Theology and the Concept of 'A Public Person,'" in

While my analysis certainly sustains this view, it avoids its implicit reductionism by arguing that clerics were motivated to incorporate these practical precedents in their divinity because it enabled them to resolve organizational problems. There is not a simple causal relationship between
economic life and Puritan beliefs about a heavenly contract; organizational features of Puritanism mediate actively between economic and ideological realities.

Finally, I confront a more general methodological issue that divides
historians: the validity of generalization in historical research. This is of
course an old issue, but it has been particularly evident in debates among
historians of early modern England. In recent years a methodologically
conservative position has gained ground and become almost a new orthodoxy for some English historians who mistrust generalization, preferring
instead to document, with certainty, less and less about less and less. In
studies of the English Reformation, this historiographic tendency leads
away from what is novel about lay intellectual initiative and focuses attention on underlying continuities, regional variations, and reverses or set-
backs that hindered reform. The argument I present in this study clearly
runs against this tendency.

Synopsis

Any interdisciplinary work confronts potentially serious audience problems, and this one is no exception. It may therefore be helpful to readers
to outline briefly the organization of this study. I begin with a discussion
of the historical preconditions that facilitated the widespread dissemination of popular dissent. Then I discuss the impact that lay initiatives in
popular dissent had on Puritanism, and I establish the relevance of these
initiatives for the development of Puritan covenant theology. I conclude
with an examination of the content of this theology. Thus my analysis of
Puritan covenant theology proceeds from its broad social and historical
context to its more immediate organizational context and, finally, to the
theology itself. Analysis of the sociohistoric and organizational contexts of
Puritan theology occupies chapters 2–4; in chapters 5 and 6 I examine
first the development and then the content of Puritan covenant theology.

In chapter 2, I discuss the historical preconditions that facilitated the
widespread dissemination of popular dissent in sixteenth-century England. My discussion identifies three sets of changes that created *social-*

Alkis Kontos, ed., *Powers, Possessions and Freedom: Essays in Honor of C.B. Macpherson*
(Toronto, 1979), pp. 3–4; Miller, *New England Mind*, p. 399.

structural, technical, and *cultural* sources of popular dissent. These made widespread dissemination of popular dissent objectively possible, though they did not, of course, in any way make it inevitable.

Social-structural preconditions concern the creation of an audience that is receptive to critical ideas of dissent. My analysis of this factor looks at changes in the nature and distribution of vocations that occurred as part of early capitalist development in sixteenth-century England. Rather than emphasize urban developments, I concentrate on the penetration of market forces into the countryside. I do so because England was and remained throughout this era a predominantly rural society. The relevance for the dissemination of dissent is this: the commercialization of agrarian communities recreated in the countryside the vocational conditions that had long been present among artisans, craftsmen, and merchants in urban centers. These conditions included the high degrees of economic autonomy and practical rationality that were responsible for the affinity between these groups and certain types of heretical movements in the late medieval era. Diffusion of these economic circumstances into the countryside, where the vast majority of the population resided, thus unleashed popular dissent from its previous confinement in urban centers and made possible its appearance on a vastly greater scale.

Technical preconditions concern the medium by which ideas are transmitted and its bearing on an audience's ability to assimilate and articulate these ideas. The effects of the printing revolution are important here— namely, the appearance of a popular press, which created a flourishing literary culture, and the growth of literacy and semiliteracy (the ability to read but not write). A general consequence of these developments was a steady laicization of culture, and this was especially pronounced in the area of religion.

Cultural aspects concern the intellectual processes that supply the critical and skeptical ideas that provide a favorable mental environment for dissent. Analysis of connections between ideas and their external contexts is unavoidable, but no less important is the fact that systems of ideas have immanent tendencies that cannot be reduced to economic or social forces. Here I follow the broad outlines of Max Weber's remarks on intellectual rationalization as an immanent tendency in intellectual life.

These are three distinct preconditions, but they are related in many ways. After all, printing developed as a capitalist enterprise; literacy became increasingly important as economic life shifted to production for markets; and rationalization of beliefs created a demand for vernacular Bibles. The powerful impulse imparted to popular dissent by the combined effects of these changes presents a striking example of overdetermination. In addition, the normative structure of popular dissent was strongly influenced by these changes. Its mixture of material skepticism, anticlericalism, and emphasis on edification is very evident in the subsequent evolution of popular dissent as it gradually developed along doctrinal lines during the century before the Civil War.

In chapter 3 our attention moves from popular to clerical aspects of the Reformation. A different type of dissent appears in pastoral and polemical writings by clerics; here dissent assumed a far less hostile stance toward the larger social world in which it fought for recognition and legitimacy. Its critical and emancipatory sentiments receded behind the elements of obedience and submission that were stressed by clerics. Critical ideas that originated in popular dissent—ideas about the importance of edification and the sanctity of conscience—were taken over and developed by clerical reformers as the foundation of a policy that they thought would secure popular submission to temporal authority. This policy addressed problems of authority that troubled social and political elites in sixteenth-century England, and it was the means by which clerical proponents of Protestant reform sought to make it palatable to these elites. More than this, it was a way to gather protection, support, and patronage from the powerful. In order to forge alliances with leaders of church and state and to gather aristocratic patronage, clerical reformers argued that creation of a preaching ministry would not merely edify the faithful but would also serve as a powerful instrument of social control.

It is not at all unusual for a dissident movement to take on different shades of meaning and emphasis when it is viewed from above, by its nominal leaders, and from below by its members. Remarks on godly edification by university-educated clerics to monarchs, privy councillors, justices of the peace, town burgesses, aristocratic supporters, and church officials emphasized its contribution to obedience and order. Popular interest in godly edification emphasized, instead, elements of intellectual independence and initiative which had radically democratic implications for religious life. In contrast to this, arguments by clerical reformers indicated how preaching as an instrument of social control would stabilize gross inequalities in social life.

In chapter 4 we return to popular aspects of the Reformation and encounter the various relations and tensions between Puritan clerics and three different groups in the popular Reformation: the lay Puritans, the Separatists, and the radical heretics. These groups display the different ways in which diffuse sentiments of popular dissent crystallized into distinct doctrinal and liturgical positions. Divisions between these groups in the popular Reformation were not firm, and therefore a precise denominational history cannot be extended much before the beginning of the Civil War. Prior to this time, popular dissent was very much in flux and subject to local and national contingencies. An archbishop like Edmund Grindal, who was sympathetic to Puritanism, could do much to retain a lay religious vanguard within the church. Policies instituted by a monarch like Charles virtually pushed the zealous laity out of the church. The local presence of a powerful aristocratic patron of Puritanism might forestall outright separation from the church by promoting activities, such as extended household services and lectureships, that supplemented church services.

Puritan clerics were the main link between an ongoing process of popular Reformation and a church whose doctrine and liturgy were fixed by the Elizabethan Settlement in 1559. The problem confronting these clerics was to develop the popular Reformation in ways that were compatible with their pastoral authority as ordained ministers in a comprehensive church. This required them to keep the zealous laity within the church and to retain their own positions. Gradually the gap widened between the popular Reformation and the church, and Puritan clerics confronted a formidable organizational dilemma in occupying two incompatible roles. As ordained ministers in the church, subject to its canons and liturgy, and as leaders of a popular movement, the Puritan clerics were caught between the conflicting demands of their ecclesiastical superiors and their restive lay followers.

This organizational dilemma played a major part in the overall development of Puritanism in pre-Revolutionary England. For example, many of the celebrated controversies over clerical nonconformity, regarding wearing the surplice and use of the cross in baptism, turn out to have been animated not merely by clerical conscience but by the demands of indignant laypersons, who literally extorted nonconformity from clerics as the price of their loyalty. Another instance is the extent to which Puritan clerics worked to dissuade a lay vanguard from doctrinal heresy and from following the Separatist path out of the church. Their anguished temporizing when ordered to conform and their efforts to combat radical trends in the popular Reformation indicate the extent to which Puritan clerics were unwilling to forgo the resources that were available to them as ministers in a comprehensive church.

The Puritan clergy's opposition to heretical and Separatist groups was unyielding, but matters were more complex in their relationship to lay Puritanism. Different priorities characterized clerical and lay Puritanism; lay Puritanism reflected concerns of popular dissent which sometimes militated against the priorities of Puritan clerics educated at Cambridge and Oxford. Puritan cleric and Puritan layperson held in common the fundamental tenets of Calvinism, but they could and did interpret them in different ways.

Chiefly responsible for this divergence were the intellectual initiative and independence that characterized lay Puritanism. This independence and initiative rested on the Puritan laity's attachment to a literate, edifying style of religion that displayed a high degree of what Weber called ethical religiosity. Lay Puritans greeted sacramental aspects of religion with skepticism, preferring instead to gain salvation by acting in conformity with the ethical postulates of an abstract system of beliefs. All this led to a democratization of knowledge and criticism in religious life, and eventually it undermined the principle of lay subordination to clerics. Neither the Puritan clergy, who encouraged ethical religiosity, nor the Puritan laity intended this outcome. Only after the collapse of church control during the Civil War did sectarian congregations openly appear in England and proclaim the principle of lay choice of ministers.

The organizational development of pre-Revolutionary Puritanism represents a transitional stage in the evolution of this principle—a stage in which groups of lay Puritans traveled across parish lines in search of clerics whose ministrations they found edifying. This organizational structure was not only transitional but also ambiguous in nature. Clerical and lay Puritans remained committed in principle to the idea of a comprehensive church; yet their activities injected a measure of voluntarism as groups of the godly pursued their religious life in the interstices of the church.

Another clerical response to these organizational problems was to channel lay initiative in directions that were compatible with continuing clerical supervision, and in chapter 5 I show how covenant theology developed as a consequence of clerical efforts to achieve this goal. Development of a distinctively Puritan version of Calvinism followed in the wake of clerical efforts to resolve organizational problems in their dealings with the popular Reformation. Contractarian themes in Puritan divinity had several uses, corresponding to the different kinds of challenges presented by radical heretics, Separatists, and lay Puritans. My analysis shows how Puritan clerics produced their covenant theology by using intellectual *precedents* in response to these *pressures*.

Puritan use of contractarian ideas was not entirely original. It was least original in conjunction with clerical attacks on radical heresy. The earliest use of such ideas in reformed theology was intimately linked to the efforts of continental clerics to combat the Anabaptist heresy at the beginning of the Reformation. These ideas underwent some elaboration when Puritan clerics later used them to dissuade the laity from Separatism. For the most part, however, the covenant concept in anti-Separatist polemics remained similar to that found in antiheretical formulations. Puritan clerics emphasized the unilateral aspects of the heavenly contract, describing it as an inheritance that heretics and Separatists spurned. In both cases the agreement between God and humanity accorded well with clerical interests, for it required an ordained ministry and a comprehensive church but not the kinds of individual initiatives that Separatists and heretics argued were the marks of a godly life.

Markedly different uses of contractarian ideas emerged in Puritan theology in conjunction with lay Puritanism. Puritan writers make far more extensive use of them with regard to a wide range of pastoral rather than narrowly polemical issues. These issues include Bible-reading, hearing sermons, household religion, and, above all else, the introspective search for evidences of election. The use of contractarian themes in discussions of these issues offered wide scope for individual initiative. For this reason bilateral rather than unilateral aspects of the heavenly contract received greater emphasis. This conceptual shift reflects efforts by Puritan clerics to channel lay initiatives instead of trying to suppress them, as they had tried to suppress radical heresy and Separatism.

My analysis further suggests that this development occurred when Puritanism encountered perhaps its greatest crisis in the pre-Revolutionary era. Between 1570 and 1590 clerical reformers became increasingly involved in lobbying for an alteration of church polity along presbyterian lines. This lobbying abruptly ended when, under Elizabeth's prodding, church leaders instituted disciplinary proceedings against these clerical reformers. At this point the limits of reform became painfully evident: it would not be allowed to alter the episcopal structure of the church. What emerged after 1590 was a renewed emphasis on the moral and spiritual reform of individuals. This of course had been the ultimate objective of seeking a presbyterian polity, because a prominent feature of this polity was the disciplinary apparatus of the eldership, which clerics hoped to use to enforce godliness. Such a disciplinary apparatus would not be necessary, however, if the laity were themselves prepared and able to monitor godliness, both in themselves and in others.

After 1590 Puritan clerics devoted their energies directly to this goal and paid scarcely any attention to the issue of church polity. They developed a popular divinity that guided the laity in the performance of those evaluative tasks formerly associated with a disciplinary apparatus. This was the era in which Puritan clerics produced their elaborate casuistries and perfected their talents as preachers and prolific writers of religious treatises. Puritan casuistry described the signs and evidences that were indications of reprobate or elect status, and the doctrinal basis of this casuistry was the idea of a heavenly contract. This idea united the pastoral and doctrinal facets of religion in a relatively simple system of divinity. It not only presented all that was essential to the Calvinist economy of grace and salvation but also explained the proper place and use of Bible-reading, communion, prayer, and introspection.

Puritan clerics used contractarian ideas to create a popular version of Calvinist divinity because these ideas met conceptual as well as social requirements. They were sufficiently complex to be useful for explaining the major doctrinal and pastoral tenets of Puritan Calvinism. They were also common objects of knowledge among the laity, especially among the groups that formed the social basis of lay Puritanism: the small employers and the self-employed in both town and country. In chapter 6 I discuss the contractarian sources of covenant theology and the cogency of this theology for ordinary laypersons.

Having suggested in chapter 5 that Puritan clerics resolved certain organizational dilemmas by equipping their parishioners with a compact system of Calvinist divinity that took the form of covenant theology, I now explain why this theology was intelligible to laypersons. Evidence of this intelligibility is, of course, indirect. It derives chiefly from remarks made by Puritan clerics that explicitly or implicitly make it clear that the general principles and practices of worldly contracts were familiar objects of knowledge among their parishioners. In explaining why this was so, I cite the expansion of market relations, which led to an increasing reliance on contractual instruments of finance in economic life. These economic developments intimately involved the social groups from which Puritanism derived its greatest support. The economic independence that characterized these social groups rested on their location in price-making markets. This type of market more closely approximated a pure model of contractual interaction than the older structure of regulated fairs and trading alongside which it grew up.

General principles of contract, along with practices specific to early modern England, provided worldly exemplars for discussions of the operation of the heavenly contract. Both the general form and the content of contractual interaction—formal equality between parties who produce a voluntary agreement—inform Puritan views of the deepest mysteries of religion: the role of faith, the meaning of Christ's intercession and sacrifice, and the introspective search for evidences of election. Specific maxims and practices that surrounded contractual agreements at this time are also important. Sermons and popular treatises by Puritan clerics relied on a distinctive rhetoric and imagery to explain the essence of the heavenly contract and its import for religious life. This rhetoric and imagery derived directly from maxims about what is and is not reasonable in contractual relations and from practices such as the giving of "earnests" to signal agreement.

Equally important for Puritan theology are examples of behavioral
qualities that contemporaries thought were necessary for success in economic contracts—for example, the disciplined and methodical use of
time, and careful record-keeping. Popular knowledge of the instrumental
utility of these behavioral qualities provided Puritan clerics with a resource for explaining how one ought to conduct a religious life. They
urged laypersons to extend the diligence and methodicalness they displayed in their use of worldly contracts to religious activities under the
operation of the heavenly contract. Thus the normative structure and rationality evident in contractual interaction in everyday life served as pastoral exemplars for Puritanism. It is from this evidence that I develop, in
chapter 7, the implications of this study for Weber's thesis on the relationship between religion and economic life.

A final theme that emerges from my examination of covenant theology
concerns the much-debated issue of "individualism." I have suggested
that contractarian themes in Puritan theology followed principles similar
to those evident in worldly contracts. At the core of these principles is a set
of assumptions about equity, justice, ownership, and accumulation. In a
seminal work C.B. Macpherson suggests that these assumptions form a
coherent doctrine, which he calls "possessive individualism." He further
argues that this doctrine unites in a fundamental way certain writings by
Hobbes, Locke, and other authors whom he identifies as progenitors of
classical liberalism.[15] In the concluding portion of chapter 6, I show that
the doctrine of possessive individualism is central to Puritan covenant theology. All major assumptions of this doctrine appear in Puritan explanations of how the saints come to acquire grace under the terms of the heavenly contract. In view of this analysis it becomes possible to locate the
proper place of Puritanism in the context of the broader social and philo-
sophic developments that produced the individualistic world view of classical liberalism.[16] Reflections on this issue also appear in chapter 7 as part
of my summary statement on the theoretical issues raised by this study.

Definitions

Several key terms ought to be at least provisionally defined, for they have
variable and much-debated meanings. The utility of the term "Puritan"

15. C.B. Macpherson, *The Political Theory of Possessive Individualism* (Oxford, 1962).
One need not accept all of Macpherson's remarks about the Levellers and the franchise in
order to appreciate the more general implications of his work.
16. Cf. Winfried Förster, *Thomas Hobbes und der Puritanismus: Grundlagen und*

has been questioned, because it was used in the pre-Revolutionary era primarily as a hostile epithet. An extensive discussion of this issue occurs in *Society and Puritanism in Pre-Revolutionary England* by Christopher Hill, who notes that the term Puritanism "is an admirable refuge from clarity of thought." Nonetheless, he argues that it is susceptible to definition, and in my study I follow his widely accepted definition of Puritans: those who sought a more evangelical and Protestant style of worship than that offered by the Church of England but who rejected outright separation from the church before the Civil War.[17]

Thus the history of Puritanism began with the ascension of Elizabeth and the creation of the Church of England in 1559. It emerged from earlier Calvinist, Lutheran, and Zwinglian currents and from an older tradition of Lollard heresy. Puritanism itself remained Calvinist in inspiration, although its system of divinity developed along new lines in response to conditions in England. Until the reign of Charles I, the Church of England generally supported Calvinist doctrine, especially during the early years of Elizabeth's reign—when many Marian exiles returned from Basle, Frankfort, Geneva, Strasbourg, and Zurich—and during the reign of James I, who held staunchly to Calvinist doctrine, though he disliked its pastoral implications in lay Puritanism. It is therefore somewhat misleading to regard Anglicans and Puritans as opposites, for Puritans were in a sense Anglicans, committed to the concept of a state church, ruled over by a godly monarch. What separated Puritan from non-Puritan during most of the pre-Revolutionary years were differences over ceremonial and pastoral practices that principally affected the reality of religion for pastor and parishioners at the parish level.

In chapter 4 I discuss in detail the differences among Separatists, radical heretics, and lay Puritans, who collectively represent the *popular Reformation*. The term popular Reformation refers to lay developments occurring outside aristocratic circles, i.e., to the penetration of Anabaptist, Calvinist, Familist, and Zwinglian ideas in town and country and their impact on religion as it was practiced in parish churches and within families. In contrast to this Reformation, the official Reformation refers to religious developments sanctioned by law in a series of statutes enacted principally between 1529 and the Elizabethan Settlement of 1559. Doctrinal and liturgical positions fixed by the Elizabethan Settlement remained

---

Grundfragen seiner Staatslehre (Berlin, 1969), who argues that Hobbes's work was a reaction to the type of covenant theology developed by Henry Jacob.

17. Hill, *Society and Puritanism*, p. 13. For those who question the utility of the word Puritanism, see C.H. George and K. George, *The Protestant Mind of the English Reformation, 1570–1640* (Princeton, 1961), pp. 399–407.

fairly constant until the reign of Charles I and Archbishop Laud, when far-reaching innovations in these positions were imposed on the church.

I use the word "dissent" in order to link Lollard heresy prior to the Reformation with Puritanism. Moreover, the meaning I attach to this word is a substantive one, and this requires some explanation. Formal definitions of dissent raise questions about its status as a civil right: the extent to which religious or social criticism is immune to prosecution. Substantive definitions concern the content of such criticism. References to dissent as the Dissenting Tradition or, more broadly, as a valuable feature of Western culture implicitly invoke a substantive definition. A substantive definition involves debatable historical judgments because in this view not all criticism constitutes dissent, although it may enjoy formal immunity from prosecution. The word dissent acquired its contemporary meaning in the latter part of the seventeenth century, when it came to denote nonconformity to the Church of England. Even then definitions were perilous, as in the case of "conformable nonconformists," of whom one observer, in 1673, remarked, "some were for three-fourths conformity, some for one-half, some for one-fourth, and a few for none at all."[18] A substantive definition is not readily available. Highly abstract definitions, equating dissent with any expression of disagreement or lack of consensus, are too broad: they gloss over the cultural significance of dissent. For dissent is not simply a negative orientation to cultural goals or to institutional means. But too narrow a view would confine dissent to its religious origins, which it shares with other words that describe various aspects of public discontents—for example, alienation, protest, reform.

While the expression of dissent in Western culture has outgrown the religious circumstances of its origins, certain issues have remained central to it in all its phases as it has moved from religious tolerance to political democracy and to social and economic rights. Some of these issues refer to the desired consequences and actual goals of dissent; others refer to the way these consequences and goals are defined and achieved. Chief among the former is the presentation of alternative forms of religious, political, or economic organization that propose to remedy what are perceived to be public problems and that are justified by universalistic ideologies. A cumulative expansion of the meaning and practice of democracy has been a principal outcome of this. But in addition to its democratic goals and consequences, dissent has also democratized criticism and upheld a style of criticism that values reason and skepticism. Max Weber's phrase "the charisma of reason" describes this commitment to a critical rationality

18. Douglas R. Lacey, *Dissent and Parliamentary Politics in England, 1661–1689* (New Brunswick, 1969), p. 18.

that holds that reason can make society not only more efficient but also more just.

It is this latter aspect of dissent with which I am concerned in this study. The democratization of criticism that is inspired by critical rationality appears initially in a series of lay intellectual initiatives in religious matters. In England these initiatives antedated the Reformation in the form of the Lollard heresy, and they became far more widely disseminated during the popular Reformation. I think they merit our attention because of their intrinsic importance as well as for their relevance for our understanding of Puritan theology.

Sources

A study of lay religious opinion in early modern England confronts formidable problems of evidence and sources. I have obtained direct and indirect evidence of such opinion from primary and secondary historical sources. My use of these sources has been guided by the analytic goals of this study: to explain organizational and ideological developments with reference to focal concerns that characterized lay Puritanism and other groups in the popular Reformation. Primary and secondary sources have been gathered partly to document these concerns, and not to explain why lay Puritans or other groups in the popular Reformation appeared in a particular region at a certain time.

My research thus strikes a compromise between, on the one hand, uncritical reliance on secondary historical sources and, on the other, the narrow use of intensive local histories of Puritanism, based on primary sources which reconstruct the complex web of relations among godly clerics and laypersons, aristocratic patrons, and ecclesiastical officials. I have used intensive local histories of Puritanism, but my goals are different from those of *histoire totale*. My references to primary and secondary sources are made in view of analytic issues posed by the relationship between ideology and organization in a social movement. I think these references are adequate for a historical sociology that grapples with analytic issues relevant to sociological studies of social movements and beliefs and that also restates, revises, or refutes the conclusions reached in previous historical studies.

It is relatively easy to document clerical attitudes, given the fact that most of the religious literature of the time was composed by clerics, and also because they were most exposed to ecclesiastical supervision. Thus we have at our disposal their sermons and doctrinal treatises, their subscriptions to conformity, and the reasons they gave for not subscribing. Matters are quite different when it comes to the attitudes of ordinary laypersons, including those who composed an articulate vanguard in the church. Their writings are scarce, and their opinions were easily concealed from church authorities because of inadequacies in the disciplinary apparatus of the church. The detection of deviant opinion was entrusted principally to churchwardens. When churchwardens shared a deviant opinion, it was likely to go unreported. It is a commonplace among local historians of Puritanism that church records are therefore unreliable guides to the incidence of lay Puritanism.[19] Most recently, historians have attempted to ascertain the extent of changes in lay opinion by analyzing bequests in wills.[20] This seems to be the best way of gauging growth in popular support for Protestantism over time in different regions.

My research, however, requires different kinds of knowledge about lay opinion than that provided by wills. My focus is not on the relative incidence of lay Puritanism but on the concerns that characterized lay Puritanism wherever it emerged and with the impact these concerns had on Puritan clerics and on the overall development of Puritanism. Formulations of faith in wills do not include opinions on specific liturgical issues which are recorded in church documents. For this reason I have relied on church records, even though they do not sample lay Puritan opinion uniformly by era or region. I have obtained these records from manuscript sources located at the Bodleian Library, the British Library, and the Public Record Office and from recent local histories of Puritanism.

Lay opinion can also be studied indirectly from clerical writings. A wide range of admonitions, complaints, and praises aimed at parishioners in sermons by Puritan and non-Puritan clerics provides valuable evidence on lay Puritan activities and opinions. Further evidence emerges from clerical correspondence, from petitions and polemical writings composed by Puritan clerics and their aristocratic supporters, and from other manuscript sources. More direct evidence of lay opinion in the popular Reformation exists in polemical writings by Separatist leaders and radical heretics, along with a few manuscript treatises written by ordinary laypersons, such as the one by a London pewterer in 1620 (BoL, *MSS. Rawls. C765*), which I cite in chapter 5.

My analysis of covenant theology and its links to organizational devel-

---

19. For discussions of this problem see R.C. Richardson, "Puritanism and the Ecclesiastical Authorities," in Brian Manning, ed., *Politics, Religion, and the English Civil War* (New York, 1973), pp. 26–30; Margaret Spufford, *Contrasting Communities: English Villagers in the Sixteenth and Seventeenth Centuries* (Cambridge, 1974), pp. 257–58, 265–71.

20. The study of wills for this purpose was developed by A.G. Dickens, *Lollards and Protestants in the Diocese of York, 1509–1558* (Oxford, 1959).

opments in Puritanism relies on both printed and manuscript sources. It is based on a comprehensive survey of doctrinal and pastoral writings—one that includes far more than the usual handful of clerics mentioned in previous studies of covenant theology, e.g., William Ames, William Perkins, John Preston, Richard Sibbes, and Thomas Taylor. Examination of several hundred sermons and treatises reveals the conceptual and rhetorical consistency of Puritan covenant theology; writings on this subject by lesser Puritan divines are fully congruent with those written by more prominent Puritans. Criteria for identifying a clerical writer as Puritan include any one of the following: evidence of ceremonial nonconformity in primary church records or in local histories of Puritanism,[21] internal textual dedications and references to other authors by known Puritan writers,[22] and entries in the *Dictionary of National Biography*.

21. The following local histories have been most helpful: C.D. Chalmers, "Puritanism in Leicestershire, 1558–1633" (M.A. thesis, Leeds University, 1962); Ian W. Gowers, "Puritanism in the County of Devon between 1570 and 1641" (M.A. thesis, University of Exeter, 1970); Roger B. Manning, *Religion and Society in Elizabethan Sussex* (Leicester, 1969); Roland A. Marchant, *The Puritans and the Church Courts in the Diocese of York, 1560–1642* (London, 1960); W.H. Mildon, "Puritanism in Hampshire and the Isle of Wight from the Reign of Elizabeth to the Restoration" (Ph.D. dissertation, University of London, 1934); R.C. Richardson, *Puritanism in North-West England: A Regional Study of the Diocese of Chester to 1642* (Manchester, 1972); W.J. Sheils, "The Puritans and the Diocese of Peterborough, 1558–1640," *NRS* 30 (1979); William Urwick, *Nonconformity in Herts.: Being Lectures upon the Nonconforming Worthies of . . . the County of Hertford* (London, 1884).

22. See Franklin B. Williams, Jr., *Index of Dedications and Commendatory Verses in English Books before 1641* (London, 1962).

2

Popular Dissent and Its Historical Preconditions

There are many ways in which the Reformation can be described as an epochal event. What I find most intriguing are the alterations that occurred in relations between clerics and laypersons. More specifically, I am interested in the intellectual origins and consequences of this alteration. Authority, criticism, dissent, and submission are among the topics that are relevant to this interest in clerical-lay relations, and with regard to these topics the Reformation can justly be described as epochal because it produced a shift in the balance between cleric and layperson that steadily favored popular intellectual initiatives and independence in religious life. This initiative and independence occurred at the expense of clerical authority and undermined a principle that long had dominated religious life: lay subservience to clerics.

Innovations that were radically democratic in nature resulted from this development, and they affected the intellectual as well as the organizational aspects of religious life. One of the chief organizational innovations was the congregational ideal, with its emphasis on voluntarism and free lay choice of ministers. An important intellectual innovation was the notion of dissent, which in effect democratized criticism. These two innovations are closely intertwined, because voluntarism and free lay choice of ministers presuppose a doctrinal competency that enables laypersons to make critical judgments about doctrinal and liturgical issues.

To be sure, the elevation of the laity at the expense of the clergy had administrative and economic as well as purely intellectual dimensions. Lay impropriation of benefices and the role played by aristocrats in enforcing religious change provided numerous opportunities for the laity to impose its demands on the church. I do not discuss these issues, for they are largely irrelevant to my interest in the doctrinal consequences of an increasingly assertive and independent laity.

Establishing these doctrinal consequences is a matter of uncovering the reciprocal influences between elite and popular cultures. Doctrinal developments were the work of university-trained clerics, while lay intellectual initiatives appeared in a tradition of popular dissent whose practitioners, though frequently able to read, lacked the formal education necessary to participate in learned discourse. My analysis of the influence of popular dissent on doctrinal developments in Puritanism follows the lead of social historians who have described these reciprocal influences in medieval and early modern Europe and demonstrated that the boundaries between elite and popular cultures are not as fixed and easily demarcated as they were once thought to be.[1] In England the influence of popular culture on its elite counterpart has been studied with reference to the rise of Baconian science and the writings of Bunyan and Milton, and the opposite flow— the way an elite culture sought to modify popular culture—has been documented by Keith Thomas in his *Religion and the Decline of Magic*.[2] Social historians in France have also described the various ways in which the two cultures overlapped and borrowed from each other in the medieval and early modern era.[3]

Demonstrating the influence of popular dissent on doctrinal develop-

1. Jacques Le Goff, *Pour un autre Moyen Age: Temps, travail et culture en Occident* (Paris, 1977), p. 44, describes the existence of "ce dialogue divers, fait de pressions et de répressions, d'emprunts et de refus, que la culture savante et la culture populaire entretinrent pendant dix siècles." See also Peter Burke, *Popular Culture in Early Modern Europe* (New York, 1978); Natalie Zemon Davis, *Society and Culture in Early Modern France* (Stanford, 1965); Robert Mandrou, "Cultures Populaire et Savante: Rapports et Contacts," in Jacques Beauroy et al., eds., *The Wolf and the Lamb: Popular Culture in France from the Old Regime to the Twentieth Century* (Stanford, 1976).

However, some historians minimize reciprocal influences between elite and popular cultures and emphasize instead the encapsulated nature of the latter; see, e.g., Geneviève Bollème, *Les Almanachs populaires aux 17ᵉ et 18ᵉ siècles* (Paris, 1968); Richard Cobb, *The Police and the People* (Oxford, 1972); Peter Laslett, *The World We Have Lost* (New York, 1965); Gerald Strauss, *Luther's House of Learning: Indoctrination of the Young in the German Reformation* (Baltimore, 1978).

2. Hill, *Intellectual Origins of the English Revolution* (London, 1972), pp. 14–22, 63–66, 95–96, 292–99, and *The World Turned Upside Down: Radical Ideas during the English Revolution* (New York, 1972), pp. 231–46, 320–36, and *Milton and the English Revolution* (New York, 1977); Charles Webster, *The Great Instauration: Science, Medicine and Reform, 1626–1660* (New York, 1976), pp. 337–38, 345–46.

3. E. Le Roy Ladurie, *Montaillou: The Promised Land of Error* (New York, 1978), pp. 231–44; George Rude, *The Crowd in the French Revolution* (Oxford, 1967), pp. 210–17; Albert Soboul, *Les sans-culottes parisiens en l'an II* (Paris, 1958), pp. 457–547. The same point has been made for Italy; see Carlo Ginzberg, *The Cheese and the Worms: The Cosmos of a Sixteenth-Century Miller* (Baltimore, 1980).

ments in the Reformation extends this previous work to new terrain. However, this can be done only if it is possible to show that popular dissent was in some way independent of clerical efforts to promote religious reform. In this chapter I demonstrate this to be the case. Clerical ideas were of course important for popular dissent, for heterodox writings by clerics were eagerly read by lay dissenters. But lay interpretation of these ideas did not always lead in directions anticipated or approved of by their authors.[4] Popular dissent in the early years of the Reformation harbored rather raw forms of anticlericalism as well as an attachment to Bible-reading. In order to understand what was new in the nature and extent of popular dissent in the Reformation, it is necessary to see how secular circumstances affected lay reception of heterodox ideas. What was new in this dissent was the doctrinal competency and intellectual assertiveness of the laity. These astounded many contemporary observers, who accurately saw them to be incompatible with the existence of a religion whose continuity relied on Latin worship and lay subservience, both of which effectively isolated doctrinal and liturgical issues from lay influence.

DISSENT IN A RECOGNIZABLY MODERN FORM FIRST APPEARED IN THE Reformation. No longer was it exclusively the property of cultural elites or confined to the wranglings of scholars and clerics. Nor did it lead a restricted and fugitive existence among the laity in isolated heretical groups. Dissent had openly entered lay intellectual life, and to contemporaries surveying the progress of Protestantism this was either its highest or its lowest achievement. What many found more surprising than the assertion that dissent from orthodoxy was a right belonging to ordinary men and women was the ideological competency of lay dissent. This development seemed to turn the world upside-down, because it marked the advent of democratic patterns of dissent from orthodoxy—a dissent that was at first religious but became political in nature.

Popular dissent lay at the heart of debates and prosecutions occurring at the onset of the English Reformation. More than a century before the Civil War and Interregnum, new attitudes of ordinary laymen undermined distinctions between clerical and lay aspects of worship and between elite and popular cultures as these affected religion. These new attitudes attached great importance to lay initiative and self-help in religion, and at all levels of society the laity usurped the traditional prerogatives of clerics. One such prerogative was religious instruction. Catherine Parr's

---

4. On this lay modification of heterodox doctrines, see Herbert Grundmann, "Hérésies savantes et hérésies populaires au moyen âge," in Jacques Le Goff, ed., *Hérésies et Sociétés dans l'Europe pré-industrielle, 11ᵉ-18ᵉ siècles* (Paris, 1968), p. 210.

fondness for reading, with others, scripture and sermons offended King Henry's conservative instincts, and he rebuked but did not behead the queen, telling her, "You are become a doctor, Kate, to instruct us (as we take it), and not to be instructed or directed by us." At the same time, worry about commoners' efforts to instruct themselves and others is evident in the lofty sneer with which the vernacular Bible was called "the book of Arthur Cobbler" and in the prosecutions, in 1541, of London parishioners for "brabbling of the New Testament" and "for busy reasoning on the new learning."[5]

What were the historical factors that made possible the widespread occurrence of "brabbling," "busy reasoning," and other forms of lay intellectual initiative in the Reformation? I suggest that three preconditions are most important, and I will argue that in their absence it is difficult to see how these intellectual initiatives could have arisen in the popular culture. My discussion of these initiatives focuses on two outstanding features: the critical skepticism and high levels of doctrinal competency that characterized popular dissent in the early years of the Reformation.

The three preconditions of popular dissent refer to its *social-structural*, *technical*, and *cultural* dimensions. Social-structural dimensions determine the nature of an audience that is receptive to critical ideas of dissent. Technical dimensions concern the medium by which ideas are transmitted and its bearing on an audience's ability to assimilate and articulate these ideas. Cultural dimensions refer to a mental environment favorable to dissent and to the intellectual processes and trends that make skepticism plausible. The specific changes that I associate with these three preconditions are, respectively, vocational changes in early capitalism, printing and popular literacy, and intellectual rationalization. No doubt there are other important factors. But the vocational, communicative, and intellectual developments discussed here are, I think, the most important social-structural, technical, and cultural sources of popular dissent in early modern England. Together they account for an unprecedented distribution of dissent in terms of its doctrinal competency and critical skepticism.[6]

Printing and literacy are not concerned with critical skepticism per se

---

5. James Kelsey McConica, *English Humanists and Reformation Politics* (Oxford, 1968), p. 226; *Foxe*, V. 443–44.

6. Max Weber's remarks on the strength of Puritanism are worth recalling: "What gave the Puritans . . . their insuperable power of resistance was not the intellectualism of the elite but rather the intellectualism of the plebeian and occasionally even the pariah classes . . . The unparalleled diffusion of knowledge about the Bible and interest in extremely abstruse and ethereal dogmatic controversies . . . created a popular religious intellectualism never found since" (*Economy and Society* [Berkeley and Los Angeles, 1978], p. 514).

but with the possibility of becoming a competent critic. In this sense communicative developments are enabling factors: they determine the potential for popular dissent and facilitate it, but they cannot supply a motive for it except in the following, rather general, way. The shift from an oral to a literate, and especially to a print, culture seems to promote individualistic outlooks that are compatible with critical skepticism.[7] Though England's early modern population generally inhabited an essentially oral culture, popular dissent was a religion of the literate.

Nonetheless, the existence of an audience receptive to critical outlooks cannot be explained by the availability of printed works. Seldom in cultural affairs can supply be said to create its own demand. Equally important is the nature of socioeconomic groups whose vocational activities inclined them toward dissent. Finally, we must also take account of the dissenting ideas themselves. After all, thought systems have their own dynamics, which cannot be reduced to developments in communications technologies or to economic influences. Rationalization of belief systems is one dynamic of crucial importance for understanding dissent.

Taken together, these three factors—vocation, communication, and rationality—comprise the essential preconditions for the diffusion of popular dissent in the Reformation. They are distinct factors, but they are interrelated at a number of levels. Consider the following: printers were early capitalist entrepreneurs; the rationalization of belief structures created a demand for vernacular Bibles; capitalism encouraged a practical rationalism that had a strong affinity for highly rationalized belief systems; printing promoted more rationalized outlooks. In early modern Europe these three factors first appeared together in a historically specific configuration whose combined effects provided powerful impulses to the generation of popular dissent. This is not to suggest that there is something inherent in this configuration that restricts it to Western civilization. Quite the opposite is the case. But it is equally evident that the historical circumstances in which popular dissent on a massive scale first appears are peculiar to Western Europe.

To sort out the different effects of the social-structural, technical, and cultural preconditions, I first discuss technical developments associated with the shift from an oral to a print culture and show their general importance for early dissent. Then I empirically assess the effects on dissent

---

7. This point has been made with regard to writing and, more specifically, to printing. For the former, see Jack Goody and Ian Watt, "The Consequences of Literacy," in Jack Goody, ed., *Literacy in Traditional Societies* (Cambridge, 1975), pp. 44–45; Michael Stubbs, *Language and Literacy* (London, 1980), pp. 104–5. On printing see Elizabeth Eisenstein, *The Printing Press as an Agent of Change* (Cambridge, 1979), pp. 84, 132, 230–31.

that printing and increased popular literacy produced in England. Next I turn to intellectual rationalization, presenting an abstract analysis of its importance for early dissent and an empirical assessment of its impact in England. I then discuss vocational changes associated with early capitalism in order to trace the way the technical and intellectual developments in cultural life were connected to specific social groups.

Communication

The importance of printing and literacy for popular dissent involved more than the mere dissemination of critical ideas. Equally important was their role in facilitating the high levels of ideological competence that is inherent in popular dissent. Dissent depends on this competency. Dissent is heresy made legitimate in varying degrees by the recognition that it is normatively wrong or practically impossible to repress it. This is so because dissent and orthodoxy can refer to the same or similar abstract beliefs and values in order to define and justify their contrary tenets. For example, socialists often derive economic democracy from the same doctrine of natural rights used by proponents of free enterprise to defend capitalism. Modern dissent presupposes that its contention with orthodoxy relies on marshaling normative rather than physical force.

Normative force requires ideological competence, the ability to utter and possibly write critical judgments about an alternative form of religious, political, or social organization. These judgments must be justified to contemporaries in terms of a more abstract system of ultimate values. Ideological competency in this dissenting activity is closely connected to printing's ability to disseminate ideas. Such competence requires that dissenters have direct access to crucial debates and doctrines that define and justify critical ideas of dissent. Both aspects of communication—dissemination and ideological competency—are thus historical preconditions of popular dissent in the sense of being technical means for its existence.

One way of gauging the impact that printing and popular literacy had on dissent is to compare them with the modes of communication alongside which they grew up: speaking and hearing. There is an important link between lay literacy and the kind of religious dissent in which rank-and-file dissenters are able to make convincing and critical normative judgments. Compared to oral instruction by priests, reading contains much greater potential for promoting assertive and independent styles of thought among laymen.

There are two reasons why reading rather than hearing can be a more critical form of religious instruction. First, the physical and social setting in which oral instruction occurs tends to diminish its potential for cultivating the ideological competence of its audience. Oral instruction has both a local context, determined by the composition and loyalties of a specific audience, and a universal context, which structures the general features of all audience settings. Among the latter is the fact that oral communication tends to elevate speakers above or otherwise set them apart from the audience. Speakers may stand on a stump, tub, or pulpit, from which they look down on their auditors, or they may be separated from them by different dress, a retinue of assistants, or the deference of the devout. These features of oral instruction give off subliminal messages that attest to the authority of the speaker and otherwise lend an aura of authority to his message. In addition, orally delivered messages must compete with other messages given off by the audience in reaction to the speaker's explicit message. Competing messages such as these are far weaker in printed works, not least because of the absence of the audience setting. True, the printed word may give off its own subliminal messages, but these tend to recede behind the explicit content, as they do not in oral instruction. Reading is a relatively context-free medium for which the reader must supply a context formerly given by the audience setting.[8]

The superior capacity of reading to promote ideological competency among laymen is also due to the fact that the printed word decisively overcomes "the transitoriness of oral communication." Readers can turn back to review arguments, can turn ahead to examine the conclusions toward which the author is moving, and can pause to deliberate or consult with others. In so doing they can acquire three critical capacities that are effectively barred in all but the most restrictive settings of oral instruction: they can gain knowledge of the conceptual core and the complexities of a belief system; they can learn to utter convincing and correct normative judgments in accord with the tenets of a belief system; and they can check for consistency and internal discrepancies. In some settings, oral instruction can cultivate ideological competency when it occurs between expert and initiate. But this relationship applies to a small, restricted audience to whom specialists impart priestly knowledge considered too esoteric or valuable for popular dissemination. Dissemination of popular dissent is clearly incompatible with this restrictive setting.[9]

With the growth of modest levels of popular literacy, books, broad-

---

8. Eisenstein, *Printing Press*, pp. 132, 148–49; Stubbs, *Language and Literacy*, p. 109; Josef Vachek, *Written Language* (The Hague, 1973), pp. 15–16.

9. Jack Goody, "Introduction," in Goody, ed., *Literacy in Traditional Societies*, p. 1; Robert Mandrou, *Des humanistes aux hommes de science, XVI' et XVII' siècles* (Paris, 1972), p. 22; S.H. Steinberg, *Five Hundred Years of Printing* (Harmondsworth, Eng., 1966), p. 9.

sides, pamphlets, and petitions made the content of dissenting ideologies accessible to many persons from social classes ordinarily excluded from the world of intellectual work. Now they became not only spectators in the arena of ideological contention but also the audience to whom such contention was directed. Attempts to justify existing institutional orders or to mobilize opposition were produced and received under new conditions. Competing elites had to calculate carefully the reception of their claims and counterclaims by potential adherents drawn from more popular social circles. Formation and dissemination of ideologies thus came to involve an inherent social calculus, taking into account the separate aspirations and mutual interrelations of different audiences.

In this way the growth of literacy and a popular press transformed dissent, making its internal organization far more democratic than it had been. This democratization affected not simply the goals of dissent but the intellectual processes by which dissenting ideas became defined and disseminated. Consider, for example, the following historical examples.

In medieval Europe, many revolutionary movements shared the same millenarian ideology, which had been formulated by clerics on the basis of their apocalyptic interpretations of the eschatologies presented in the Revelation of Saint John and in the book of Daniel. The continuity of this ideology is truly remarkable, for it sporadically emerged and disappeared in the course of half a millennium. The vision of a perfect society, signs of chaos forecasting its inauguration, the identity of prophets bearing tidings of these signs, proofs that verified this identity—these are found in major chiliastic revolts occurring in locales widely separated in space and time. This continuity probably reflects the domination of such movements by the charismatic qualities of their messianic leaders. Often they were clerics who alone had access to writings containing the millenarian eschatology.[10] For half a millennium, and extending on into the modern world, self-proclaimed prophets appeared during times of urban or rural unrest and rapidly gained uncritical support from unemployed townsmen or uprooted peasants, to whom the eschatology was presented orally. The unilinear influence of these prophets on their supporters is evident in the belief that the prophetic leader is deified, a belief based on the invincibility,

10. Guy Fourquin, *Les soulèvements populaires au moyen âge* (Paris, 1972), pp. 21, 98–101.

The rest of this paragraph relies on Norman Cohn, *The Pursuit of the Millennium* (London, 1970); Christopher Hill, *Antichrist in Seventeenth-Century England* (Oxford, 1971); Rodney Hilton, *Bond Men Made Free* (London, 1977), pp. 96–134; E.J. Hobsbawm, *Primitive Rebels* (New York, 1965), pp. 57–107; Keith Thomas, *Religion and the Decline of Magic* (Harmondsworth, Eng., 1973), pp. 166–71. Cf. Robert Lerner, "Medieval Prophecy and Religious Dissent," *P&P* 72 (1976), who stresses the continuity of chiliasm in the Middle Ages.

healing powers, or secret marks of the prophet. These facts suggest why the content of millenarian ideology was largely independent of the context of its appearance.

Very different dynamics of popular dissent appeared in the revolutionary movements that arose in England in the seventeenth century and in France in the eighteenth. Leadership now depended less on the quasi-sacral qualities perceived in the spokesman for dissent than on adherence to and promotion of important tenets of a belief system shared by a mass following. More democratic patterns of dissent emerge when leadership is legitimated no longer by personal charisma but by what Max Weber called the charisma of reason.[11]

Symptomatic of this new style of dissent is the central place of debates on the subject of popular participation in political and religious life during the early years of the English Civil War. Control over local church affairs "more directly, and perhaps more deeply, concerned the common people, and also the gentry" than the more general question of the merits of episcopacy. Equally pressing were the propriety and implications both of Parliament's appeals to public opinion in protestations and remonstrances and of popular petitions presented to Parliament. An astonished parliamentarian, Sir Edward Dering, complained, "I did not dream that we should remonstrate downward, tell stories to the people, and talk of the King as a third person."[12]

11. Weber, *Economy and Society*, pp. 266–67: "The basically authoritarian principle of charismatic legitimation may be subject to an anti-authoritarian interpretation, for the validity of charismatic authority rests entirely on recognition by the ruled, on 'proof' before their eyes . . . But when the charismatic organization undergoes progressive rationalization, it is readily possible that, instead of recognition being treated as a consequence of legitimacy, it is treated as the basis of legitimacy." See also Guenther Roth, "Charisma and the Counterculture," in Guenther Roth and Wolfgang Schluchter, *Max Weber's Vision of History* (Berkeley and Los Angeles, 1979), p. 134.

12. Brian Manning, "Puritanism and Democracy, 1640–1642," in Donald Pennington and Keith Thomas, eds., *Puritans and Revolutionaries: Essays in Seventeenth-Century History Presented to Christopher Hill* (Oxford, 1978), p. 140; Christopher Hill, *Change and Continuity in 17th-Century England* (London, 1974), p. 193. See also Brian Manning, *The English People and the English Revolution, 1640–1649* (London, 1976). Cf. the views of some historians who minimize the democratic implications of popular protests in the English Revolution, regarding them instead as products of aristocratic intrigue, instigation, and patronage, e.g., Alan Everitt, *The Community of Kent and the Great Rebellion, 1640–1660* (Leicester, 1966), pp. 61, 86–87, 95–107; James Farnell, "The Social and Intellectual Basis of London's Role in the English Civil Wars," *Journal of Modern History* 49 (1977), pp. 654–55, 659. Strong objections to these views have been voiced by Christopher Hill, "Parliament and People in Seventeenth-Century England," *P&P* 92 (1981); David Underdown, "Community and Class: Theories of Local Politics in the English Revolution," in Barbara C. Malament, ed., *After the Reformation: Essays in Honor of J.H. Hexter* (Philadelphia, 1980).

Another sign of this new style of dissent is the well-known phenomenon of polarization and radicalization within the revolutionary movement. New intellectual conditions of dissent make divergent interpretations of a shared ideology a political factor of central importance in determining inner developments in revolutionary movements. In the English and French revolutions, expressions of grievance were ideological; they referred to a universally valid set of beliefs, such as natural-law doctrines of native birthrights or of the rights of man. Grievances were justified and generalized by dissident elites who cited universalistic tenets that seemed applicable to all, regardless of social and economic divisions. However, dissemination of the ideology by the printed word, its popular appeal, and the different interest situations of elite and mass components of the revolutionary movement combined to produce different interpretations of the ideology.

The doctrine of natural rights that justified opposition to Charles I and Louis XVI permeated rank-and-file support as it filtered through the popular press, through newspapers such as *Mercurius Britannicus* and *L'Ami du Peuple*, and through printed copies of speeches and sermons by opposition MPs and Puritan preachers. Literate activists in the New Model Army and among the sans-culottes read these publications to less literate comrades in taverns and on street corners. In the Long Parliament, natural law justified rule by the propertied classes; but for Levellers and agitators in the New Model Army, "every man born in England cannot, ought not, neither by the Law of God nor the Law of Nature . . . be exempted from the choice of those who are to make laws for him." In France, moderate Republicans cited natural law to defend laissez-faire; but for the sans-culottes, natural law meant *l'égalité des jouissances* and the *maximum général*.[13]

These divergent interpretations of highly abstract beliefs point to new patterns of dissent made possible by popular access to a mobilizing ideology. Intellectual dependency no longer characterizes the rank-and-file supporters of dissident positions, for they can now adopt critical views of the policies and pronouncements of their ostensible leaders. The process of political polarization that is so familiar a feature of modern revolutionary movements is a direct consequence of this development. In the absence of the printing press and of modest levels of popular literacy, this type of popular initiative in dissent is literally unthinkable.

The Reformation reflected the first widespread victory of popular dis-

---

13. For France, see W. Markov and A. Soboul, eds., *Die Sansculotten von Paris: Dokumente zur Geschichte der Volksbewegung 1793–1794* (Berlin, 1957), pp. 104, 138, 158; Rude, *The Crowd in the French Revolution*, pp. 196–99, 207–209, 228; Souboul, *Les sans-culottes parisiens*, pp. 458, 474, 670–72. For England, see A.S.P. Woodhouse,

sent.[14] To go beyond the unsuccessful anticipations of dissent in medieval heresies, lay initiatives in religious life had to await the invention of printing and the consequent growth of popular literacy. This much seems clear enough in the abstract. What remains to be seen is how a popular press and a broad distribution of literacy in sixteenth-century England facilitated the kinds of intellectual initiatives that characterized popular dissent in the early years of the Reformation.

Literacy, Printing, and Dissent in England

It is difficult to disentangle the cultural, economic, and technical dimensions of the revolution wrought by the printing press. The broad cultural implications of printing became apparent in Germany between 1520 and 1525, during the so-called "pamphlet war." Opponents and proponents of Lutheran reform flooded the market with cheaply printed broadsides and pamphlets that sought to enlist popular support for Catholicism or for the new religion. The economic implications must have been equally evident, because "when the clergy stopped writing these tracts the bottom dropped out for the printers."[15] This episode illustrates some of the complex interconnections between the capitalist basis of printing, lay literacy and religious debate in the Reformation.

For the printing industry to realize its technical ability to mass-produce relatively inexpensive books, there had to be a stable market for them, constituted by a literate public. From its inception, printing was a business that did not depend, like manuscript production, on individual patrons or institutional sponsors but on a large, anonymous audience. Evidence of the size of this lay audience throughout early modern Europe is offered by the rapid growth of printing, which produced 35,000 editions of different works by the year 1500 and an additional 150,000 to 200,000

---

ed., *Puritanism and Liberty: Being a Record of the Army Debates, 1647–9* (London, 1938), p. 56, and see pp. 24–28, 52–95; Hill, *The World Turned Upside Down*, pp. 18–20, 48.

14. An orthodox Marxist version of this thesis portrays the German Reformation and the Peasants' War as an "early bourgeois revolution" and stresses their unity by depicting the latter as a radical consequence of the former. See Max Steinmetz, "Der geschichtliche Platz des deutschen Bauernkrieges," *Zeitschrift für Geschichtswissenschaft* 23 (1975), pp. 254–55; Günter Vogler, "Revolutionäre Bewegung und frühbürgerliche Revolution," ibid. 22 (1974), passim. For two collections of articles on this Marxist interpretation of the Reformation see Rainer Wohlfeil, ed., *Reformation oder frühbürgerliche Revolution?* (Munich, 1972) and *Der Bauernkrieg, 1524–26* (Munich, 1975).

15. Miriam Chrisman, "From Polemic to Propaganda: The Development of Mass Persuasion in the Late Sixteenth Century," *AfR* 73 (1982), p. 181.

editions—i.e., about 75,000,000 to 100,000,000 books—by 1600. A recent estimate places the number of clandestine copies of Tyndale's New Testament in circulation in England at 64,000 by the year 1530 (when the total population was about three and a half million). These figures not only provide clues about the size of the literate lay audience but also point to new conditions governing cultural production, to a laicization of culture. By the time printing established itself as the major vehicle for the transmission of knowledge, "intellectual impetus and economic power had long since become a property of the laity."[16]

It was the capitalist basis of printing that shifted intellectual impetus to the laity in print culture. To gain and maintain competitive advantages, printers produced relatively inexpensive works in addition to costly folio volumes destined for an educated elite. Competitive pressures held down book prices in England, which were stable from 1560 to the Civil War. In addition to producing cheaply printed works, printers also had to anticipate lay interests. These two facets of publishing strongly reinforced each other. Competitive pressures were most pronounced in the area where lay interest was keenest: in religion. In Germany, a printed version of Luther's vernacular Bible first appeared in 1522, and, over the next two years, fourteen authorized and sixty-six pirated editions were published. Tyndale experienced the same problem when publishing his clandestine version of the English Bible. Later, after Cromwell secured approval for an English Bible, the appointed publisher complained to the Privy Council of being undersold by unauthorized rivals.[17] Apparently, lucrative opportunities existed for publishers who would cater to popular tastes in religion.

More direct evidence exists on the extent of popular literacy in En-

16.   Lucien Febvre and H.J. Martin, *L'Apparition du Livre* (Paris, 1958), pp. 377, 396–97; J.F. Davis, "Lollardy and the Reformation in England," *AfR* 73 (1982), p. 230; Mandrou, *Des humanistes aux hommes de science*, pp. 42–51; Steinberg, *Five Hundred Years of Printing*, pp. 43–46. Cf. H.S. Bennett, *English Books & Readers, 1475–1557* (Cambridge, 1952), pp. 43–50, who stresses the continuing importance of patronage in the early printing industry.

17.   *L&P*, XII, pt. 2, p. 489; Louis A. Schuster et al., eds., *The Complete Works of St. Thomas More* (New Haven, 1973), VIII. 1090; Steinberg, *Five Hundred Years of Printing*, pp. 142–44, 202.

Tyndale's New Testament sold for about three shillings in England. Lollards had earlier paid from twenty to fifty-five shillings for manuscript editions of vernacular New Testaments, roughly the price of a horse in the period 1450–1500. Multiple editions of inexpensively printed bibles appear yearly after 1575. See Peter Bowden, "Statistical Appendix," in Joan Thirsk, ed., *The Agrarian History of England and Wales, 1500–1640* (Cambridge, 1967), p. 869; *Foxe*, III. 597, IV. 237; Alfred Pollard, *Records of the English Bible* (Folkstone, 1974), pp. 6, 44.

gland. Like other countries where the popular Reformation gained a foothold, late Tudor and early Stuart England could boast of a substantial minority of inhabitants who could read. Contemporary estimates range from Sir Thomas More's better than half to Stephen Gardiner's "not the hundredth part of the realm." We do know that from 17 percent to 38 percent of the signatories to the 1642 protestation oath in each parish were able to sign their names. Lawrence Stone estimates that by the third quarter of the seventeenth century nearly 40 percent of adult males could read, a high watermark not equaled again for some two centuries.[18] David Cressy's important study documents the decline of illiteracy in the century before the Civil War. To acquire semiliteracy—the ability to read but not write—was not difficult during this era. There were many opportunities to do so, far more than are indicated by the records of endowed grammar schools and universities. Intermittent schooling often occurred in villages; the teachers were frequently clerics without benefices. At this level the ability to read varied by social class and, to a lesser extent, by region.[19]

Economic activities created a demand for reading and writing. Contracts, bonds of debt, and other simple financial instruments were important aspects of rural as well as urban life, and they required an ability to read them. A contemporary writer defended the rudimentary education available in villages, observing that "this is all we go to school for: to read common prayers at church; and set down common prices at markets; write a letter and make a bond; set down the day of our births, our marriage day; and make our wills when we are sick . . . these are the chief matters that we meddle with."[20]

Further evidence exists on the social dimensions of the growth of popu-

18. Joy Adams, "The Extent of Literacy in England in the Fifteenth and Sixteenth Centuries," *Transactions of the Bibliographic Society* 2d ser. 10 (1929); Spufford, *Contrasting Communities*, pp. 183–91, 207; Lawrence Stone, "Literacy and Education in England 1640–1900," *P&P* 42 (1969), pp. 100–101, 125; Raymond Williams, *The Long Revolution* (New York, 1961), p. 157.

19. David Cressy, *Literacy and the Social Order* (Cambridge, 1980). Conclusions similar to Cressy's also emerge from several local studies, e.g., Jay P. Anglin, "The Expansion of Literacy: Opportunities for the Study of the Three Rs in the London Diocese of Elizabeth I," *Guildhall Studies in London History* 4 (1980); Peter Clark, "'The Ramoth-Gilead of the Good': Urban Change and Political Radicalism at Gloucester 1540–1640," in Peter Clark et al., eds., *The English Commonwealth, 1547–1640* (New York, 1979), pp. 182–83; D.M. Palliser, *Tudor York* (Oxford, 1979), pp. 173–74; Keith Wrightson and David Levine, *Poverty and Piety in an English Village: Terling, 1525–1700* (New York, 1979), pp. 146–51.

20. Mildred Cambell, *The English Yeoman under Elizabeth and the Early Stuarts* (London, 1967), p. 265, and see also pp. 266, 378, 418; Peter Clark, *English Provincial Society from the Reformation to the Revolution* (Hassocks, Eng., 1977), p. 188; Spufford, *Contrasting Communities*, pp. 80, 212; Wrightson and Levine, *Poverty and Piety*, pp.

lar literacy in early modern England. We can intuit the social aspects of the audience for whom popular authors thought they wrote, and we can look at contemporary reaction to the growth of a popular market for books. From the sheer numbers of religious works—40 percent of all books published in this era—we can infer certain characteristics of their readers. About a thousand editions of vernacular sermons by English and foreign divines appeared in Elizabeth's reign; most of these were inexpensive quartos.[21]

In addition to sermons, there appeared many catechisms, doctrinal treatises, and translations of foreign religious works, constituting a large vernacular literature clearly intended for a popular audience. Anthony Gilby translated Beza's work on the psalms of David for his "unlearned countrymen"; he was delighted by the thought that "now even the simplest poor man for a small piece of money may by diligent reading in this book . . . attain to a better understanding of these holy psalms of David than in old time . . . the great learned men were able by the perusing of many of the great doctors of the Church." Many other sixteenth-century translations of works by foreign authors, such as Erasmus, Luther, and Calvin, were undertaken, according to their translators, for "unlearned readers," for "the gross and rude multitude as . . . [for] curates and teachers," and these translators "shaped and ordered" their translations "as might be most meet and agreeing to the capacity of those that are simple."[22]

Translators and paraphrasers of scripture omitted difficult passages that might be "stumbling blocks" to "simple" readers. They also instructed them to read the work in order, diligently, reviewing the sentences more than once, as did the translator of Luther's commentary on Paul's Epistle to the Galatians, a work whose English title concludes: *"now out of Latine faithfully translated into English for the unlearned."* Frequently, the presumed reader was termed "illiterate" or "unlearned," but these terms, like "rude," "simple," or "gross," indicate not illiteracy but lack of a university education and an inability to read Latin and foreign languages. A biblical concordance published in 1550 begins with a table "expressing by plain letters the number of the figures contained in this book," the assumption being that its readers are familiar with roman but not arabic

151–52. See also Thomas Laqueur, "The Cultural Origins of Popular Literacy in England, 1500–1850," *Oxford Review of Education* 2 (1976).

21. H.S. Bennett, *English Books & Readers, 1558–1603* (Cambridge, 1965), pp. 145, 148–49, 269.

22. Theodore Beza, *The Psalmes of David* (1580), sig. 6; Anon., *A playne and godly exposytion of the commune Crede* (1533), Sig. A2ʳ; Desiderius Erasmus, *Apophthegmes* (1542), Sigs. *2ᵛ-3ʳ, *The first tome or volume of the Paraphrase of Erasmus* (1548), Sigs. B4ʳ, B6ʳ.

numerals. Still, these allusions to the rudimentary literacy of this popular
audience should not lead us to minimize its abilities or ambitions in reading religious material. Luther's commentary, cited above, though intended for "simple" readers, ran to 560 folio pages![23] Sometimes more
specific social attributes of this audience are mentioned. A typical one occurs in the following title: *The Seconde parte of the Domesticall or house-
holde Sermons, for a godly householder, to his children and familie.* The audience alluded to by the term "householder" corresponds rather closely to
the "industrious sort of people," i.e., to the social stratum in between the
wealthier gentry and nobility and the ranks of husbandmen, servants, and
laborers.[24] Many religious works in sixteenth-century England were
produced for this audience, whose abilities bordered on semiliteracy.

Popular access to printed works generated great alarm, for a new literary culture developed as authors and printers attempted to cater to a market composed of commoners generally lacking a grammar-school and university education. The stimulus provided by the printing industry to a
popular literary culture affected many aspects of cultural production and
not just religion. Defenders of high cultural standards heaped a chorus of
abuse on popular writers and had nothing but contempt for the common
reader. Poets were dismayed by the appetite of "ignorant dunces" and
"every dull mechanic" for ballads, and they, too, scorned such readers:

> Readers too common, and plentiful be;
> For readers
> they are that can read a,b,c.
> And utter their verdict on what they doe view,
> Though none of the Muses they yet ever knew.

The popular literary culture created by printing produced a predictable
backlash which attached a stigma to authorship of books, a stigma sufficiently troublesome to prompt another poet to request:

> Let not each Pesant, each Mecannick Asse,
> That neer knew further than his Horn-booke crosse,

23. William Baldwin, *The Canticles or Balades of Salomon* (1549), Sig. A1ᵛ; Martin
Luther, *A Commentarie of M. Doctor Luther Upon The Epistle of S. Paul* (1575), Sigs. *5ʳ,
*6ʳ; John Marbeck, *A Concordance* (1550), Sig. A5ʳ. For another example of a long tome
intended for simple readers, see H.S. Bennett, *Books & Readers, to 1640* (Cambridge,
1970), p. 96.

24. Christopher Hill, *Society and Puritanism in Pre-Revolutionary England* (New York,
1967), pp. 447, 456, 470–71, 475; Louis B. Wright, *Middle-Class Culture in Elizabethan England* (London, 1964), pp. 237–38, 260–61. The title is from the English
version of a book by Hegendorf (1549). For another example, see Wrightson and Levine,
Poverty and Piety, p. 153.

> Each ravin-Rusticke: each illiterate Gull:
> Buy of my Poesie, by pocket full.[25]

These are instructive complaints, for they show that a semiliterate culture among commoners provided a popular and even somewhat critical audience for printed materials. Ignorance of the "muses" and a lack of all but the most rudimentary education were hardly barriers to the growth of a lay reading public. Later, the appearance of England's first newspapers, the corantos, costing about two pence, also prompted denunciation, because they catered to the presumption of the "vulgar" sort to be informed of foreign developments.[26]

The implications of printing for popular culture were most sharply drawn in religious matters. At issue was not merely lay access to religious writings but popular access to and knowledge of the Bible. For lay religious literacy itself was neither new nor necessarily greeted with clerical hostility. Among educated elites, a favorable climate existed for the reception of vernacular Bibles. Erasmian teachings had created in aristocratic circles an intellectual atmosphere supportive of early Protestant reform. Recent research dispels the belief that state policies on religion under Henry VIII were merely so many ecclesiastical expediences dictated by royal politics. Under Thomas Cromwell such policies followed a steadier course than the vagaries of politics; they followed the *philosophia Christi* and received support from elite groups committed to the ideals of humanist reform. A renewed emphasis on the lay role in religion, even the vision of a church dominated by the laity, was a central theme of this reform, along with a Pauline emphasis on inner religion and a decided lack of concern with the sacramental aspects of worship.[27]

Reform also found ready support in the lower and middle reaches of lay society. Here also there was an interest in greater lay participation in religion, expressed by a desire for access to vernacular Bibles. But this desire merged with sentiments that were either absent or more moderately expressed in elite circles: anticlericalism. Religious edification *and* a virulent anticlericalism were prominent features of popular dissent at the onset of the Reformation.

Popular literacy is intimately linked in several ways to this popular dissent. Obviously, a desire to read the Bible became more plausible in the

---

25. Richard Speght, *Mortalities Memorandum* (1621), Sig. A3ᵛ; Wright, *Middle-Class Culture*, p. 97, and see also pp. 91–99.

26. Joseph Frank, *The Beginnings of the English Newspaper* (Cambridge, Mass., 1961), pp. 12, 276–77.

27. G.R. Elton, *Reform and Renewal* (Cambridge, 1973), pp. 9–37, and "Thomas Cromwell Redivivus," *AfR* 68 (1977); McConica, *English Humanists and Reformation Politics*, pp. 11–12, 23, 199.

context of a flourishing literary culture. Moreover, opposition to this development by clerics put them in a position of appearing to oppose lay
enlightenment. For these reasons the printing revolution facilitated a style
of popular dissent that was characterized by anticlericalism and a pro-
found commitment to edification.

But printing and popular literacy cannot by themselves account for the
broad appeal of this popular dissent. They can facilitate dissent, but they
do not supply the motive for it. Indeed, in the absence of other factors,
the appearance of printing and popular literacy can leave intact the
conventional demarcations between a priestly class, possessing esoteric
knowledge, and a largely illiterate laity. Where printing is an adjunct to
preexisting modes of oral instruction, highly restricted forms of literacy
often emerge.[28] Other factors determine whether printing is to become an
enabling factor in the development of popular dissent. One of these other
factors concerns the cultural processes that supply an intellectual setting
supportive of the critical skepticism of dissent.

Rationality

Rationalization refers to three distinct but related tendencies in intellectual systems. It encourages the systematic organization of ideas, calculation in selecting efficient means to attain goals, both ideal and material,
and comprehension of the world through the use of abstract concepts.[29] In
sixteenth-century England these tendencies were sufficiently advanced to
support popular dissent. In discussing them, however, it is important not
to conflate rationalization and secularization in this era. The dissent initially generated by intellectual rationalization was essentially religious in
nature. The eclipse of theological world views by secular ones occurred at
a later time, after the rise of Baconian science, deism, and natural religion. Earlier there was no simple relationship between rationalization and
secularization. The former developed within belief systems whose theo-

28. Goody explores the idea of restricted literacy in "Restricted Literacy in Northern
Ghana," in Goody, ed., *Literacy in Traditional Societies*, pp. 199–264. Kathleen Gough
provides an interesting example of this in "Literacy in Kerala," ibid., p. 154. Eisenstein,
Printing Press, pp. 77–78, makes a related point in her discussion of the "transformation
of occult and esoteric scribal lore after the advent of printing." She notes that "one should
not think only about new forms of enlightenment when considering the effects of printing
on scholarship. New forms of mystification were encouraged as well." See also Davis, *Society and Culture in Early Modern France*, pp. 224–25.

29. Max Weber, "The Social Psychology of the World Religions," in H.H. Gerth and
C.W. Mills, eds.. *From Max Weber* (New York, 1958), pp. 293–94.

logical presuppositions remained largely intact. Thus, a paradoxical consequence of intellectual rationalization in the Reformation was its simultaneous accentuation of ethical religiosity and secular attitudes.[30]

Rationalization led away from unitary world views, from magical outlooks in which empirical and spiritual realities, the mundane and supernatural, mingled indiscriminately. Instead, the two became sharply separated in dualistic world views that are more abstract in nature and comprehensive in scope. Intellectual rationalization transformed the limited vision of magically infused religion[31] in medieval Catholicism, whose unitary world view attended principally to mundane matters—to specific problems such as childbirth, crop failure, drought, or illness—and thereby limited its scope.

Rationality and ethical religiosity advanced together in the transition from unitary to dualistic world views, with their characteristic qualities of iconoclasm, suspicion of ritual, and denunciation of magic as the devil's sorcery. This is an advance in rationality because it portrayed the universe "as a cosmos governed by impersonal rules." Capricious gods gave way to a divine providence conceived as a first cause or prime mover of a lawful world. Acknowledgment of a lawlike order created by a God of, but not in, this world disenchanted empirical reality. It discounted the existence of spiritual entities previously thought to be corporeally present in animals, plants, inanimate objects, and people. It militated against efforts to manipulate sacred forces through magic, demanding instead obedience to a divine will revealed in the ethical postulates of an abstract system of beliefs. No longer were evil, suffering, and life-threatening situations associated with the weakness or caprice of spiritual entities. They became the consequence of human weakness and sin, of human violation of divinely ordained ethics. In place of magical practices, employed to acquire specific commodities, there was the ethical pursuit of salvation, which followed prescribed courses of action, defined in accordance with a generalized system of beliefs. Consequently, religious life became intellectualized at the expense of the ritual dimensions of worship. As its conceptual structure became more systematic, integrated, and internally consistent, the ritualistic validation of beliefs became less important as a commitment mecha-

30. See Bryan R. Wilson, *Magic and the Millennium* (New York, 1973), p. 497. Eisenstein, *Printing Press*, pp. 79, 130, discusses "contradictory developments" promoted by printing, namely, the "intensification of religiosity and secularism."

31. According to Thomas, *Religion and the Decline of Magic*, pp. 761–62, magic "never offered a comprehensive view of the world . . . It was a collection of miscellaneous recipes, not a comprehensive body of doctrine." Durkheim also made this distinction between religion and magic in his *The Elementary Forms of the Religious Life* (London, 1915), pp. 44–47.

nism. Religion could be understood only with reference to ethical norms, based on an abstract system of generalized beliefs.[32]

Initially, in the medieval period, this process did not efface all of the magical aspects of Christianity. Intellectual rationalization, and its implications for dualist world views, left its mark on the institutional church and on official dogma long before it penetrated to, and transformed, the mental attitudes of the laity. It merely reserved all efforts to manipulate sacred forces to the institutional church, which was thus set off as an enchanted preserve in an otherwise profane world. The rational core implicit in Christian religion, its ethical religiosity, barely extended to the medieval laity.[33] Institutionally sanctioned activities by clerics sought goals formerly attended to by magic. Auricular confession and penance, indulgences, perambulations, veneration of saints, cults of images and relics—these efforts to bend divine will to send a good crop or recovery from illness were sublimated forms of magic.

In the Reformation, however, intellectual rationalization did extend to lay attitudes toward religion. Rationalization of lay beliefs led to ethical religiosity in place of older forms of worship that were encrusted with magical practices. Important features of popular dissent at the onset of the Reformation and later displayed high levels of rationality: a strong perception of a lawlike cosmos, reflecting divine providence; a dualist vision of heaven and earth, with the disenchantment of the latter; and a desire to gain heaven by following a virtuous course of conduct on earth.

The influence of rationalization on lay beliefs doomed the medieval forms of popular worship and the overall conception of the church as an enchanted preserve. No longer could the church and its official emissaries presume to do that which, previously, it had forbidden all other agencies to do: manipulate divine powers. This led to the disenchantment of the church itself and then to the collapse of the intellectual foundations of a religion that elevated clerics above laymen in a sacral sense. Aspects of worship involving mediation of the priesthood became incompatible with pastoral implications to be drawn from a rationalized system of ethical beliefs. In view of these implications, clerical claims to mediate spiritual powers appeared as an intolerable threat to the laity.

The heightened rational content of lay dissent explains not only why

32. James T. Borhek and Richard F. Curtis, *A Sociology of Belief* (New York, 1975), p. 27; Weber, "Social Psychology of the World Religions," p. 282, and *Economy and Society*, pp. 422–39. See also Robert N. Bellah, *Beyond Belief* (New York, 1976), pp. 32–37; Wolfgang Schluchter, "The Paradox of Rationalization," in Roth and Schluchter, *Max Weber's Vision of History*, pp. 35–45.

33. See Weber, "Social Psychology of World Religions," p. 273: "The premises of the religions of salvation at first remained tied to ritualist rather than to ethical preoccupations."

"magic was eradicated even in the sublimated form of sacraments and symbols" but also why dissent developed at the expense of clerical interests. Weber's remarks on the relationship between popular religion, with its magical qualities, and the patrimonial bureaucracy in China apply with equal force to the threat confronting ecclesiastical hierarchies in the age of the Reformation: "Any rationalization of popular beliefs would inevitably have constituted an independent power opposed to officialdom."[34] Just as the initial rationalization of belief systems established the autonomy of the church in western Europe, so its later development detached the spiritual interests of the laity from those of the institutional church and its priestly orders. In the following section I provide evidence on intellectual rationality in early popular dissent and discuss the intimate links between its attachment to edification and its anticlericalism.

Anticlericalism and Critical Skepticism

Popular anticlericalism had many sources, including conflicts of a purely economic nature between clerics and laymen; social resentment; and crude forms of materialist skepticism.[35] The materialist skepticism encouraged by intellectual rationalization made anticlericalism a prominent part of popular dissent. This anticlericalism consisted of diverse sentiments with roots in fifteenth- and sixteenth-century Lollardy. By joining these sentiments to the Protestant cause, clerical efforts to gather popular support for the new religion were partly assured of success. But this was a two-edged sword. Anticlerical sentiment was certainly channeled against Rome by Protestant publication of vernacular Bibles, but this also helped to change heretical eddies and currents among isolated groups into waves of lay insurgency against priestly authority.

Opposition by ecclesiastical officials to vernacular Bibles further ensured that anticlericalism would figure prominently in the popular Reformation. In effect, clerics appeared to be standing between forward-looking elements of the laity and religious edification. And, ironically,

34. Max Weber, *The Religion of China* (Glencoe, Ill., 1951), pp. 144, 226; and see also Weber, *Economy and Society*, p. 447.

35. Clark, *English Provincial Society*, pp. 28–29; Christopher Hill, *Economic Problems of the Church: From Archbishop Whitgift to the Long Parliament* (Oxford, 1956); J.F. Maclers, "Popular Anticlericalism in the Puritan Revolution," *Journal of the History of Ideas* 17 (1956); Emma Mason, "The Role of the English Parishioner, 1100–1500," *JEH* 27 (1976). A.G. Dickens, *Lollards and Protestants in the Diocese of York, 1509–1558* (Oxford, 1959), p. 245, observes that Lollardy united with more worldly forms of anticlericalism and facilitated a favorable reception of early Protestant propaganda.

this was a great help to popular dissent. The church inadvertently provided concrete symbols for the highly abstract beliefs of the Lollards and early Protestants by making clerics the obstacles to lay religious edification. In the course of its conflicts with the ecclesiastical hierarchy, lay dissent appeared as enlightenment. Attacks on magical and ritualistic elements in worship and on the mediating roles of the clergy that were incompatible with dualistic outlooks found highly visible targets in the institutions of the mass and the sacral priesthood and in other aspects of traditional worship.

The advance of dissent over orthodoxy obtained forceful expression in a combination of anticlerical and skeptical sentiments. Polemics against the mass, in tracts such as *A new Dialogue Called the Enlightenment agaynst Mother Messe,* depict it as being tantamount to sorcery, as claiming a magical ability to "make fair weather & rain & heal all sickness." For lay dissidents, only one plausible conclusion could be drawn from the church's insistence that it, its buildings, burial grounds, ceremonies, and officials had sacral power: the conception of the church as an enchanted preserve was a cloak with which clerics concealed their covetousness for wealth and status. The rationality of dissent thus inclined it to skeptical views that were wholly compatible with anticlerical grievances fueled by strictly economic issues. When a fifteenth-century Lollard asserted that the burial of "a corpse in consecrated ground does the soul of the dead man no more good than if the corpse had been thrust into a bog," an anticlerical conclusion readily followed: "The solemnities of funerals were invented to provide fees for money-loving priests."[36]

Why else invent such solemnities if the mundane world, including its cemeteries, was disenchanted? Accordingly, Lollards denounced the priesthood because its members "falsely and cursedly deceive the people with their false mammetries and laws, to extort money from the simple folk." It is not difficult to see how Lollardy must have seemed to its adherents to be a rational liberation from the magical world views of "simple folk." Inquisitorial records contain Lollardy's confident dismissal of all priestly and ceremonial appurtenances of a church that sought to impress ordinary laymen with its sacral control over a divine order, thought to be corporeally present on earth. Auricular confession could serve only to "exalt the pride of priests"; "pilgrimages were nothing worth, saving to make the priests rich"; "priests ordained all holy days . . . to have offerings and tithes of the people"; and even the sacrament of the altar, derisively called

---

36. William Punt, *A new Dialogue called the Enlightenment agaynst Mother Messe* (1548), Sigs. A4ᵛ-A5ᵛ; Andrew Clark, ed., "Lincoln Diocese Documents, 1450–1544," *EETS* 1st ser. 149 (1914), p. 93.

"the baken God" by a grocer, was not immune to this reasoning. According to one Lollard, "It should be to the great honor of priests, that the bread really were changed into the body of Christ . . . thereby they get a little worldly and transitory honor."[37]

However, Lollard beliefs went beyond mere anticlericalism and attached positive importance to reading the Bible. Crudely skeptical sentiments are intertwined with a strong commitment to edification. When Lollards, such as the wife of a wheelwright, reasoned that,

> if every such sacrament were God, and the very body of Christ, there should be an infinite number of Gods, because that a thousand priests, and more, do every day make a thousand such Gods, and afterwards eat them, and void them out again in places, where, if you will seek them, you may find many such Gods,

they were, in effect, arguing, as did a tailor in 1410, that any godly person "had as much power to do, as had the priest." Properly speaking, such power consisted in knowing and obeying the divine will revealed in scriptures and teaching others to do the same. To go beyond instruction and exhortation to mediation of divine power was considered illegitimate for both layman and cleric. Thus, a Lollard or Protestant woman in 1543 asserted not only that "her daughter could piss as good holy water as the priest make any," but also that "it cannot be read in Scripture that Our Lady should be in heaven."[38] Lay recourse to the Bible equipped Lollards with an unshakable assurance in their denial of orthodox practices.

Above all else, Lollardy was a literate religion whose practice involved circulating and reading prohibited texts, chiefly the Gospels. The doctrinal edifice of Lollardy rested on this literary foundation and provided room for lay initiative with its Pauline concern with inner faith and its belief in the priesthood of all believers. The importance of literacy in Lollardy was known to church officials, whose efforts to detect and repress it were informed by the long-standing association in late medieval thought between vernacular books and lay dissent.[39] Interrogations of suspected Lollards focus on possession or use of English books. Reports of a Nor-

---

37. *Foxe*, III. 175, 205, 595, IV. 177, and see also III. 185 and IV. 135; Norman P. Tanner, ed., "Heresy Trials in the Diocese of Norwich, 1428–31," *CS* 4th ser. 20 (1973), p. 153. See also Simon Fish, *A Supplication for the Beggers* (1529) J. Meadows Cowper, ed., *EETS* extra ser. 13 (1871), p. 10.

38. *Foxe*, III. 237, 594; *L&P*, XVIII, pt. 2, p. 307.

39. Herbert Grundmann, "Ketzerverhöre des Spätmittelalters als quellenkritisches Problem," *Deutsches Archiv für Erforschung des Mittelalters* 21 (1965), pp. 555–57, *Religiöse Bewegungen im Mittelalter* (Hildesheim, 1961), pp. 447–48.

wich man who, in 1424, "keeps schools of Lollardy in the English
tongue" and receives from "a certain parchment maker . . . all the books
containing that doctrine from London," attest to the accuracy of this perception. So does the remark of a London woman, accused in 1529 of publicly saying that a laborer "was very expert in the Gospels . . . and could
express and declare them, and the Paternoster in English, as well as any
priest." In prosecuting Lollards in 1528, the bishop of London discovered a bricklayer who "kept in his house a man named John to write the
Apocalypse in English, the expenses being born by . . . [a] grocer."[40]

Lollardy's commitment to edification fully harmonized with and further reinforced its anticlerical sentiments. In a slightly later era, this mixture of positive and negative sentiments would strongly characterize lay
Puritanism; it too evoked from its adherents a commitment to religious
edification and an almost instinctual revulsion against all forms of worship
that were incompatible with an edifying style of vernacular religion.

As a source of popular dissent, intellectual rationalization is clearly an
independent factor. Lollard attacks on clerical efforts to manipulate sacred
forces preceded the Reformation by a century and a half and preceded the
advent of printing in England by nearly a century. These facts, plus our
knowledge that Lollardy attached crucial importance to Bible-reading
when only manuscript versions were available, ought to caution us against
regarding the invention of printing as the chief factor in creating an audience receptive to highly rationalized beliefs.[41]

The familiar view of magic as a surrogate technology might suggest
that technological advances were responsible for the decline of magic and
the rise of ethical religiosity in Lollardy. Yet from Wyclif's work in the late
fourteenth century to the gradual merger of his early sixteenth-century
followers with the newer Protestant groups, there were no technological
advances that provided effective solutions to the kinds of life-threatening
problems—of childbirth, disease, crop failure, mental illness—that were
addressed by magical practices in the old religion.[42]

40. *Foxe*, III. 585, IV. 582; *L&P*, IV. 1788. See also Dickens, *Lollards and Protestants*, pp. 16–52; John Fines, "Heresy Trials in the Diocese of Coventry and Lichfield,
1511–1512," *JEH* 14 (1963), pp. 164–65; Ann Hudson, "Some Aspects of Lollard
Book Production," *SCH* 9 (1972), pp. 148–49; Tanner, "Heresy Trials in Norwich,"
p. 29; John A.F. Thomason, *The Later Lollards, 1414–1520* (Oxford, 1967), pp. 62,
242–43.

41. Eisenstein's discussion of the implications of printing for religious developments
sometimes overemphasizes this factor (*Printing Press*, pp. 353–55, 368, 370). See also
Margaret Aston, "Books and Beliefs in the Later Middle Ages," *Papers Presented to the
Past & Present Conference on Popular Religion* 7 July 1966; Febvre and Martin, *L'Apparition du Livre*, p. 433.

42. For more on this issue, see Thomas, *Religion and the Decline of Magic*, pp. 787,
794.

These considerations indicate why intellectual rationalization must be seen as an independent factor. Nonetheless, ideas require bearers, and intellectual trends persist when they receive support from other developments. The social groups who had been receptive to the Lollard heresy grew rapidly in the sixteenth century, and this fact, along with the printing revolution, explains why popular dissent was far more widespread in the Reformation than under Lollardy. Though Lollardy anticipated many crucial doctrinal tenets of Puritanism and much of its lay initiative, it remained an "abortive Reformation."[43] The subsequent success of Puritanism owed much to social-structural developments that created a lay audience with an affinity for ethical religiosity rather than magical religion.

Capitalism and the Civic Strata

Three questions must be answered in order to explain the existence of an audience receptive to highly rationalized belief systems. First, which socioeconomic groups provided major support for belief systems characterized by lay initiative? Second, what economic attributes of these groups account for this support? Third, did these groups grow in number and wealth during the era here under consideration? Answers to these questions show that the same social basis that provided popular support for Lollardy and Puritanism underwent rapid expansion during the century that began with the onset of the English Reformation and ended with the Civil War.

In the later Middle Ages, diverse heretical movements often had one aim in common: an attempt to make religious life more accessible to the laity. Of the major movements that foreshadowed Protestantism—the Lollards, the Taborites, and the Waldensians—only the last originated among the laity. The other two were the creation of clerics, but the survival of these heresies depended on obtaining popular support. To obtain this, heterodox doctrines—initially reflecting clerical concerns—changed in ways that made them more compatible with lay aspirations. As we have seen, these lay aspirations included a strong attachment to highly rationalized beliefs, which demanded considerable lay initiative and self-help in the pursuit of religious goals. They had a long historical association with what Weber called the civic strata: artisans, traders, and entrepreneurs. Descriptions of the social basis of Lollardy as "mobile elements in the lower and middle reaches of society" and of Puritans as the "industrious sort of people" also point to this association.[44] It may not be possible to

43. A.G. Dickens coined this phrase in his *The English Reformation* (London, 1964), p. 37.

44. On the social basis of Lollardy see J.F. Davis, "Lollard Survival and the Textile

define this social basis more precisely, given the complex class structure created by early capitalist development. More important than terminological precision is our understanding of the links between these social strata and highly rationalized beliefs, between vocation and rationality in early modern dissent.

To see these links, we must find elements of practical rationalism in the vocational activities of specific social strata. This practical rationalism provides specific points of attachment to highly rationalized beliefs. Thus it is not sufficient to suggest, as I have elsewhere,[45] that these intermediary social strata were bearers of dissent because they possessed sufficient socio-economic autonomy to be capable of some intellectual initiative and reflection. This refers to the intellectual independence facilitated by economic autonomy. It does not indicate why there existed a positive *affinity* between autonomy and rationalized beliefs. After all, subsistence agriculture provides considerable autonomy, yet, historically, agriculture is associated not with ethical religion but with magical outlooks.

A source of positive support for rationalized beliefs can be found in those social strata whose economic autonomy depends on their location in "price-making" markets. Weber's discussion in *Economy and Society* provides indispensable guidance on this point. He describes how economic independence based on market transactions cultivates a degree of practical rationalism in mental attitudes that greatly surpasses that found in simple agriculture. Practical rationalism involves calculation and an ethos of self-help, which were prerequisites for success in price-making markets.

Industry in the South-East of England," *SCH* 3 (1966); Dickens, *Lollards and Protestants*, pp. 24, 35; Fines, "Heresy Trials in Coventry and Lichfield," pp. 162–63. Christopher Hill has most thoroughly explored the "industrious sort of people" as the social basis of Puritanism in *Society and Puritanism*, pp. 133–34, 207–9, 235, 477–78, 499. See also Brian Manning, "Religion and Politics: The Godly People," in Brian Manning, ed., *Politics, Religion, and the English Civil War* (New York, 1973); R.C. Richardson, *Puritanism in North-West England: A Regional Study of the Diocese of Chester to 1642* (Manchester, 1972), pp. 7–15; David Underdown, *Somerset in the Civil War and Interregnum* (Hamden, Eng., 1973), p. 22. The absence of this economically independent stratum is held responsible for the slow advance of the Reformation in Sussex by Roger Manning, *Religion and Society in Elizabethan Sussex* (Leicester, 1969), p. 239.

On the social basis of early Huguenot dissent in different parts of France, see Philip Benedict, *Rouen during the Wars of Religion* (Cambridge, 1981), pp. 49, 73–81; Emmanuel Le Roy Ladurie, *Les Paysans de Languedoc* (Paris, 1966), p. 342, who writes: "Structure classique: on retrouve là une sorte d'éternelle sans-culotterie des villes traditionnelles, tantôt hérétique, tantôt révolutionnaire, au gré des siècles, mais toujours recrutée dans l'échoppe ou dans la boutique."

45. "Ideology and Organization in Puritanism," *European Journal of Sociology* 21 (1980), p. 86.

> The tendency towards a *practical* rationalism in conduct is common
> to all civic strata; it is conditioned by the nature of their way of life,
> which is greatly detached from economic bonds to nature. Their
> whole existence has been based upon technological or economic cal-
> culation and upon the mastery of nature and man, however primitive
> the means at their disposal. The technique of living handed down
> among them may, of course, be frozen in traditionalism . . . But pre-
> cisely for these, there has always existed the possibility—even though
> in greatly varying measure—of letting an ethical and rational regu-
> lation of life arise.[46]

Here is the vocational source of support for intellectual rationalization. In
addition to economic autonomy, the members of these intermediary strata
developed, through their everyday experience in markets, a practical rationalism that predisposed them to highly rational beliefs as well, and
hence to early modern dissent.

It is true that this affinity between vocation and rationality antedated
capitalist development in sixteenth-century England. The kinds of economic situations that fostered practical rationalism were no more unique
to capitalism than were market transactions. Dissent and highly rationalized belief structures appeared, as in Lollardy, well in advance of a large-
scale movement toward capitalism.[47] Yet to the extent that early capitalist
development reoriented economic activities to production for a market, it
also unleashed critical and dissenting outlooks from their previous con-
fines in small artisan communities. It did so precisely because it produced
a broad stratum whose attributes of economic autonomy and practical rationalism were similar to those of the older artisan communities. Early
capitalism thus fostered popular dissent by extending the conditions of an
urban, artisan way of life to the countryside, where the bulk of England's
population resided. This not only stimulated urban economies but also
facilitated the flow of ideas between London and the far corners of
England.[48]

46. Weber, "Social Psychology of World Religions," p. 284, and see his *Economy and
Society*, pp. 479, 482–84. For a discussion of differences between price-making and more
primitive markets in economic history, see Walter Neale, "The Market in Theory and
History," in Karl Polanyi et al., eds., *Trade and Market in the Early Empires* (New York,
1957).

47. See Thomas, *Religion and the Decline of Magic*, p. 794: "We do not know how the
Lollards were able to find the self-reliance necessary to make the break with Church magic
of the past. The most plausible explanation seems to be that their spirit of sturdy self-help
reflected that of their occupations. Few of these early heretics were simple agriculturalists
dependent on the uncontrollable forces of nature. In the fifteenth century most of them
were artisans."

48. On London's economic importance for the rest of England, see F.J. Fisher, "The

In the sixteenth century, regional and national markets rapidly expanded, along with many opportunities for individuals to become either self-employed or small employers in the countryside as well as in towns. The result was a broad basis of support for capitalist development. What made this possible was the fact that commercial impulses historically associated with towns had penetrated and begun to transform the countryside in response to demographic pressures associated with a 75 percent increase in population in the century and a half prior to the Civil War.[49] Evidence of these developments exists in the transformation of farming in response to expanding regional and national markets. A new division between specialized forms of agriculture followed and further reinforced commercial impulses in the countryside. That farming regions tended to specialize in growing crops or in raising livestock was hardly new. But in the sixteenth century this specialization between arable and pastoral farming achieved not merely local but national significance for economic affairs.

Divisions between arable and pastoral farming began to follow new lines laid down by stable markets for certain kinds of produce. In the sixteenth century, some regions, better suited to pastoral farming, converted from grain production; a traditional balance between arable and pastoral activities was upset in others; and some well-established pastoral areas further specialized in dairy products.[50] This specialization depended on the

Development of the London Food Market," *EcHR* (1935). For a modification of Fisher's argument, see Alan Everitt, "The Marketing of Agricultural Produce," in Thirsk, ed., *Agrarian History of England and Wales*, pp. 515–16. On the intellectual influence of London on the countryside, see Christopher Hill, *Change and Continuity*, pp. 3–77.

49. A seminal article on this is by Joan Thirsk, "Industries in the Countryside," in F.J. Fisher, ed., *Essays in the Economic and Social History of Tudor and Stuart England* (Cambridge, 1961). See also John Merrington, "Town and Country in the Transition to Capitalism," in Rodney Hilton, ed., *The Transition from Feudalism to Capitalism* (London, 1976). Two historians emphasize that the influence of demographic growth was mediated by developments in markets and property relations; see Robert Brenner, "Agrarian Class Structure and Economic Development in Pre-Industrial Europe," *P&P* 70 (1976), and "The Agrarian Roots of European Capitalism," *P&P* 97 (1982); Victor Skipp, *Crisis and Development: An Ecological Study of the Forest of Arden, 1570–1674* (Cambridge, 1978), p. 65.

50. David Hey, *An English Rural Community: Myddle under the Tudors and Stuarts* (Leicester, 1974), pp. 30, 57, 67; D. Rodden, "Field Systems of the Chiltern Hills," in Alan R.H. Baker and Robin A. Butler, eds., *Studies of Field Systems in the British Isles* (Cambridge, 1973), p. 364; V.H.T. Skipp, "Economic and Social Change in the Forest of Arden, 1530–1649," *AHR* 18 (1970) suppl., p. 110; R.B. Smith, *Land and Politics in the England of Henry VIII* (Oxford, 1970), p. 19; Thirsk, "Farming Regions of England," in *Agrarian History of England and Wales*, pp. 69, 86, 94, 110, 211; E.M. Yates, "Enclosure and the Rise of Grassland Farming in Staffordshire," *North Staffordshire Journal of Field Studies* 14 (1974), pp. 55–58.

availability of marketed grain, grown elsewhere.[51] Farmers in arable regions supplied this by increasingly consolidating their landholdings in order to produce a marketable surplus. Severe population pressure in arable regions, due to this disincentive to partition holdings, found an outlet in cities and pastoral communities.[52]

In pastoral regions, commercialization of handicrafts accompanied these changes. Handicrafts were important sources of secondary employment for small farmers and for recent migrants into the unintensive farming systems of pastoral regions. Perhaps half to three-fourths of these farmers and migrants participated in handicraft work as weavers, metalworkers, leather-workers, potters, and so on.[53] Again, these activities were not new; rural handicrafts obviously antedated this era. But in the course of the sixteenth century they were commercialized: production transcended purely local needs, and merchandizing became separated from production. Handicrafts in the northern pastoral regions began to produce for the London market, and large numbers of craftsmen specialized in one line of products.[54] It may safely be assumed that this specialization occurred somewhat earlier in areas closer to London. In addition, commerce in the countryside led to entirely new rural industries. Integration of urban and rural markets changed the occupational characteristics of both markets; for the urban guilds borrowed techniques pioneered by rural handicraft workers, while the latter began to produce cheaper versions of guild products. New rural industries produced many luxury goods, originally supplied by guilds for the export trade, for an internal, lower-quality mass market.[55]

51. Everitt, "Marketing of Agricultural Produce," pp. 493–94, 499; M.R. Postgate, "Field Systems of East Anglia," in Baker and Butlin, eds., *Field Systems*, pp. 284–86; Skipp, *Crisis and Development*, p. 56; Joan Thirsk, "Seventeenth-Century Agriculture and Social Change," *AHR* 18 (1970) suppl., p. 168.

52. Alan R.H. Baker, "Field Systems in the Vale of Holmesdale," *AHR* 14 (1966), p. 22; Phillip A.G. Pettit, "The Royal Forests of Northamptonshire," *NRS* 23 (1968), pp. 142–43; Postgate, "Field Systems of East Anglia," pp. 287–88; Spufford, *Contrasting Communities*, pp. 49, 79, 90, 101, 118; Thirsk, "Farming Regions," pp. 58–59, 65, 92–96.

53. Alan Everitt, "Farm Labourers," in Thirsk, ed., *Agrarian History*, pp. 428–29; Pettit, "Royal Forests of Northamptonshire," pp. 161–62; Skipp, "Economic and Social Change," pp. 109–110; Thirsk, "Farming Regions," pp. 48, 58–59, 79.

54. L.A. Clarkson, "The Leather Crafts in Tudor and Stuart England," *AHR* 14 (1966), pp. 27–28; David Hey, "The Rural Metalworkers of the Sheffield Region," *Leicester University Occasional Papers* 2d ser. 5 (1972), pp. 8, 24; Norman Lowe, *The Lancashire Textile Industry in the Sixteenth Century* (Manchester, 1972), pp. 17, 20, 59; D.M. Woodward, "The Chester Leather Industry, 1558–1625," *Transactions of the Historical Society of Lancashire and Cheshire* 119 (1968), pp. 80–83.

55. D.C. Coleman, "An Innovation and Its Diffusion," *EcHR* 22 (1969), p. 421;

Sixteenth-century commerce in the countryside thus involved handicrafts as well as agriculture in higher levels of specialization. Internal markets in the countryside, along with trade between town and country, stimulated further specialization. This led to growth of a large and diverse class of economically autonomous producers, who took advantage of opportunities presented by regional and national markets. In addition to many members of the gentry, numerous persons in strata located just below them also seized entrepreneurial opportunities. During the "long" sixteenth century, from 1500 to 1640, yeoman farmers became wealthier, both absolutely and relatively, than husbandmen. Stratification between yeomen, husbandmen, and cottagers advanced as wealthier farmers benefited from a sixfold increase in prices through their ability to produce marketable surpluses, while poorer farmers suffered.[56] Individuals in rural industries also prospered, such as tradesmen and brewers. The accumulation of wealth by these intermediate social strata created a rapidly rising volume of testamentary business in the sixteenth century.[57]

The economic transactions engaged in by members of these strata followed the logic and procedure dictated by a market rationality. Strictly private transactions closely approximated a pure model of contractual interaction and grew up alongside the older structure of fairs and markets, which were still subject to official regulation. Between 1570 and 1640 there was a marked expansion in "that type of bargaining which was most nearly 'free,' or emancipated from official conrol," which used contracts to

---

S.D. Chapman, "The Genesis of the British Hosiery Industry," *Textile History* 3 (1972), pp. 11, 16, 40; G.F.R. Spenceley, "The Origins of the English Pillow Lace Industry," *AHR* 21 (1973), pp. 82–84; Joan Thirsk, "The Fantastical Folly of Fashion," in N.B. Harte and K.G. Ponting, eds., *Textile History and Economic Growth* (Manchester, 1973), pp. 52, 72.

56. Peter Bowen, "Agricultural Prices, Farm Profits, and Rents," in Thirsk, ed., *Agrarian History*, pp. 600, 608; Cambell, *English Yeoman*, pp. 156–220; Alan Everitt, "Farm Laborers," pp. 399, 401; Skipp, "Economic and Social Change," pp. 107–9; Spufford, *Contrasting Communities*, pp. 48–53, 116; Thirsk, "Seventeenth-Century Agriculture," p. 166; Wrightson and Levine, *Poverty and Piety*, pp. 36–39.

The yeomanry, along with members of the gentry and aristocracy, participated in the enclosing and engrossing of lands and experimented with new agrarian techniques; see Cambell, *English Yeoman*, p. 78; Patricia Croot and David Parker, "Symposium: Agrarian 'Class Struggle and Economic Development in Pre-Industrial Europe," *P&P* 78 (1978); Margaret Spufford, "A Cambridgeshire Community," *Leicestershire University Occasional Papers* 20 (1965), pp. 37–38.

57. Roland Marchant, *The Church under the Law* (Cambridge, 1969), p. 88, notes a fivefold increase in testamentary business of the diocese of York between c. 1550 and c. 1615. See also Baker and Butlin, "Introduction," in Baker and Butlin, eds., *Field Systems*, p. 17; Christopher Haigh, *Reformation and Resistance in Tudor Lancashire* (Cambridge, 1975), p. 227n.

buy and sell products that were produced as marketable surpluses. Contemporaries were well aware that taverns adjacent to fairs and regulated markets provided a setting for drawing up private contracts that eluded official regulations as to price and product quality.[58] Gentlemen, yeomen, brewers, and millers were prominent among the ranks of these contractors, who used "bipartite bonds and bills" to ratify private agreements. Credit was also an important element in agricultural transactions, for both crops and pastoral products were often sold before they were actually available.[59]

Capitalist development was thus an important factor in the sixteenth-century countryside, despite the absence of major technological innovations. In response to regional and national markets, economic differentiation and specialization developed and led to the growth of a diversified group of independent producers and small employers engaged in both agriculture and crafts. This created highly ramified strata of buyers and sellers, for whom contractual interactions in pursuit of profit were familiar features of everyday life. Conditions long present in the urban economy had now become more general features of the English economy as a whole, and in their wake followed intellectual outlooks that also originated in an urban milieu but now traveled along the path of trade throughout England. By promoting economic autonomy and helping to sow intellectual independence, early capitalist development ensured the existence of an audience receptive to rationalized beliefs disseminated by the printing press.

Lay Dissent and Early Protestantism

The intellectual and social dimensions of popular dissent discussed so far are very evident in the opposition it provoked in the rulers of church and state at the onset of the Reformation. For example, opposition among clerical and secular elites to early Protestant reform was motivated by the association of vernacular religion with popular dissent and anticlericalism. This opposition was further stiffened when confiscation of Tyndale's New Testament, by church officials, was met with denunciation of the authorities by

58. Anon., *A Discourse, Tendered to the High Court of Parliament* (1629), p. 29; Everitt, "Marketing of Produce," pp. 532, 543, 559–64, 587. Cf. Fernand Braudel, *Afterthoughts on Material Civilization and Capitalism* (Baltimore, 1977), p. 28.

59. Everitt, "Marketing of Agricultural Produce," pp. 544–45, 553, 557, and "Farm Labourers," p. 423; Lowe, *Lancashire Textile Industry*, p. 20; Smith, *Land and Politics*, p. 15; R.H. Tawney, editor's Introduction to Thomas Wilson, *A Discourse upon Usury* (London, 1925), p. 26. On notaries and scriveners in provincial towns, see Everitt, "Marketing of Agricultural Produce," p. 555.

dissenters, who argued that the church refused to countenance English
Bibles lest laymen discover ecclesiastical traditions to be fronts for clerical
avarice.[60] These sentiments were nearly identical to those voiced in earlier
heresies, such as Lollardy. But what worried ecclesiastical officials was not
simply the specter of a religiously literate laity, for that was hardly new; it
had appeared earlier, when Erasmian humanism took hold among cultural elites. What worried them now was the appetite of *unlearned* laymen
for religious works.

This concern followed the path of religious reform throughout Europe
and is recorded in a not untypical report by the vicar general of Constance
in 1521: "Through the wrongdoing of irresponsible printers all kinds of
unlearned people have read or have had read to them the teachings of
Luther." It is a concern satirized in Protestant polemic, as in a play that
appeared in Lyon in 1562 and had its priest lament exaggerated accom-
plishments of the reformed laity:

> Quoy vous verrez un mecanique,
> Un cordonnier, ou serrurier,
> Un orfévre ou un cousturier,
> Savoir le Testament par coeur
> De Jesus Christ! O quel erreur,
> O quel poison, ô quel diffame!
>
> Mesmes vous verrez une femme
> Qui vous respondra coup sur quille,
> A tous propoz, d l'Evangile,
> Soit en françois ou en latin.[61]

Like their counterparts on the Continent, English divines opposed to
the new faith directed their attacks against its vernacular format. That a
sizable portion of the unlearned could read was hardly questioned; indeed, it was a principal topic in debates over religious reform. The common medieval association of popular literacy with heresy animated the opposition of ecclesiastical officials to the *scriptura sola* doctrine of reform,
according to which religious beliefs should be based solely on the Bible.

60. Simon Fish, *A Supplication for the Beggers* (1529), in J. Meadows, ed., *EETS*
extra ser. 13 (1871), p. 11.

61. Putnam, *Books and Their Makers*, p. 245; stanzas quoted in Emile Picot, "Le
Monologue dramatique dans l'ancien théatre français," *Romania* 17 (1888), pp. 252–53.
A partial translation of these stanzas can be found in Davis, *Society and Culture in Early
Modern France*, p. 6, and see also pp. 77–78, 220–21; Alastaire Duke, "The Face of
Popular Religious Dissent in the Low Countries, 1520–30," *JEH* 26 (1975), p. 45;
Strauss, *Luther's House of Learning*, p. 128.

As the bishop of London testily remarked in 1536, "You are far deceived if you think that there is no other word of God, but that which every souter and cobbler does read in his mother tongue." The association of vernacular religion, popular dissent, and anticlericalism led to two conclusions: vernacular Bibles and other religious literature created heresy, and possession of such literature revealed heresy. On the one hand, arguments over English Bibles turned on the issue of whether "the rude, simple, and unlearned" would misunderstand them. On the other, inquiring clerics sought evidence of lay dissidence in the simple fact of possessing English books, as in the following dialogue, composed about 1534, between a Scottish priest and a servant girl:

> Quod he, ken ye na heresie?
> I wyt nocht quhat that is, quod she.
> Quod he, hard ye na Inglis bukis?
> Quod she, my maister on them lukis.
> Quod he, the bishop that sall knaw
> For I am sworne to schaw.[62]

Fierce debates over the issue of reform at this time raged in simply written pamphlets that explicitly sought the support of the "common sort." With this explicit objective, Sir Thomas More's polemical career was launched. Bishop Tunstal enlisted his aid in 1528 as a propagandist on behalf of orthodoxy, telling him, "You can rival Demosthenes in our vernacular as well as in Latin" and therefore ought to publish "in English for the common man [simplicibus et ideotis hominibus] some books" to fortify the laity against the new heresies of Luther and Tyndale. More did this in masterful works clearly intended for widespread dissemination. *The Confutation of Tyndale's Answer* (1532–33) attempts to convince "the people unlearned" not to read heretical works by Tyndale, Frith, and Barnes but, instead, "such English books as most may nourish and increase devotion." Written as a dialogue, More's work cleverly appeals to a popular audience and triumphantly concludes with the goodwife of the Bottle of Botolph Warf rebuking the heretical Barnes. More observes, "Lo thus might a wise woman that could no more but read English, re-

---

62. *Foxe*, V. 383; John Standish, *A discourse wherein is debated whether it be expedient that the scripture should be in English* (1555), Sig. D4; F.S. Ferguson, "Relations between London and Edinburgh Printers and Stationers (to 1640)," *Transactions of the Bibliographic Society* 2d ser. 8 (1928), pp. 148–49. For additional arguments by religious conservatives, see Stephen Gardiner, *A Declaration of Such True Articles* (1546), Sig. F2ʳ; John Strype, *Memorials of Cranmer* (Oxford, 1848), I. 71. For religious reformers, see Edward Arber, ed., *Thomas Lever: Sermons, 1550* (London, 1870), p. 29; William Turner, *The huntyng and fynding out of the Romysche foxe* (Basle, 1543), Sig. F8ʳ.

buke and confound Friar Barnes." For the other side, simple pamphlets denounced the Catholic mass and boldly appealed to curiosity and open judgment:

> Reade me first from toppe to toe
> And afterward judge me a friend or a foe.

Other pamphlets warned against the idolatry of the mass, invoking the sentiments of materialist skepticism. In support of their claims, these pamphlets boldly state, "& if you will not believe us herein, search these scriptures following," and they then list appropriate biblical references.[63]

Slightly later in the reign of Henry VIII the evident desire of ordinary laymen to read English Bibles surfaced in complaints that poured into the Privy Council. Cromwell learned of clerics who maintained the old religion and sought to dissuade lay reading of scripture: a Stamford cleric accused young men of hideous sin "who carried the New Testament in their hand or at their girdles, especially those who explain it in taverns"; another cleric "despises servingmen and craftsmen" for reading New Testaments. Controversy over this raged among laymen as well as between pastor and parishioner. Leases were terminated because of landlords' displeasure with tenants who read scriptures; quarrels broke out when a goldsmith's wife who read English books rebuked Catholics; brawls occurred in a tavern when on a market day a minstrel exhorted a saddler to read the Bible. In 1533, an apprentice to a London merchant got into trouble for telling a friend "my mind on that part of St. James' Epistle, how Abraham was justified by works." He reported that several merchants questioned him: "They asked me if I thought that I was wiser than other men. I replied, I counted myself altogether naught, and desired to conform my wit to scripture."[64]

Public disputes in markets and taverns testify to lay involvement in doctrinal debates promoted by publication of vernacular Bibles and controversial literature. Cautious remarks by proponents as well as opponents of reform reveal deep concern with this development. A prolific Protestant translator, Nicholas Udall, declared that his purpose in translating Erasmus's paraphrase of the New Testament was not to encourage laymen to be "curious searchers of high mysteries . . . to be troublesome talkers

---

63. *Complete Works of More*, pp. 37, 896, 1139, 1265–66; Antoine de Marcourt, *A declaration of the Masse* (1547), Sig. A1ʳ; Anon., *An Epistle exhortatorye* (c. 1549), p. [4]. See also Anon., *The dysclosyng of the Canon of ye popysh Masse* (1548), Sig. A4ᵛ.

64. *L&P*, VI. 39, IX. 207, XIII, pt. 1, p. 227, pt. 2, pp. 101, 330, XIV, pt. 1, p. 204, and see XIII, pt. 2, pp. 51, 326, XIV, pt. 1, p. 415, pt. 2, p. 349; John Nichols, ed., "Narratives of the Days of the Reformation," *CS* 1st ser. 72 (1859), pp. 61–63.

of the Bible . . . unreverent reasoners in holy scripture . . . curious disputers in the gospel." At about the same time, a spokesman for religious conservatives, Stephen Gardiner, decried biblical discussions by the "rude and unlearned" because of "the facility and easy understanding of scripture, which many do arrogantly presume to have by themselves attained." [65]

When official approval was finally given for the printing of English Bibles, clerics were carefully instructed to urge parishioners to read them with the caveat that they not "be presumptuous in judging matters without perfect knowledge." Moreover, they were "not to reason about doubtful passages of the book in taverns and alehouses." Such prohibitions were subsequently reconfirmed but had little effect. Presumptuous laymen continued to debate controversial matters in taverns and markets, and they openly contested clerical practices when they seemed to violate scriptural precepts. This prompted an act of Parliament, 34 & 35 Henry VIII, c. i, that prohibited all servingmen under the rank of yeoman, all nonaristocratic women, and all artificers, apprentices, journeymen, husbandmen, and laborers from even privately reading the scriptures. But this effort to institute a sumptuary law on religion was futile. Too much popular demand existed for the vernacular Bibles that had already appeared in many editions. The futility of this effort is evident in Henry the Eighth's famous last speech to Parliament in 1545, when he observed that he had the Bible printed with the hope that his subjects would read it privately, "not to dispute and make Scripture a railing and taunting stock against priests and preachers, as many light persons do. I am very sorry to know and hear how unreverently that most precious jewel, the word of God, is disputed, rhymed, sung and jangled in every alehouse and tavern." [66]

Many other aspects of worship were read about and contested by ordinary laypersons. A royal proclamation against "seditious books" sought to dissuade those who "argue and dispute in open places, taverns, and alehouses" about baptism and communion. While debates over baptism may reflect the foreign influence of Dutch Anabaptists, those over communion follow critical arguments well established by Lollardy, as is evident in a later proclamation, issued in the reign of Edward VI. [67]

65. Udall, preface to Erasmus, *The first tome*, Sig. C1ʳ; Gardiner, *Declaration of True Articles*, Sigs. A1ᵛ, F2ᵛ-3ʳ.

66. *L&P*, XIII, pt. 1, pp. 407, 480, XVI. 390, XX, pt. 2, p. 535. See *Foxe*, V. appendix 11.

67. Paul L. Hughes and James F. Larkin, eds., *Tudor Royal Proclamations* (New Haven, 1964), I. 271. The proclamation issued under Edward (ibid., pp. 411–12) forbids public discussion of communion that displays materialist skepticism, for example, discussion of "whether his blessed body be there, head, legs, arms, toes, and nails, or any other way, shape, and manner, naked or clothed; whether He is broken or chewed, or He is always whole."

With due allowance for royal hyperbole, these complaints clearly illustrate why vernacular religious literature, especially the Bible, met with so much official opposition. Fed by this literature, lay religious intellectualism proved to be a wellspring of popular dissent. And such dissent pointed ineluctably to a future in which a new balance between layman and cleric would reverse traditional lay subservience in religious matters. As one of Cromwell's protégés boasted in 1539, "the people begin to know what they that be curates ought to preach." Gardiner asked in 1546 why laymen would defer to clerics if, as reformers argued, truth lay in scriptures, available to all in vernacular form. That same year witnessed the martyrdom of Ann Askew, who had boldly affirmed what Gardiner feared: "She had rather read 5 lines in the Bible than hear five masses, for the one edified her and the other not at all." Gardiner's fears had, in fact, been uttered earlier by a priest in a satirical dialogue attacking the old religion:

> If these hobbes and rusticals be suffered to be thus busy in reading of English heresy and to dispute after this manner with us which are spiritual men, we shall be fain to learn some other occupation, or else we are like to have but a cold broth.

An anti-Protestant tract, composed in 1548 but not published until Mary had succeeded her Protestant brother, denounced impudent laypersons "presuming to affirm themselves (having certain texts of the new or old testaments) that they were as well learned as they that had studied divinity xl years." This was, according to a Marian cleric, "one of the greatest inconveniences that has these wretched years sprung [up] by having the Bible in English"; for "many . . . have presumptuously taken upon them, being most unmeet thereunto, the offices of doctors and teachers in corners & conventicles, being not sent."[68]

Ecclesiastical officials accurately foresaw that religious life, as they understood it, would end if lay insurgency and vernacular religion established themselves. Orthodoxy and Latin worship were so closely linked in conservative criticism of religious reform that one often stood as a proxy for the other. According to Stephen Gardiner, the English language "has not continued in one form of understanding 200 years, and without God's work and special miracle, it shall hardly contain religion long."[69] Clearly,

---

68. Richard Morison, *An Invective Ayenste . . . treason* (1539), Sig. D6ʳ; Gardiner, *Declaration of True Articles*, Sig. L3ᵛ; *A goodly dyalogue & dysputacyon* (1530), quoted in Bennett, *Books & Readers, 1475–1557*, p. 74; Miles Hogarde, *The displaying of the Protestants* (1556), Sig. K7; *L&P*, XX, pt. 1, p. 174; Standish, *A discourse*, Sig. K2ᵛ-K3ʳ.

69. James A. Muller, *The Letters of Stephen Gardiner* (Cambridge, 1933), p. 289.

what was at stake was not religion itself but a religion that separated clerics and laity in terms of access to and knowledge of core doctrine. Lay subservience and Latin worship were twin pillars of orthodoxy and of the continuity of medieval Catholicism precisely because they effectively confined edification and doctrinal discussion to clerics.

This became evident for all to see at the onset of the Reformation in England. By this time, broad developments in vocation, communication, and rationality had combined to promote a doctrinal competency among laymen drawn from the middling strata, a competency that provided the basis for the appearance of popular dissent on a wide scale. Vocational developments created a social-structural basis for early dissent, supplying an audience receptive to critical skepticism and capable of expressing skeptical sentiments in a competent and convincing manner. Printing and the growth of popular literacy were enabling factors, technically facilitating an audience's ability to assimilate and articulate complex ideas. Cultural developments associated with intellectual rationalization provided a mental environment favorable to the critical ideas of dissent. What remained uncertain were the precise doctrinal and liturgical forms which this dissent would eventually take. Up to the middle of the sixteenth century, popular dissent was still in its infancy, and its sentiments, favoring edification and opposing clerical prerogatives, had not yet found coherent and systematic expression.

The major legacy of early popular dissent in the Lollard tradition was its contribution to Protestantism. During the reign of Henry VIII, Lollardy became infused with newer ideas as English Bibles, Lutheran slogans, and books by Tyndale were smuggled into England from the Continent. This process continued during the subsequent reigns of Edward and Mary.[70] Though our knowledge of this process is limited by the secrecy that surrounded it, its implications for subsequent developments in the popular Reformation are clear enough.

The infusion of new ideas into Lollardy was superintended by an educated elite in the church and university who had taken a leading role in disseminating the ideas of continental reformers to an English audience. Relations between these early Protestant leaders and the older Lollard tradition appear to have been symbiotic. In areas that had been centers of

---

70. Margaret Bowker, *The Henrician Reformation: The Diocese of Lincoln under John Longford, 1521–1547* (Cambridge, 1981), pp. 145–47; J.F. Davis, "Lollardy and the Reformation in England," pp. 223–27; Dickens, *Lollards and Protestants*, pp. 17–29; Ralph Houlbrooke, *Church Courts and the People during the English Reformation, 1520–1570* (Oxford, 1979), pp. 225–26, 235; Diarmaid MacCulloch, "Catholic and Puritan in Elizabethan Suffolk," *AfR* 72 (1981), pp. 263–64; J.E. Oxley, *The Reformation in Essex to the Death of Mary* (Manchester, 1965), pp. 7–14.

Lollard activity—especially in parts of Buckingham, Essex, Kent, and Suffolk—clerical reformers encountered audiences favorably impressed by critical and skeptical arguments that scorned what were deemed the idolatrous and superstitious elements in Catholicism. However, clerical reformers also transformed popular dissent. When they became its nominal leaders, they provided it with a far more precise identity and with specific doctrinal and liturgical commitments that tempered its anticlericalism and shaped its diffuse sentiments—for edification; against ritualism—into a Calvinist religion. After the ascension of Elizabeth, in 1559, sentiments of popular dissent in a Calvinist guise acquired the pejorative connotation of Puritanism.

3
Puritan Preaching and Social Control

To surceasse al sedicion to punish
false teachers
And to stablishe true doctrine god
send us good preachers.

Edmon Becke, *A brefe confutacion of this most detestable Anabaptistical opinion* (London, 1550)

When the herts of the people
be wonne to their prince,
Than can no Commotioners
do hurte in hys province.

Robert Crowley, *One and thyrtye Epigrammes* (1550)

During the Reformation, clerics committed to reform became the nominal leaders of popular dissent. Dissent thus gained a measure of respectability, and a new and more complex relationship developed between it and the prevailing powers. Central to this development was, of course, the legal redefinition of the faith of the English Church—a redefinition that had begun under Henry VIII. What was formerly heretical had, in part, become the official faith of the realm. This redefinition occurred over three decades in a halting manner; there were sudden reversals in the last years of Henry VIII and under Mary. It acquired its final form in the Elizabethan Settlement of 1559 and owed much to clerical reformers who sought aristocratic patronage and official support for the new religion.

Acquisition of this patronage and support helped to transform the meaning of dissent. The critical ideas originally associated with early popular dissent—on edification and the sanctity of conscience—became the foundation of policies now proposed by clerical reformers, who claimed that these policies would secure popular submission and obedience to temporal authority. The centerpiece of these policies was a preaching ministry, and the edifying effects of preaching included alignment of individual conscience with external authority. This secular benefit of preaching was consistently cited by early clerical reformers during the reigns of Henry and Edward and by the Puritan clergy during the Elizabethan era. Much evidence indicates that their efforts bore fruit: they secured official allies and aristocratic patrons, who greatly valued the secular benefits of godly preaching and feared that its suppression would pose a threat to their own wealth and power.

Aristocratic patronage and official support for clerical reformers had, of course, several dimensions. One involved dynastic considerations and foreign policy, for which the domestic establishment of Protestantism was an extension of statecraft. Another involved the proximity to wealth and power enjoyed by clerical reformers who were members of England's educated elite. At Cambridge, Oxford, and the Inns of Court, the sons of the aristocracy could develop an appreciation for the spiritual benefits of a style of worship advocated by clerical reformers. But equally important for the task of gaining the support of the powerful were the efforts that reformers made to convince monarchs, privy councilors, town burgesses, and justices of the peace that the doctrine and practice of a reformed religion—one that incorporated popular dissent—would best serve the political as well as the religious interests of the kingdom.

On this point a firm bond of interest united clerical reformers and the secular powers. Both regarded social unrest among the lower classes with great alarm, for deviation there from the true religion merged with a host of economic grievances, and the eruption of sporadic revolts convinced many sixteenth-century contemporaries that restive behavior among the lower classes posed a serious threat to the Tudor establishments of Henry, Edward, and Elizabeth. It was specifically this threat that animated Puritan reflections on the secular benefits of preaching as an instrument of social control. In addition to promoting godliness, preaching was intended to stabilize the existing social order by teaching the lower class the virtues of conscientious obedience to local and national leaders.

The importance of preaching for clerical leaders of reform in the sixteenth century thus derived from two considerations.[1] First, it was the major means by which the laity could acquire religious knowledge. Preaching as the centerpiece of worship was the visible result of Puritanism's emphasis on edification to the neglect of the sacramental aspects of religion. The Puritan clergy regarded preaching as an ordinary means of salvation from which the godly learned about spiritual freedom and the comforts of *renewing* grace. It was also a way to instruct the unregenerate about God's provision of *restraining* grace so that social order might continue. Strictly speaking, the doctrines of renewing and restraining grace were to be taught to all, because one's religious status was, in theory, independent of one's worldly estate. In practice, however, the clerical reformers, in their reflections on the social utility of preaching, tended to fuse religious and political concerns, and to transpose theological and social categories, so that lessons applicable to the unregenerate became targeted

1. See Godfrey Davis, "English Political Sermons," *Huntington Library Quarterly* 3 (1939); Christopher Hill, *Society and Puritanism in Pre-Revolutionary England* (New York, 1967), chap. 2.

on England's unruly lower classes. To wage laborers, cottagers, and the parish poor, Puritan preaching presented a far grimmer visage than that which greeted godly members of the more respectable social classes.

Dissent in the Reformation thus entered into a complex and ambiguous relationship with the larger society. The popular dimensions of dissent remained a potent threat to the existence of a church whose rigidly hierarchical order reflected and supported the social hierarchy. As we saw in chapter 2, edification and literate religion produced forms of lay initiatives that were incompatible with a religion which expected its parishioners to submit to clerical authority. For clerical reformers, dissent's emphasis on edification through preaching provided a valuable resource for social control. These clerics expressed an ambivalence toward the church that only gradually crystallized into outright opposition under the reign of Charles. Conformity to temporal authority and the gross social divisions it protected generated few second thoughts. For cleric and layperson alike, Puritanism was a higher form of patriotism: it was an affirmation of loyalty to the Elizabethan Succcession, of hostility to Catholic interests at home and abroad, and of support for an active foreign policy in conjunction with beleaguered Protestant nations on the Continent.

These remarks indicate that it is impossible to regard dissent simply as an oppositional force in pre-Revolutionary England. An ambiguous relationship between dissent and society, however, is not at all uncommon, for dissent seldom exists in outright hostility to prevailing values and institutions. A more complex relationship exists when the nominal leaders of dissent claim to have solutions to pressing social problems. This is a familiar phenomenon: dissent as a loyal opposition that seeks to defend values and institutions that appear to be threatened or neglected. Dissent can simultaneously involve opposition to some dominant values and to the normative deficiencies of the existing order. This is certainly the case with early Protestantism, under Henry and Edward, and, later, with Puritanism, for they expressed a higher form of patriotism as well as value conflict.[2]

This conclusion contradicts the one-sided views that stress only the points of opposition between Puritanism and the prevailing powers. Such views appear in influential studies by historians and social scientists who depict Puritan clerics as alienated intellectuals, as prototypes of modern radical intelligentsias. In *The Revolution of the Saints*, Michael Walzer argues that the major features of Puritanism were shaped by the ways in which clerics responded to social and political disorder. This disorder re-

2. For this reason the well-known sociological distinction between norm-oriented and value-oriented social movements does not apply to Puritanism in pre-Revolutionary England.

flected broad changes in social structure and specific political crises, such as the persecution and flight of clerical reformers during the reign of Mary. Fanatical concern with discipline was, according to Walzer, the product of clerical experiences of such disorder. Central to his analysis are notions of marginality and structural rootlessness, which have also been applied to Puritan clerics by Mark Curtis, who cites overproduction of university-trained clerics and the resulting lack of career prospects as the cause of clerical alienation. Both accounts discern the same etiology of intellectual dissension in Puritanism that later led to Jacobinism and Bolshevism. Both portray Puritan clerics as "angry and isolated" men who existed in the "interstices" of society, "alienated . . . especially from its inner circles."[3]

Neither of these views can be sustained, because marginality and alienation were not constant features of clerical Puritanism. Impeded mobility cannot be held to be a cause of clerical dissent, because it was Puritan convictions that precluded clerics from advancing within the church. Moreover, recent work has shown that Curtis provides far too pessimistic an account of career prospects for clerics.[4] Walzer is certainly correct in calling attention to the repressive features of Puritanism, but these were an essential part of clerical efforts to gather official support and aristocratic patronage. In their policies and pronouncements on preaching, clerical reformers were not fleeing from or reacting against the prevailing powers but were seeking, rather, to become their servitors.

Via Media *and the Lower Classes*

Puritan views on the secular benefits of preaching as an instrument of social control focus on the problem of revolt and insubordination among the lower classes. On this point Puritan rhetoric displays a pervasive anxiety about the possibility that chronic grievances among the lower classes might erupt in outright rebellion. It was the "rude people," "the simple sort," that provoked so much alarm. They lurked in "dark corners," which Puritan clerics hoped to illuminate with their preaching. To be

3. Mark H. Curtis, "The Alienated Intellectuals of Early Stuart England," *P&P* 23 (1962), p. 28; Michael Walzer, *The Revolution of the Saints: A Study in the Origins of Radical Politics* (Cambridge, Mass., 1965), pp. 121–27. See also Reinhard Bendix, *Kings or People: Power and the Mandate to Rule* (Berkeley and Los Angeles, 1978), pp. 294–95; Bruce Mazlish, *The Revolutionary Ascetic* (New York, 1976); Lawrence Stone, *The Causes of the English Revolution* (New York, 1972), p. 114.

4. Ian Green, "Career Prospects and Clerical Conformity in the Early Stuart Church," *P&P* 90 (1981).

sure, some of the danger lurking in these corners reflected only the exaggerated fears felt by the upper classes of an acutely class-conscious society. But some of the danger was real, and it instilled in Puritan clerics and their powerful lay supporters a sharp sense of anxiety.

These dangers and anxieties appeared at the onset of the Reformation, when reform was under popular attack by diametrically opposed forces: those committed to the old religion and those who wanted more radical reforms. Clerical discussion treated this division as evidence of the irrationality of the lower classes. From the earliest days of the Reformation, proponents of reform wrestled with the problem of *via media:* establishing a middle way between extremes. Identification of these extremes as popular Catholicism and radical heresy appeared in the earliest formulations of *via media* in the writings of Thomas Starkey, who advised Henry VIII to steer a middle course "betwixt the old & blind superstition and this light & arrogant opinion lately entering here among us."[5]

In Elizabethan England, powerful lay supporters of the Puritan ministry denounced in one breath doctrinal deviations committed by Catholics and those committed by members of the heretical sect known as The Family of Love.[6] For their part, clerical reformers pointed to the lower-class milieu of both popish superstition and radical heresy. It was "the simple sort of common man," declared Laurence Chaderton, who was most amenable to either the old faith or familism.[7] The same argument was advanced by John Vernon, a prolific translator of works by continental reformers. Writing during the reigns of Edward VI and Elizabeth, he described how both radical heretics and Catholics did the devil's work among commoners. Beginning with radical heretics, he observed:

> These men, sitting upon their alebenches . . . do inculcate and beat into men's heads that no Christian can lawfully execute the office of a magistrate . . . This commonly in those places where the pure seed of the gospel has been diligently sown . . . In other places where they do yet for the most part sit in darkness of ignorance . . . the Pope's darlings are the stirrers up of all mischief.

5. Thomas Starkey, *An exhortation to the people instructynge them to unitie and obedience* (c. 1540), ff. 3ᵛ, 27, 29ᵛ-32ʳ, 83ᵛ, letter to Henry VIII in S.J. Herrtage, "England in the Reign of King Henry the Eighth: Starkey's Life and Letters," *EETS* extra ser. 12 (1878), pp. lx-lxi.

6. Sir Francis Knollys told Lord Burghley that Jesuits "do follow the same scope that the deified men of the Family of Love do follow," BrL, *MSS. Lands.* 33, f. 201ʳ. In 1585, Puritan justices of the peace in Suffolk made the same point to the Privy Council, BrL, *MSS. Lands.* 109, f. 27ʳ. See also Sir Francis Hastings, quoted in Claire Cross, *The Puritan Earl: The Life of Henry Hastings, Third Earl of Huntingdon* (New York, 1966), pp. 36–37.

7. Laurence Chaderton, *An Excellent and godly sermon* (1580), Sig. C5ʳ.

Many other sixteenth-century reformers made the same point, often in sermons delivered at Paul's Cross in London, which generally were carefully selected and taken to represent official views.[8]

Identifying a lower-class milieu as the source of popular Catholicism and radical heresy reflected a more general social outlook among Tudor writers, who wrote about the irrationality of the lower classes. For them, popular challenges to existing structures of authority were evidence of this irrationality. Archbishop Warham expressed this outlook when, confronted in 1528 by East Anglia yeomen who assembled to request repayment of money lent to the king, he said: "Commonly the greater part of the multitude lack wit and discretion and yet will take upon them to rule the wiser." According to many clerical and lay writers, "the multitude given always to extremes, either to madness or fear . . . is called a beast with many heads."[9] It was this "many-headed monster" that animated clerical fears about popular Catholicism and radical heresy as deviations from *via media*.

Thomas Starkey thought that false teachers succeeded in spreading "papist or schismatic" beliefs because "the people in every commonweal are rude and ignorant." The title of an Elizabethan tract opposed to idolatry conveyed the same point: *A Mirrour for the Multitude, Or Glasse, Wherein maie be seene, the violences, the errour, the weaknesse, and rash consent, of the multitude.* Its author, John Norden, was a layman, but, like many Puritan clerics, his remarks on the many-headed monster conflated religious and social issues: "It is a deceit of Satan to allure men to consent unto the multitude." An Elizabethan preacher also made the same point in a sermon, delivered at Paul's Cross, that denounced radical heresy: "experience teaches the multitude to be a monster of many heads . . . Take away the magistrate, and let loose the bridle unto the unruly multitude, and these enormities shall by and by flourish . . . virgins shall be deflowered, ma-

---

8. John Vernon, epistle to Heinrich Bullinger, *A most necessary & frutefull Dialogue, betweene ye seditious Libertin . . . & the true obedient christian* (Worcester, 1551), Sigs. B4ᵛ-B6ʳ. See also Vernon, *A most necessary treatise of free-will, not onlye against the Papists, but also against the Anabaptists* (1561), Sig. A2ᵛ. For more remarks on the twin dangers of Anabaptism and popery in this era, see Thomas Becon, *David's Harp* (1542) and *The Common-Places of the Holy Scripture* (1564), in *PS*, II. 295, IV. 293; Albert Peel and Leland Carlson, eds., *Cartwrightiana* in *ENT*, I. 24; John Dyos, *A Sermon Preached at Paules Crosse* (1579), Sig. F4ᵛ; Edward Harris, *A Sermon Preached At Hitchin* (1590), p. 68; John Udall, *Amendment Of Life* (1584), in *Certaine Sermons* (1596), Sigs. L7ᵛ-L8ʳ; Thomas White, *A Sermon Preached at Paules Crosse* (London, 1589), p. 44.

9. *L&P*, IV. 1850; White, *Sermon at Paules Crosse*, p. 7. See also Francis Bacon, *Works* (London, 1868), VIII. 100; Becon, *An Humble Supplication* (1544), in *PS*, IV. 243; Samuel Otes, *An Explanation of the Generall Epistle of St. Jude* (1633), p. 397; John Strype, *Ecclesiastical Memorials* (Oxford, 1822), II. pt. 2, pp. 373-74. See Christopher

trons ravished, old men slain in their beds, young men in fields, infants suckling at their mothers' breasts, children playing in their nurses' laps." [10]

Difficult though it may be for us to regard these alarms seriously, they did reflect the social prejudices of clerical reformers, who identified the dangers posed by popular Catholicism and radical heresy with the unruly behaviors and irrationality that they attributed to the lower classes. The riotous activities associated with doctrinal deviations in popular circles corresponded closely to fears about the many-headed monster. Certainly, gentlemen were known to commit adultery, rape, and murder. But in their discussions of popular Catholicism and radical heresy, the clerical reformers explicitly point to the denial of all social bonds and boundaries by the many-headed monster.

Preaching in the Early Reformation

Emphasis on preaching as a solution to problems posed by lower-class unruliness was a product of attitudes formed in the earliest years of the Reformation. Clerical reformers, aristocratic sympathizers, and government officials regarded preaching as the chief way to gather support for the political decisions in the 1530s that legally established the Reformation in England. In many ways these were unpopular decisions, and their enforcement produced a serious challenge to the authority of both church and state.

After 1533, government maneuvering with Rome over the king's divorce gave way to an ambitious attempt to legislate social change. A series of acts and injunctions defined new allegiances in spiritual and temporal affairs and altered traditional forms of worship. Clerical hostility and bawdy derision of the king's affairs greeted the Act of Supremacy (1534), the First Act of Succession (1534), and the Act Abolishing Papal Authority in England (1536). More incredulous and hostile reactions confronted the alteration of religious life ordered in 1536 by the Ten Articles and Thomas Cromwell's Injunctions, by the Act for the Dissolution of the Lesser Monasteries (1536), and by Cromwell's Injunctions of 1538. For commoners, royal supremacy was "a peripheral issue" compared to the changes in religious practice, which were met with "disaffection, disobe-

---

Hill, "The Many-Headed Monster in Late Tudor and Early Stuart Political Thought," in *Change and Continuity in 17th-Century England* (London, 1974), pp. 181–204.

10. Starkey, *An exhortation*, f. 34ʳ; John Norden, *A Mirrour For the Multitude* (1586), Sig. *5ᵛ; John Stockwood, *A verie godlie and profitable Sermon* (1587), Sig. B3. See also Arthur Dent, *A Sermon of Repentance* (1585), Sig. D5.

dience and disturbance." [11] One of Cromwell's protégés, Thomas Starkey, informed the king that it was not "this defection from Rome" but fear of the decline of "all old rites & rules of our religion" that created "great fear and suspicion." Cromwell himself heard from the archbishop of York that proclamations about "the King's matters" were heard "reverently" by northern laymen, but at "novelties they grudge much." [12]

The attack on traditional forms of worship and the institution of "novelties" in their place occurred in a number of stages, beginning in 1536–38 with prohibitions against pilgrimages, superstitious excesses in the worship of saints, and abuses associated with purgatory. Shrines and images were dismantled, some holy days were abolished, youths were taught the *pater noster* and Articles of Faith in English, and Bibles, "of the largest volume in English," were installed in every church. Moreover, priests were told to urge laymen to read the Bible and to admonish them "that images serve for none other purpose but as to be books of unlearned men, that ken no letters." [13] A second wave of reforms under Edward VI, between 1548 and 1550, abolished or abridged more ceremonies, rescinded more holy days, replaced altars with communion tables, and led to vernacular prayer books.

It is not difficult to understand why these "novelties" provoked so much popular unrest. Many of Thomas Cromwell's reforms attacked the same religious practices that the Lollards had earlier denounced. These included the ceremonies and rituals that were associated with sacerdotal magic: pilgrimages, rogation processions, prayers for the dead, and the worship of images, saints, and relics. Some regarded Cromwell's reforms as Lollard heresy. [14] These reforms also had the practical consequence of prohibiting parishioners from using practices thought to possess supernatural power in achieving worldly commodities.

Equally important was the expressive and symbolic function of these practices. Much of the ceremonial encrustation of pre-Tridentine Catholicism contained communal symbols of village life and provided for its ritual integration. Many ceremonial practices varied from village to village, their idiosyncratic nature reflecting and affirming local custom. One of these practices was the rogation procession, which in altered form survived the Reformation. Originally this procession was fused with sacer-

11. G.R. Elton, *Policy and Police* (Cambridge, 1972), p. 45 and see p. 34; Christopher Haigh, *Reformation and Resistance in Tudor Lancashire* (Cambridge, 1975), p. 113.

12. Herrtage, "Starkey's Life and Letters," p. lx; *L&P*, X. 172.

13. Gilbert Burnet, *The History of the Reformation of the Church of England* (London, 1679), pt. I, appendix, pp. 160–61, 178–81.

14. See Margaret Bowker, *The Henrician Reformation: The Diocese of Lincoln under John Longford, 1521–1547* (Cambridge, 1981), p. 141.

dotal magic before it became the perambulation ceremony of the Anglican Church. A good crop was thought to be ensured by this procession across the fields and along the boundaries of a parish. Prayers recited along the way were variously combined with curious customs. In one Linconshire parish, boys were put head first into holes on parish boundaries; in Huntingdonshire it was the vicar who was held "upside down with his head in a waterhole." [15]

The unpopularity of the reforms ordered by Cromwell and Henry VIII thus presented them with a formidable challenge to their authority. In areas committed to the old religion—many of them far from London and not easily controlled by the central government—these reforms visibly threatened the symbolic identity of local communities, an identity more salient than that of an embryonic national community. From Yorkshire, Cromwell heard about northerners' commitment to "frantic fantasies and ceremonies, which they regard more than either God or their prince." [16]

But an attachment to the old religion was not the only source of popular opposition to Cromwell and his policies. Two other developments in the early years of the English Reformation also challenged the ability of the central government to enforce its authority on the country, and both of these were linked intimately to popular developments. One was the rise of radical heresy, alluded to above. Official concern with this was animated by the example of the 1535 Anabaptist revolt in Münster. The second development involved secular grievances of an economic nature. The engrossing and enclosing of land at this time intensified the impoverishment of the poorer segments of the rural population. Periodically, pockets of resentment exploded in open rebellion, and most of these rebellions also championed the Catholic religion. Two notable exceptions to this were the Norfolk rebels in 1549 (Kett's Rebellion) and Sir Francis Bigod's role in the Pilgrimage of Grace in 1537: here religious grievances were radical, not conservative, in nature. The other rebellions, however, linked Catholicism with memories of an era supposedly characterized by prosperity. This mingling of economic and religious grievances is evident in the complaint that "It was a good world when the mass was up, for then all things were cheap." [17]

It was in view of these problems that William Paget in 1549, during the

---

15. Dorothy M. Owen, *Church and Society in Medieval Lincolnshire* (Lincoln, 1971), pp. 108–9; Keith Thomas, *Religion and the Decline of Magic* (Harmondsworth, Eng., 1973), pp. 73–74.

16. *L&P*, VIII. 375.

17. Christopher Haigh, "Puritan Evangelism in the Reign of Elizabeth I," *EHR* 92 (1977), p. 56. See Thomas, *Religion and the Decline of Magic*, p. 483, who observes that

reign of the boy king, Edward VI, issued his famous warning to the Lord
Protector regarding the dire consequences of an unfinished Reformation:

> Society in a realm . . . is maintained by means of religion and laws.
> And these two or one wanting, farewell all society, farewell kings,
> government, justice, all other virtue . . . Look well, whether you
> have either law or religion at home, and I fear you shall find neither.
> The use of the old religion is forbidden by a law, and the use of the
> new is not yet printed: printed in the stomachs of eleven of twelve
> parts of the realm.[18]

No easy or single solution to these problems was available. Enforcement
of the early Tudor Reformation, suppression of conservative and radical
opinion, and forestalling rebellion required the government to use every
available local authority. Bishops were to implement changes in traditional worship and have them justified in sermons to parishioners; members of the local gentry were to report to Cromwell on the bishops; and
local justices were to examine those suspected of seditious sentiments.
Cromwell also supervised the publication of popular and learned tracts
that justified the divorce, the royal supremacy, and the novelties of the
new religion.[19]

Yet none of these measures was thought to possess quite the same
efficacy as preaching for preventing, as opposed to detecting, disaffection
and disturbance. This political use of preaching had special relevance to
the task of influencing the popular mind. For commoners in early modern
England preaching was a primary medium for news and official an-
nouncements as well as for moral propaganda. This situation was not, of
course, markedly different from that which had existed throughout the
Middle Ages. But political uses of the pulpit increased as the result of two
developments in the Reformation. First, Protestantism heightened concern with preaching by its emphasis on sermon attendance as an ordinary
means of salvation. Second, by a process of default, preaching inherited
some of the social functions of the traditional rites and rituals that were
abolished by the Reformation. As the most popular form of Protestant
propaganda, aside from interludes and stage plays,[20] preaching filled a
vacuum created by the demise of auricular confession.

Political use of auricular confession as an agency of control was well

---

"popular radicalism could sometimes underlie the recusant myth of the utopia . . . which
would come with the restoration of Popery." See below, p. 97.

18. Strype, *Ecclesiastical Memorials*, II. pt. 1, p. 431.

19. Elton, *Policy and Police*, passim.

20. Joseph Block, "Thomas Cromwell's Patronage of Preaching," *Sixteenth-Century*

known in this era. William Tyndale denounced the misuse of confessional secrets by kings and popes: Henry VII was said to have spied on notable persons with information culled from their confessions.[21] Priests opposed to changes ordered by Cromwell advised laypersons during their confession against use of vernacular worship.[22] Cromwell ordered priests to use confession to monitor lay progress in adopting vernacular religion.[23]

But the progress of the Reformation quickly eliminated this resource of control: auricular confession contravened too many fundamental tenets of Protestantism. It was denounced as a corrupt invention that promoted both church revenues and sexual misconduct by clerics. In addition, its spiritual efficacy was denied because priests unjustly presumed to "sit in the conscience of men, where as God alone should sit."[24] At the same time, however, some clerical reformers worried about the abolition of auricular confession. This reflected their awareness of its secular uses as an instrument of social control that helped preserve communal tranquillity by detecting and reconciling conflicts. Early Protestant leaders such as Becon, Latimer, and Ridley hoped to retain the institution of priestly confession by separating it from the abuses associated with auricular confession. Six years before auricular confession ceased to be mandatory, Becon asked, "How many, think you, are there, which, if this auricular confession were taken away, would not care how they lived . . . not once having respect unto the correction of their old and wicked manners?"[25] But the logic of the Reformation strongly militated against auricular confession, and any substitute for it had to be more compatible with Protestant dogma. That substitute was preaching.

Journal 8 (1977), p. 37; J.J. Scarisbrick, *Henry VIII* (Berkeley and Los Angeles, 1968), pp. 367–68.

21. William Tyndale, *The Obedience of a Christian Man* (1528), in *PS*, XLII. 281, 336–37, and *The Practice of Prelates* (1530), in *PS*, XLIII. 305.

22. Elton, *Policy and Police*, pp. 27–30. *L&P*, X. 130; XIII. pt. 1, p. 385, pt. 2, p. 51; XVIII. pt. 2, p. 293.

23. Burnet, *History of the Reformation*, pt. 1, appendix, p. 179; A.J. Slavin, ed., *Thomas Cromwell on Church and Commonwealth: Selected Letters, 1523–1540* (New York, 1969), p. 171. See Stephen Gardiner's remarks on this, *L&P*, XIII. pt. 2, p. 168.

24. Henry Brinklow, *The Complaynt of Roderyck Mors* (c. 1542), in J.M. Cowper, ed., *EETS* extra ser. 22 (1874), p. 65. See also Miles Coverdale, *The Defence of a Certain Poor Christian Man* (1545), in *PS*, XIV. 482; A.G. Dickens, *Lollards and Protestants in the Diocese of York, 1509–1558* (Oxford, 1959), pp. 47–49, 232–33, 243, 245; Strype, *Ecclesiastical Memorials*, I. pt. 2, pp. 262–63.

25. Becon, *The Potation for Lent* (1542), in *PS*, II. 101. See also John Bossy, "The Social History of Confession in the Age of the Reformation," *Transactions of the Royal Historical Society* 5th ser. 25 (1975), pp. 24–27; Thomas, *Religion and the Decline of Magic*, pp. 184–88.

Popular Catholicism, Radical Heresy, and Revolt

Many contemporary observers cited the same causes when explaining popular challenges to both spiritual and temporal rulers in the early years of the Reformation. According to John Hales, in 1549, "it is for three sundry causes that they make these insurrections. Some be papists, and would have again their old popery. Some be Anabaptists and libertines, and would have all things in common. And the third be certain poor men that seek to have again their revenues that have been by power taken from them." Clerical reformers at this time uniformly blamed sin for the "unnatural disposition" of the king's subjects. According to Archbishop Cranmer, "The general cause of these commotions is sin." Somewhat more helpfully, he added that there were "certain special causes," which included enclosures, "subtle papists," and "arrogant gospellers."[26]

Interest in preaching as a solution to these problems can be traced to Cromwell's efforts to control the pulpit in order to gain popular support for the Henrician Reformation. In 1535 and 1536 he ordered bishops to have the priests in all churches of their dioceses deliver sermons that defended royal supremacy and denounced the usurped power of "the bishop of Rome" (no longer referred to as pope in official documents). All licenses to preach were to be called in, and only conformable clerics were to be allowed access to the pulpit. Cromwell kept in close correspondence with Archbishop Cranmer, reviewing drafts of sermons that were to be distributed throughout the realm. The style of desired sermons invariably was described as "sincere," meaning not only loyal but plain preaching, as opposed to "the allegorical and analogical artificialities of late-medieval preaching."[27] Clerical reformers supported a simple, expository style because it facilitated godly edification. Cromwell supported it for the obvious reason that it was more suitable to the task of influencing popular opinion. From York Cathedral, Cromwell heard the following report on the archbishop of York's preaching in defense of government policy: "It was in a plainer fashion than was ever heard there before."[28]

26. John Hales, *The defence of John Hales* (1549), in Elizabeth Lamont, ed., *A Discourse of the Common Weal of This Realm of England* (Cambridge, 1954), p. lvii; Becon, *The Fortress of the Faithful* (1550), in *PS*, III. 593; Thomas Cranmer, *Sermon on Rebellion* (1549), in *PS*, XVI. 191–96. See also Robert Crowley, *The Way to Wealth* (1550), in *The Select Works of Robert Crowley*, edited by J.M. Cowper, *EETS* extra ser. 15 (1872), pp. 132–33, 140, 142.

27. Elton, *Policy and Police*, pp. 211–16, 232–34; Cranmer, in *PS*, XVI. 314. The contrast between the simple, expository preaching of Protestantism and medieval preaching should not be overdrawn; see G.R. Owst, *Literature and Pulpit in Medieval England* (Cambridge, 1923).

28. *L&P*, VIII. 393.

This official concern with preaching was further heightened by rural insurrections against certain real or imagined policies of Henry VIII. The Lincolnshire Rebellion of 1536 was repeated in 1537 by the Pilgrimage of Grace, the most dangerous popular challenge to Henry VIII. Following so closely upon the official inception of the English Reformation, they revealed the wide gulf that divided the government's commitment, however modest, to religious reform from the people's attachment to the old religion in many parts of the country. Grievances of other types are equally evident in these rebellions. In addition to economic grievances, mentioned earlier, some administrative innovations of the Tudor state also provoked opposition. All three sources of unrest appear in rumors about the parish registers, ordered by Cromwell to be kept in every church, in which all christenings, marriages, and burials were to be recorded. It was said that the king would have three shillings twopence of fees for burials and christenings.[29]

The Lincolnshire Rebellion and the Pilgrimage of Grace demonstrated a pressing need for more "sincere" preaching. Postmortems of these revolts held lack of "sincere" preaching to be the principal cause of popular disaffection with the Henrician Reformation. For want of such preaching, Catholic loyalty among northern commoners went unchecked, and the justice of the king's proceedings went unproclaimed. Contemporaries were aware that rebellious commoners received aid and direction from some clerics and gentlemen; but the government regarded these two rebellions as popular uprisings, despite the fact that neither amounted to anything like a *jacquerie*. Official views focused on the role of popular economic and religious grievances: culpable clerics and gentlemen were, with some exceptions, allowed to plead that they had been coerced by the mob to act as its spokesmen.[30]

It was in this context that "sincere" preaching acquired greater importance as a resource for influencing the popular mind. In 1537, a future archbishop, Mathew Parker, declared that "no ways better can we deserve of the commonwealth" than by preaching "to continue the commons in a quiet subjugation and obedience toward their governors." After the 1536–37 revolts and the 1549 revolt, during Edward's reign, reformers argued that lack of preaching was the cause of "all the insurrection, commotion, [and] dissension which has arisen or begun" since the reign of Henry VIII. Preaching was necessary if the king's subjects were to obey his "ordinances,

29. *L&P*, XIV. pt. 1, pp. 197, 214.

30. Dickens, *Lollards and Protestants*, pp. 53–113; M.E. James, "Obedience and Dissent in Henrician England: The Lincolnshire Rebellion, 1536," *P&P* 48 (1970); R.B. Smith, *Land and Politics in the England of Henry VIII* (Oxford, 1970), pp. 165–212.

commandments and laws without grudge or murmuration." Evidence in support of this assertion was seen in the "quietness that was among them" who had sincere preachers.[31]

Powerful members of the government apparently placed some credence in these claims on behalf of the secular merits of "sincere" preaching. They included Thomas Howard, duke of Norfolk, a man of very conservative views on religion. He commended to Cromwell the efforts made by several preachers to resecure the loyalty of the Yorkshire commons after the Pilgrimage of Grace: "If three or four such preachers had been continually in these parts instructing the unlearned, no such follies would have been attempted." After these "follies" subsided, the Council of the North sought "discreet and learned personages to preach and teach the word of God that the people may better know their duties." Similar policies were put into effect after the 1549 revolt, during Edward's reign, and after the 1569 Northern Revolt, during Elizabeth's reign, when the Privy Council ordered the earl of Sussex to have offenders brought before "discreet preachers to instruct them in open sermons."[32]

Arguments stressing preaching as an antidote to revolt were, of course, quite useful to clerical reformers already committed to a program of reform based on a preaching ministry. The self-serving nature of these arguments undoubtably explains why they continued to be made during the reign of Elizabeth, when Puritan clerics increasingly came under attack from conservative forces in the Church of England. The claim of Protestantism's early leaders, in the reigns of Henry and Edward, that "sincere" preaching would prevent popular revolt became a standard feature of Puritan rhetoric. During the last decades of the sixteenth century, arguments by Puritan clerics in defense of their activities routinely discussed their preaching as an antidote to insurrections like the 1569 revolt, the last serious challenge from the North to the ascension of Elizabeth and to the religious settlement of 1559.

Archbishop Grindal, suspended by Elizabeth from his office for supporting moderately Puritan policies, defended his efforts to create a preaching ministry in the church by warning the queen:

31. John Strype, *The Life and Acts of Matthew Parker* (Oxford, 1821), III. 4; Richard Tracy, *A supplycacion to our moste soveraigne lorde kynge henry the eyght* (np, 1544), Sigs. A5ʳ-A6ᵛ; Robert Crowely, *The Way to wealth*, p. 140. See also Bernard Gilpin, *A Sermon Preached In The Court* (1552; reprinted 1630), p. 22; Richard Morison, *An Invective Ayenste . . . treason* (1539), Sig. D7ʳ.

32. *L&P*, XI. 561, XII. pt. 1, p. 534; *CSPD-addenda* 1566–79, p. 251. See also Sam Haynes, ed., *A Collection of State Papers left by William Cecil, Lord Burghley* (London, 1740), p. 559; Strype, *Parker*, I. 561.

Where preaching wants, obedience fails . . . what bred the rebellion in the north? Was it not papistry, and ignorance of God's word, through want of often preaching? . . . one poor parish in Yorkshire, which by continual preaching had been better instructed than the rest (Halifax I mean) was ready to bring three or four thousand able men into the field to serve you against the said rebels.[33]

This reasoning subsequently reappeared in defense of Puritan preachers who came under attack by Archbishop Grindal's more conservative successors. Because Puritan preachers were outspoken proponents of preaching, an attack on them could be equated with a threat to the security of the Tudor state. The most powerful member of Queen Elizabeth's government, Lord Burghley, heard about this threat from a Rutlandshire cleric who, faced with suspension for nonconformity, remarked that the 1569 revolt would not have happened if every parish had had a preacher, like himself, "to beat into their heads what obedience faithful subjects owe, first to God, and next to their prince." For the Puritan mind, the 1569 revolt showed that "where the people are not taught, they cannot serve God, [and] the prince is not so dutifully obeyed."[34]

CLOSELY ALLIED WITH THE PROBLEM OF RURAL INSURRECTIONS WAS the problem of popular Catholicism. Long after the Elizabethan Settlement, adherence to Catholicism remained widespread in many places—e.g., Yorkshire, the northwest, Hampshire, and Sussex—that had strategic importance as potential invasion routes for foreign forces aligned with the Catholic powers of Europe. The view that recusants were also foreign agents, sent to "stir up the Queen's subjects . . . to animate them to rebel against her own person," was a familiar Elizabethan sentiment.[35] But aristocratic recusants, seminary priests, foreign intrigue, and the Counter-Reformation were one issue. Persistence of old rituals and superstitions among commoners was another.

33. Edmund Grindal, *Remains*, in *PS*, XIX. 379–80. The same argument was made with reference to the attempted Spanish invasion of 1588: eight thousand "valient fighting men" gathered in one day in Kent, where "the great number of reverend preachers" had taught "Christian subjection to the higher powers" (John Seller, *A Sermon Against Halting Betweene Two Opinions* [1611], Sigs. A2ᵛ-A3ᵛ).

34. Anon., *An Humble Motion With Submission Unto The . . . Privie Counsell* (n.p., 1590), pp. 85–86; John Strype, *The Life and Acts of John Aylmer* (Oxford, 1822), pp. 88–89. See also William Bradshaw, quoted in Hill, *Change and Continuity*, p. 10.

35. William Overton, *A Godlye and pithie Exhortation* (n.p., 1580), Sig. C8ʳ. See Carol Z. Wiener, "The Beleaguered Isle: A Study of Elizabethan and Jacobean Anti-Catholicism," *P&P* 51 (1971).

Contemporaries were well aware of the great social distance between the aristocratic world of the Counter-Reformation and the older, more insular religious world of popular Catholicism in England. Reports on English recusants in Paris in 1579 noted that all were gentlemen.[36] The danger posed by popular Catholicism was of a somewhat different nature. As we saw, attachment to old rites and rituals was stronger than loyalty to a Protestant regime. Fears generated by this state of affairs are evident in remarks attributed to a papist in a dialogue composed by William Turner, a prominent reformer in the reign of Edward VI:

> The multitude of this realm has the mass in such a reverence & takes it for such a godly thing . . . if they should once perceive the mass should be handled as a thief and a robber, that is, if she [the mass] should openly be accused before the face of the court, the rude people would make an insurrection & so should all this realm come in great jeopardy, by the breaking of inward peace.[37]

As in the case of rural revolts, government officials and clerical reformers regarded the problem of authority posed by Catholicism chiefly in terms of the existence of popular grievances which could easily be mobilized in support of insurrection. The credulous and superstitious mind they associated with popular Catholicism was thought to be susceptible to manipulation by foreign agents and domestic traitors. Influential laymen in the reigns of Henry and Elizabeth, such as Lord Burghley, Richard Morison, and Thomas Starkey, warned that the "simplicity" of commoners, combined with clerical interests in the Catholic cause, created a potent threat to England's rulers.[38]

The connection between Catholicism and secular affairs of state thus existed on two levels. A distinction was drawn between the Catholicism of aristocratic recusants and popular Catholicism: what was possibly tolerable in the former might be dangerous in the latter. This is evident in a minor public controversy, ignited by the presence of a silver crucifix in the queen's chapel. In 1565 James Calfhill, chaplain to Grindal, who was then the bishop of London, warned Catholics not to be falsely encouraged by this crucifix, for "neither her grace and wisdom has such affiance in the

---

36. *CSP-foreign* 1579–80, pp. 250–51; Bacon, *Works*, X. 262–63; Thomas, *Religion and the Decline of Magic*, p. 483. But cf. Christopher Haigh, "The Continuity of Catholicism in the English Reformation," *P&P* 93 (1981).

37. William Turner, *A newe Dialogue Wherein is conteyned the examination of the Messe* (1548), Sig. B3ʳ.

38. William Burghley, *The Execution of Justice in England* (1583), Sig. A2; Morison, *An Invective Ayenste treason*, Sig. D7ᵛ; Starkey, *An exhortation to the people*, ff. 18ᵛ, 45ᵛ, 47.

cross as you do fondly teach; neither takes it expedient her subjects should have that which she herself (she thinks) may keep without offense. For the multitude is easily through ignorance abused."[39] Lord Burghley defended harsh laws enacted against recusancy by citing the tolerance extended to sincere Catholics "of good possessions and lands" and "good credit in their countries."[40]

Distinctions between aristocratic recusancy and popular Catholicism were inspired by politics, not religion. The old religion was anathema to Puritan clerics, regardless of its social standing. But political and religious considerations merged in regard to popular Catholicism. Puritan clerics and powerful statesmen like Lord Burghley agreed that Catholic superstition in popular circles led ineluctably to treason. Sermons in which the laity was informed about this association between idolatry and treason were, according to Puritan clerics, a valuable contribution to the state. In 1565, a venerable clerical reformer, Thomas Lever, informed Burghley and Leicester of this contribution: "Now is notable papistry in England and Scotland proved and proclaimed, by preaching of the Gospel, to be idolatry and treason."[41]

For clerical reformers, the credulous and superstitious mentality in popular Catholicism reflected the irrationality of the lower classes. Popular Catholicism was, in this view, a natural religion of the lower classes, an appendage of untutored mental habits. Unlike the malignant intentions of trained seminary priests, "the ignorant and unlearned sort of people," said Bishop Jewel, "offend out of simplicity."[42] In view of the prevailing wisdom about the "many-headed monster," it was easy for clerical reformers to equate popular Catholicism and its mental qualities with a turbulent population prone to riot and insurrection. One cleric warned that "idolatry once committed, it cannot be but adultery should follow, and incest, perjury, murder, extortion, robbery." Another remarked in a sermon on the lack of preaching and the persistence of Catholicism in the north: "What springs of such contempt in these estates? Even effusion of all riot

39. James Calfhill, An Answere To The Treatise Of The Crosse (1565), Sig. B1ʳ. Seventy years later, Sir Thomas Browne made the same point: "Holy-water and crucifix (dangerous to the common people) deceive not my judgement," Religio Medici (c. 1635; reprinted, London, 1889), p. 9.

40. Burghley, The Execution of Justice, Sig. B2ᵛ.

41. Strype, Parker, III. 140.

42. John Haweis, Sketches of the Reformation and Elizabethan Age Taken from the Pulpit (London, 1844), pp. 175–76. See John Hooper, A Declaration of the Ten Holy Commandments (1548), in PS, XX. 279; John Stockwood, A Sermon Preached at Paules Crosse (1579), p. 104; Turner, A newe Dialogue, Sig. A4ʳ; John Vernon, epistle to Ulrich Zwingli, The ymage of bothe pastoures (n.p., 1550), Sig. A7ᵛ.

and running into sin of the common inferior sort."[43] These concerns, voiced alike by clerical and lay reformers, clearly refer in the first instance not to the aristocratic recusants who promoted foreign intrigues but to Catholicism in the lower social orders. The "dark corners" of England, into which Puritan preaching would bring light, were defined, not only geographically but socially, as a lower-class milieu where popular Catholicism coexisted with a predilection for restive behavior.

The ability of preaching to enlighten these dark corners had first been stressed by reformers in Henrician and Edwardian England. A lack of preachers, they argued, was among "the chief and principal causes of the blindness that yet at this present [time] rages among the simple and ignorant people."[44] Powerful laymen in the Elizabethan establishment agreed with this assessment, in spite of the fact that preachers supported by the Crown in the heavily pro-Catholic northwest were having only limited success in converting its population to Protestantism.[45] Nonetheless, Lord Burghley, the earls of Huntingdon and Leicester, Sir Francis Knollys, and Sir Francis Walsingham were convinced of the importance of Puritan preaching in winning heavily Catholic areas to the Elizabethan Settlement. In addition to providing Puritan preachers for benefices in their control and recommending them for other vacant benefices, these courtiers lobbied vigorously against efforts by conservative church officials to suspend Puritan preachers for nonconformity. Sir Francis Knollys denounced Archbishop Whitgift's measures, in 1584, against the Puritan clergy, who were "the most diligent barkers against the popish wolf." Acknowledging this importance of Puritan preaching, the Privy Council ordered the archbishop to temper his prosecution of nonconformist preachers.[46]

43. Thomas White, *A Sermon Preached at Pawles Crosse* (1578), p. 6; Christopher Shutte, *A very godlie and necessarie sermon preached before the yong countesse of comberland* (1578), Sigs. F6ᵛ-F7ʳ. See Thomas Becon, author's Preface to *Works* (1564) and *An Invective against Swearing* (1543), in *PS*, II. 9, 354; Grindal, *Remains*, p. 326; R.C. Richardson, *Puritanism in North-West England: A Regional Study of the Diocese of Chester to 1642* (Manchester, 1972), p. 5; *VCH* Cumberland, II. 75–76.

44. Vernon, epistle to Zwingli, *The ymage of bothe pastoures*, Sig. B3ʳ. See Edward Arber, ed., *Thomas Lever: Sermons 1550* (London, 1870), pp. 108, 119; Thomas Becon, *The Jewel of Joy* (1553), in *PS*, III. 421–22; Gilpin, *Sermon Preached In The Court*, p. 21; Hooper, *Answer to the Bishop of Winchester's Book* (1547), in *PS*, XX. 202, 205; Tracy, *A supplycacion*, Sig. A3ᵛ.

45. Haigh, "Puritan Evangelism," passim.

46. Thomas Fuller, *The Church History of Britain* (Oxford, 1845), V. 27–28; M.M. Knappen, *Tudor Puritanism* (Chicago, 1966), p. 275; John Strype, *The Life and Acts of Archbishop Whitgift* (Oxford, 1822), I. 507. The Puritan sympathies of men like Lord Burghley and the earl of Leicester were shaped by their appraisal of Puritan preaching as an anti-Catholic weapon; see Patrick Collinson, "Letters of Thomas Wood, Puritan,

At about this time, Lord Burghley, the earl of Huntingdon, and Sir Francis Walsingham worked closely with a pro-Puritan bishop of Chester, William Chaderton, to provide "good preachers" to reform that staunchly Catholic diocese. Walsingham urged the bishop to continue to seek preachers for benefices in his diocese:

> As by this beginning you have won many of the gentlemen of that country to an outward obedience, so I persuade myself that if these parts were well furnished with a competent number of good learned preachers, they would be inwardly in heart as conformable as they be outwardly in body.[47]

In 1612, a report of efforts on behalf of persecuted Puritan preachers in Chester reached Burghley's son from a gentleman who told him that in previous years Puritan preachers had been protected "by letters I obtained first by Sir Francis Walsingham, and after by Sir Thomas Henneage, and last by your father, to the bishop in Chester, to permit the ministers to live according to their preaching . . . being in a place so full of papists."[48] Prominent lay patrons of the Elizabethan Puritan ministry evidently thought that preaching was the major way to convert recusants, at all levels of society, to the Protestant cause. Its importance consisted in its ability to do what external coercion by the state could not: gain the inner loyalty of the queen's subjects to her temporal and spiritual regime.

IN THEIR EFFORTS TO SECURE THIS REGIME, HOWEVER, THE SPIRITUAL and temporal authorities had to contend with another challenge. Radical heresy was a by-product of the Reformation that posed problems of authority similar in scope to those presented by rural unrest and popular Catholicism. Accordingly, attacks on radical heresy complemented anti-Catholic policies of the church and state. These attacks equated, erroneously, all forms of radical heresy with Anabaptist practices in the 1525 Peasants' War in Germany, and especially with the bloody revolt in Münster. Clerical reformers and government officials associated radical heresy with a denial that scriptural justification existed for any form of

---

1566–1577," *Bulletin of the Institute of Historical Research* suppl. 5 (1960), xxxi–xxxii; Conyers Read, *Lord Burghley and Queen Elizabeth* (London, 1960), p. 294.

47. Cross, *The Puritan Earl*, p. 226; Francis Peck, ed., *Desiderata Curiosa: Or, a Collection of Diverse Scarce and Curious Pieces Relating Chiefly to Matters of English History* (London, 1779), pp. 92, 94, 130, 137–38. See also Claire Cross, ed., "The Letters of Sir Francis Hastings, 1574–1609," *Somerset Record Society* 69 (1969), p. 59.

48. HMC, *MSS. Hatfield*, p. 142. Another gentleman urged Burghley to place preachers in the north to "bridle evil before it appeared," *CSPD-addenda* 1566–79, p. 222. See also Francis Bacon's 1585 letter to the queen, in Bacon, *Works*, VIII. 49–50.

political authority. It was, however, radical heresy's social basis as much as its explicit doctrines that was responsible for this and other subversive qualities ascribed to it, such as its primitive communism, "which confound[s] all propriety [property] and dominion of goods."[49]

The radical heretic in Elizabethan England was invariably described by clerical reformers as a "common sort" of person.[50] Referring to these persons, John Stockwood noted that the "point of the necessity of magistrates should not at all need to be touched were it not that there are start-up tumultuous heads and troublesome spirits which . . . have gone about to seduce the minds of the simple and rude people."[51] Regretfully, reformers observed the role played by vernacular religious literature in spreading radical heresy: in the absence of clerical supervision, biblical parables on wealth and power were misinterpreted by the corrupt intellect of commoners. Clerical reformers argued that radical heretics allegorically expounded the Bible in order to "feed the humors of the poor and simple people, who through their corruption wonderfully delight in such a deformed handling of the word."[52] In this view, the irrationality of the lower classes combined with popular access to Bibles to produce heresy.

Puritans again cultivated official support by pointing out that preaching could influence the popular mind against heresy as well as against popular Catholicism. Suppression of radical heresy required "sincere" preaching to guide lay interpretation of scriptural passages on wealth and power. In 1549 a clerical leader of reform, Hugh Latimer, made this point to King Edward. He described a town where five hundred heretics lived, all of whom "will have no magistrates or judges." "Where is it?" he rhetorically asked, and then answered: "[It is where] the bishop of the diocese is an unpreaching prelate." The next year Thomas Lever made the same point to the king about heresy, magistracy, and preaching.[53]

Puritan clerics thus fended off an increasingly hostile episcopacy in the latter part of the sixteenth century by referring to these services of theirs

49. John Hooper, *A Godly Confession* (1550), in *PS*, XXI. 76. Allegations of subversion were routinely lodged against the most notorious group of radical heretics in Elizabethan England, the Family of Love (see below, pp. 102–3).

50. See below, pp. 100–101, for contemporary and modern opinion on the social basis of the Family of Love.

51. Stockwood, *A godlie Sermon*, Sig. B2ᵛ. Stockwood, cited several times in this chapter, received patronage from Sir Francis Walsingham; see Stockwood's epistle to John Brentius, *A Right Godly and Learned Discourse* (1584), Sig. A2ʳ.

52. Thomas Wilcox, *The Unfouldyng of sundry untruths* (1581), Sigs. A5ᵛ, A6ᵛ. See also Lever, *Sermons*, pp. 28–29; Otes, *An Explanation of St. Jude*, p. 398; John Rogers, *The Displaying of an horrible secte of grosse and wicked Heretiques* (1578), p. 55.

53. Hugh Latimer, *The Seven Sermons* (1550), in *PS*, XXVII. 151–52; Lever, *Sermons*, p. 61.

to the state. In the 1560s, after the first serious clash between Puritan preachers and ecclesiastical officials in the reign of Elizabeth resulted in suspension of nonconforming clerics, Anthony Gilby noted how these clerics "have written and preached so plainly" against radical heresy, and he predicted: "These errors will now spread, doubtlessly, seeing that so many good preachers are put to silence."[54] This defense of threatened preachers reappeared in many petitions and polemical tracts, as in the scandalous writings of Martin Marprelate, who denounced anti-Puritan prosecutions because "the people . . . already run into corners and more are like, because you keep the means of knowledge from them. Running into corners will breed Anabaptists. Anabaptists will alienate the hearts of the subjects from their lawful governors."[55]

Though these arguments helped Puritans to secure government support, they were not at all disingenuous. We shall see in the next chapter the extent to which radical heresy threatened clerical control over the popular Reformation. Puritan clerics devoted great efforts to combating radical heresy. For the moment it is sufficient to observe that Puritan preachers and their powerful lay patrons thought that "sincere" preaching was an important weapon in the battle against radical heresy, one too valuable to be lost by suspending clerics for nonconformity.

Preaching and Loyalty

Originally the social utility of preaching had been linked to the specific problems of peasant revolt, popular Catholicism, and radical heresy. By the late sixteenth century, however, more generalized claims emerged in Puritan rhetoric on behalf of preaching as an instrument of social control. These claims focused on godly preaching's cultivation of loyalty and submission to laws, local rulers, and the monarchy. This development was the consequence both of specific political problems confronting the Puritan clergy and of more general social trends.

The political problems the Puritan clerics faced consisted of official opposition that crystallized in a series of disciplinary proceedings against them in the latter part of Elizabeth's reign and in the early years of her

54. Anthony Gilby, *A Pleasant Dialogue, Betweene a Souldier of Barwicke, and an English Chaplaine* (n.p., 1581), Sig. C8.

55. William Pierce, ed., *The Marprelate Tracts, 1588, 1589* (London, 1911), pp. 98–99. See also Bacon, *Works*, VIII. 89; *CSPD* 1591–94, pp. 275–76; *An Humble Motion*, p. 84; Josiah Nichols, *The Plea Of The Innocent* (1602), pp. 118–19; Albert Peel, ed., *The Seconde Parte of a Register* (Cambridge, 1915), I. 229–30, II. 188–90; Anon., *The Unlawful Practices Of Prelates Against Godly Ministers* (1584), Sig. C8.

Stuart successor, James I. Archbishop Grindal's conservative successor, Whitgift, began a campaign in the mid-1580s to enforce clerical conformity in ceremonial matters; there followed the repression of the classis movement in 1590–91; finally, there was James the First's hostility to nonconforming clerics, which led to another campaign to enforce clerical conformity. These developments forced Puritan clerics to rely on aristocratic supporters and Parliament for protection. Such protection took the form of public and private lobbying and petitioning for less stringent definitions of conformity and for lax enforcement of conformity. The reasons advanced for this protection, by both Puritan clerics and their powerful lay supporters, focused squarely on the utility of Puritan preaching as a means for securing the political loyalty and submission of commoners.

More general social trends also heightened interest in the problem of loyalty and submission among commoners. Local levels of government dominated by lay Puritans displayed growing interest in the enforcement of piety and social discipline in the late sixteenth century. Lay jurisdiction was exercised over adulterers, fornicators, sabbath-breakers, swearers, and drunks in towns ruled by Puritan oligarchies and in rural areas where Puritan clerics allied themselves with godly justices of the peace. This initiative was prompted, in part, by Puritan contempt for the church courts, which were held to be corrupt and inefficient.[56]

It also occurred as part of a process of increasing stratification, which created in rural areas a widening gulf between wealthier yeomen farmers and impoverished groups of husbandmen and laborers. This process had cultural as well as economic dimensions. Regulatory initiatives undertaken by relatively wealthy and influential Puritans in villages and towns sought to instill discipline and piety among the poor. One recent study suggests that these initiatives replaced an older pattern of village conflict: "The sporadic interpersonal conflict of earlier years was giving way to a pattern of hostility between the ruling group of villagers and the village poor."[57] Attacks on unlicensed alehouses were a prominent feature of this regulatory initiative. Unlike more prestigious inns and taverns, alehouses were run by the poor for the poor, and they harbored an "alternative society," which became a center for old games and rituals, frowned upon by

56. Patrick Collinson, "Magistracy and Ministry: A Suffolk Miniature," in R. Buick Knox, ed., *Reformation, Conformity and Dissent* (London, 1977); Paul Slack, "Religious Protest and Urban Authority: The Case of Henry Sherfield, Iconoclast, 1633," *SCH* 9 (1972); Keith Thomas, "The Puritans and Adultery: The Act of 1650 Reconsidered," in Pennington and Thomas, eds., *Puritans and Revolutionaries*, pp. 266–67.

57. Keith Wrightson and David Levine, *Poverty and Piety in an English Village: Terling, 1525–1700* (New York, 1979), p. 140. See also Christopher Hill, *Puritanism and Revolution* (New York, 1964), p. 229, and *Society and Puritanism*, pp. 222–25.

Puritans, and "provided a focus for lower-class irreligion and igno-rance."[58] This heightened concern for social discipline also appeared in the contemporary version of a "crime wave," a steady increase in felony prosecutions, that began in the 1590s and peaked about midway through the reign of James I. This probably had some connections with the en-closure and grain riots of 1592–93, 1596–97, and 1607. But the regu-latory initiatives clearly had deeper motivations, which inspired lay Pu-ritans to cope with the real and imagined forms of disorder that they associated with the poor and their culture.[59]

THESE POLITICAL AND SOCIAL CIRCUMSTANCES HEIGHTENED INTEREST in preaching as an instrument of social control. This development, how-ever, was fully compatible with the major tenets of Protestantism, such as the importance of edification. Secular benefits of preaching were always treated as an appendage to its primary purpose, which was to proclaim the gospel. In Puritan rhetoric it was a commonplace to note the twofold uses of preaching: first, its spiritual use, as an ordinary means of salvation of souls; second, its political use, as a way to influence the popular mind.

From comments by a bishop in 1541 to the first Fast Sermon before the Long Parliament in 1640, it was often said that "beside the spiritual bene-fit, a preaching ministry is one of the best advantages to secure a state."[60] During the reigns of Henry, Edward, and Elizabeth, clerical reformers argued that preaching was "the only ordinary means of salvation of souls, and the only good means to teach your Majesty's subjects to know their true obedience."[61] At the beginning of James's reign, opponents of anti-Puritan measures predicted that suspension of Puritan preachers would have disastrous spiritual and political consequences: "The people by this means . . . shall both perish of themselves, and not yield that cheerful & conscionable obedience to his Majesty which otherwise they should and ought."[62] Powerful lay supporters of godly preaching also held this ap-

---

58. Peter Clark, "The Alehouse and the Alternative Society," in Pennington and Thomas, eds., *Puritans and Revolutionaries*, p. 65 and passim; Wrightson and Levine, *Poverty and Piety*, pp. 134–46.

59. J.S. Cockburn, "The Nature and Incidence of Crime in England, 1559–1625: A Preliminary Survey," in J.S. Cockburn, ed., *Crime in England 1550–1800* (London, 1977); Wrightson and Levine, *Poverty and Piety*, pp. 177–80.

60. Cornelius Burges, *The First Sermon, Preached To The Honorable House Of Commons* (1640), in *FS*, I. 91; *L&P*, XVI. 377. "Fast Sermons" were presented by Puritan preachers to the Long Parliament during the English Civil War.

61. Peel, *Seconde Parte*, I. 75. See also Hooper, *Later Writings*, p. 80; Grindal, *Remains*, p. 379; Lever, *Sermons*, p. 141; Tracy, *A supplycacion*, Sig. A5ᵛ.

62. BrL, *MSS. Sloan* 271, f. 26ᵛ. See also *Certaine Advertisements For The Good Of The Church And Common-Wealth* (1622?), pp. 11, 46; Hill, *Change and Continuity*, p. 14.

praisal of the twofold uses of preaching. For example, the governors of
Rye in 1591 requested permission to hire a town preacher that "thereby
the ignorant might be informed of the will and pleasure of God, and the
better sort reformed in lives and conversation."[63]

The two uses ascribed to preaching by Puritan writers clearly distinguished between two audiences. Spiritual comforts accrued to those within
the Puritan camp; dire warnings of God's wrath confronted enemies of the
godly. This is, of course, to be expected of Calvinist clerics seeking to
gather the elect from the mass of unregenerates. But Puritan discussion of
this point also reflected the broader social circumstances that heightened
concern with discipline among the poor. Discussion of the secular benefits
of preaching concerned chiefly the disposition of unregenerates, but descriptions of this disposition corresponded closely to specific forms of
lower-class unruliness.

This twofold appraisal of preaching certainly was compatible with Calvinist theology, stressing as it did the distinction between renewing and
restraining grace. For William Perkins, the most eminent Puritan divine
of this era, the latter grace "bridles and restrains the corruptions of men's
hearts from breaking forth into outward actions, for the common good,
that societies may be preserved."[64] This theological point was implicit in
Puritan pronouncements on the twofold uses of preaching. But Puritan
divines added to the theological distinction between renewing and restraining grace a social distinction: restraining grace was the solution to
the problem of restive behavior among the lower classes, while renewing
grace dispensed spiritual amenities to others. Thus, the social prejudices
of the upper classes and their fear of the threat posed to authority by the
irrationality of the lower classes, by the many-headed monster, neatly
dovetailed with Puritan views on the twofold uses of preaching.

It is, of course, difficult to gauge precisely the amount of support that
Puritan clerics managed to gain by these arguments about the usefulness
of their preaching. Certainly they overestimated the success of preaching
as a means of converting Catholics to the new faith, as I noted above. But
so did their lay supporters. Both thought, too confidently perhaps, that a
common interest linked their plans for religious reform and the Tudor
and early Stuart rulers' need for popular submission to authority.

This is evident in numerous letters, petitions, and pamphlets that defended Puritan clerics against their adversaries. A 1606 petition to Parlia-

63. HMC, *MSS. Rye*, p. 99. See also Cross, *The Puritan Earl*, pp. 47–48, and
"Letters of Sir Francis Hastings," p. 59; G. Eland, ed., *Thomas Wotton's Letter-Book,
1574–1586* (Oxford, 1960), pp. 24–25; Peck, *Desiderata Curiosa*, p. 113.

64. William Perkins, *Workes* (Cambridge, 1608–9), II. 131, and see also ibid., I.
274–75, 628, II. 289, 712.

ment cited evidence from a previous century of rural unrest and revolt: where godly clerics preached, there was "diligence in the knowledge & obedience of the people in such places . . . whereas in other places, men are for the most part ignorant of all duty to God and man . . . apt to sedition & rebellion as all experience teaches us." Sir Richard Holland's letter to the Privy Council in 1605 summarized the arguments of many Puritan clerics about those places in the realm where "his Majesty is obeyed of conscience": "the people have been most obedient to the state in those parts where they have been best instructed by the labors of these preachers."[65] Indeed, so useful was this argument thought to be for deflecting attacks by conservative church officials that it was even used by some Separatists to justify *lay* preaching: "Thus should atheists, familists, papists, traitors . . . be more discovered and sooner rooted out."[66] For their part, Puritan clerics confidently expected to obtain patronage and protection from powerfully placed laymen who appreciated the secular uses of their preaching. This can be seen in a cleric's description of the motives that prompted influential gentlemen to protest against Archbishop Whitgift's campaign in 1583–84 to enforce clerical subscription to conformity:

> These things gentlemen of all sorts took to heart . . . God's cause moved them, and honor of the Gospel drew them. Yea, the safety of her Majesty in these dangerous times even compelled them. Their own offices of justice, which by the word was so well laid, & which without it they could not steer in a storm of so great confusion, drew them to sue in all humble manner to the archbishop.[67]

Much evidence indicates that Puritan clerics succeeded in their efforts to gather support from influential and powerful laymen. Previously we saw how keenly some influential members of Elizabeth's government appreciated the secular benefits of Puritan preaching, and they had some success in defending the preachers who were under attack by Archbishop Whitgift in 1583–84. In addition, the Puritan gentry from at least nine

65. Anon., *Certain Arguments . . . To Perswade And Provoke . . . Parliament to speake for the ministers* (1606), pp. 1–2; Richard Holland, quoted in HMC, *Salisbury MSS.* XVII. 56–57; Peel, *Seconde Parte*, II. 81. See also Wiliam Attersoll, *The Pathway to Canaan* (Barbican, 1609), p. 140; Nicholas Bownde, *The Doctrine Of The Sabbath* (1595), pp. 280–81; William Bradshaw, *A Myld And Just Defence Of Certeyne Arguments* (1606), p. 61; Nichols, *Plea Of The Innocent*, pp. 172–74. For views of Puritan MPs, see *CJ*, 199–200, 784.

66. Henry Ainsworth and Francis Johnson, *An Apologie Or defense Of Such True Christians* (1604), p. 46.

67. *The Unlawful Practices of Prelates*, Sig. C3ʳ.

counties petitioned on behalf of these preachers. Referring to these petitioners, Lord Burghley told the archbishop that he was "now daily charged by councilors and public persons, to neglect of my duty in not staying of these your Grace's proceedings . . . as the papists are thereby encouraged, all ill-disposed subjects animated." Protesting gentlemen from Norfolk informed the Privy Council that, in addition to their ordinary pastoral duties, the Puritan clerics also "preach in the great towns and so urge the people to dutiful obedience." Lord Burghley apparently agreed, and he advised the queen that "the bishops, in these dangerous times, take a very ill and unadvised course, in driving them [Puritans] from their cures."[68]

The appointment of nonpreaching clerics to benefices vacated by the suspension of Puritan preachers further alarmed some gentlemen. In 1581, a member of Parliament denounced this practice of some bishops and argued that "the number of papists and the number of the Family of Love had increased under them [the bishops] by their remissness in executing their authorities."[69] But these specific evils were not the only threats combated by Puritan preachers. It was also noted that Puritan preaching had more generally cultivated the obedience of commoners to local rulers. For example, when Whitgift proceeded against the Puritan clergy, Sir Thomas Wotton presented a strong case to the Privy Council for stopping the archbishop:

> None can better tell than we that a great number of the inhabitants of this country by this good preaching . . . have been brought . . . to live quietly, and in the execution of your or her Majesty's commandments very obediently.[70]

And at the beginning of James's reign, some "religious gentlemen" testified that, due to Puritan preaching, "the magistrates in every county have found it easier to continue the common people in duties of their subjection and loyalty to the supreme power."[71] Local elites, as well as powerful fig-

---

68. Knappen, *Tudor Puritanism*, p. 269; Peel, *Seconde Parte*, I. 225; Strype, *Whitgift*, III. 105; Walter Scott, ed., *A Collection of Scarce and Valuable Tracts* (London, 1809), I. 166.

69. *Archaeologia* 36 (1855), p. 112. The same reaction greeted Whitgift's suspension of Puritan preachers in 1584: "What more pernicious councel could hell itself contrive, in a time when Jesuits, those of the family of love, and others of all sorts swarmed . . . now to thrust out godly and learned preachers" (Strype, *Whitgift*, I. 241).

70. Eland, *Thomas Wotton's Letter-Book*, p. 63.

71. Anon., *Certaine Demandes With their grounds . . . by some religious gentl.* (1605), p. 16. This plea is the same as one made by Lancashire gentlemen to the Privy Council, quoted in Richardson, *Puritanism in North-West England*, p. 146. See also Anon., *A parte*

ures at court, thus placed a good deal of credence in Puritan claims on behalf of the secular merits of their preaching.

Consent and Control

Why did Puritan clerics and their powerful lay supporters place so much credence in these claims that preaching was an effective instrument of social control? What enabled them to presume so strongly that preaching had a unique ability not merely to forestall rebellion, convert Catholics, and deter heretics but to cultivate general obedience to local and national rulers? In part, this was due to the heightened religious significance that Protestantism conferred on preaching, as mentioned above. It was also due to specific political circumstances, which forced Puritan clerics to rely on powerful lay interests for protection against conservative church forces. Equally important was Puritan appraisal of the nature of this type of social control, one that focused on the inward disposition of individuals. Their remarks on the obedience cultivated by godly preaching continually emphasized that it was an "inward" and "cheerful & conscionable" obedience. Growing awareness of the importance of consent in establishing social order underlay Puritan emphasis on the efficacy of preaching as a means of social control.

Several factors were important in shaping this view of preaching. First, the Protestant emphasis on faith and on the inner dimensions of the conversion process generally called attention to the inward disposition of individuals in religious matters. An extension of this to secular matters is evident in remarks by Sir Francis Hastings, brother of the staunchly Puritan third earl of Huntingdon: "Religion then is the true guide to every man's conscience, and holds every man's conscience within the compass of true obedience."[72]

Second, the reception of Machiavelli's thought in England, beginning in the early sixteenth century, heightened appreciation of the importance of influencing the popular mind as a policy of statecraft. Cynical manipulation of religion for political ends was, of course, anathema to Puritanism. But what England adopted from Machiavelli's writings was not a coherent doctrine, which was frequently denounced, but instead a diffuse set of ideas that emphasized the expedient features of consensual

---

of a register contayning sundrie memorable matters (1593), p. 177; HMC, *MSS. Salisbury* XVII. 56–57.

72. Francis Hastings, *A Watchword To All religious, and true hearted English-men* (1598), p. 109.

submission to authority.[73] This provided an alternative to brutal laws dealing with impiety, poverty, and sedition, which many contemporaries
knew to be ineffective.

Third, the problem of recusancy in Elizabethan England also focused
attention on the expediency of consent in political matters. As Walsingham observed (above, p. 79), the crucial issue was not outward conformity but the inner consent of England's Catholics to the Elizabethan
Settlement. It was this point that led Lord Burghley to urge the queen to
use godly preachers and loyal schoolmasters to secure her realm from papist disaffection. Puritan writers typically upheld the importance of godly
preaching by arguing that "no human laws . . . will reclaim papists without liberty of the word."[74]

These factors, and not simply political self-interest, shaped Puritan
opinion on the secular merits of their preaching, its ability to align individual conscience with the prevailing powers. In sermons before important persons and in polemical writings, Puritan clerics extolled this aspect
of godly preaching, and they did not hesitate to point out the bond of interest it forged between them and worldly rulers, despite its Machiavel-
lian connotations. In a Paul's Cross sermon, Robert Harris warned the
magistrates of England: "Did not our ministry awe men's consciences, nor
you, nor the world would be one year the older; should you cease to countenance us in our righteous causes, you should betray your right hand with
the left." A decade later, in 1632, a Puritan lecturer in Preston repeated
this message, word for word, in a sermon delivered before judges at the
Lancaster assizes. Half a century earlier, John Stockwood made the same
point in a Paul's Cross sermon: "The preacher enters into the very soul
and mind of man . . . and frames it unto inward obedience unto God, out
of which springs and issues the true outward obedience unto his civil
magistrate."[75]

Further discussion of preaching and of the consensual foundations of
obedience occurred in petitions and polemical writings on behalf of Puritan clerics who were threatened with suspension for nonconformity. An
Elizabethan tract written in defense of these clerics cited the dangers attendant upon suppression of their preaching. "The cutting of preaching
. . . is the cutting of the sinews asunder whereby the subjects in all parts of
the realm are most strongly knit to their prince." It then continued:

73. Felix Raab, *The English Face of Machiavelli* (London, 1964).

74. Scott, *Collection of Tracts,* I. 166–67; *Certaine Advertisements,* p. 34. See also
Cross, *The Puritan Earl,* p. 247.

75. Robert Harris, *Gods Goodnes And Mercie* (1631), p. 13; John Stockwood, *A very
fruitful Sermon preached at Paules Cross* (1579), Sig. C8ᵛ. For the Preston lecturer, see
Richardson, *Puritanism in North-West England,* p. 145.

And, indeed, the policy being taken away, I mean the preachers that break the first rage of men's outrageousness, what can the banks hold (I say) the ordinary justice of the land for stay of men's evil behaviors . . . The laws therefore that shall provide against these outward evils, be they never so well framed, yet if conscience stays not the inward, it shall be easier for an evil body to contrive mischief, than for the wisest and best man to devise remedies.

This argument concluded, significantly enough, with the observation, "The conscience of the subject, is the strength of the prince."[76]

These reflections on preaching display important links between secular problems of authority and efforts to promote religious reform by Puritan clerics and their powerful lay supporters. Appraisals of preaching as an instrument of social control show how critical ideas of religious dissent, stressing edification and the sanctity of conscience, came to be offered in the service of the state in late Tudor and early Stuart England. In the view of the clerical reformers and their lay supporters, the relationship between religious dissent and the social order appeared to be one of harmony, in which the former stabilized the latter.

For the clerical reformers and their elite lay supporters, religious dissent was a higher form of patriotism. Its cultivation by a ministry devoted to godly preaching appealed to important values held by local and national rulers of a society still organized along rigidly hierarchical lines. These were profoundly conservative values, and the emphasis on unquestioned obedience to constituted authorities reflected a pervasive concern with the many-headed monster of popular unrest and insurrection. Such concern was as natural for university-educated clerics, who led the movement for religious reform, as it was for their lay supporters, drawn from the ranks of merchants, yeomen, the gentry, and the peers of the realm. Puritan clerics exploited this concern to the fullest extent possible by promising that sincere preaching would make the popular mind more tractable to existing structures of authority at all levels of society.

76. *The Unlawful Practices Of Prelates*, Sigs. B5^v, B6^v-B7^r, B8^r. See also *Certaine Advertisements*, p. 23; *An Humble Motion*, p. 58; Anon., *An Humble petition of the Communalitie* (1588), Sigs. A8^r, I6^r; Peel, *Seconde Parte*, I. 76.

4

Puritan Clerics and
Popular Dissent

Scholarly convention associates the term Puritanism with the religious dissent that occurred within the church that was established by the Elizabethan Settlement in 1559. Its general aims included removal of ceremonial "abuses" in the official liturgy of the church, reform of social manners and morals, and development of an evangelical style of Calvinist religion, which upheld the importance of biblical literacy for laypersons and of preaching for ordained ministers.

The rise of Puritanism in pre-Revolutionary England, from 1559 to 1640, was not merely the result of efforts by Puritan clerics to indoctrinate the laity with their religious goals. To be sure, this was an important factor, and one that has been thoroughly explored in accounts of Puritanism, as in William Haller's classic work, *The Rise of Puritanism*. But equally important was the existence of a tradition of popular dissent, which had long-standing commitments to a literate religion and to an edifying and preaching style of worship, and which was opposed to all rituals associated with a sacerdotal priesthood. These lay commitments, together with the emergence of a cohesive clerical leadership, were the sources of the religious dissent that today is called Puritanism.

The organizational and ideological features of Puritanism thus had both clerical and lay sources. Where popular dissent existed, the pastoral activities of Puritan clerics were likely to receive a favorable reception and go unreported to church officials. But popular dissent did not always provide uncritical support for these pastoral activities, for it also posed serious challenges to the authority of Puritan clerics as leaders of religious dissent. In their broad outlines, the doctrinal tenets held by Puritan clerics and laity were similar, but lay dissenters interpreted these tenets in ways that often were unanticipated and unwelcomed by the clerics. Thus, radical challenges to the leadership of the Puritan clergy were partly a consequence of its success.

Subtle and overt conflicts between Puritan clerics and a lay vanguard played a crucial part in the rise of Puritanism. Central to these conflicts were the radically democratic implications of some of the lay initiatives in popular dissent. Although these implications varied for different factions of dissenters, all factions shared in a tendency to undermine the principle of lay subordination to clerics in religious matters. *Radical heretics* pushed the principle of edification to the point where an ordained ministry, and sometimes even the sacraments, became needless. *Separatists* argued that lay interest in godly religion required congregational control over membership and choice of pastors. All of this was incompatible with the Puritan clergy's commitment to the idea of a state church. But the *Puritan laity* presented problems as well. Its commitment to edification and literate religion, its iconoclasm and opposition to many ceremonies prescribed by the Anglican church, greatly outweighed its loyalty to parochially appointed clerics, even Puritan clerics.

The inner direction of religious reform in pre-Revolutionary England was thus guided by a complex set of tensions between Puritan clerics and a lay vanguard that existed both within and outside the church. This created a key organizational dilemma for Puritan clerics. As ordained ministers in a comprehensive church and as nominal leaders of a popular religious movement, they occupied incompatible roles. As ordained ministers, they were subject to an episcopal authority that displayed increasing hostility to the kinds of lay initiatives that were evident in popular dissent. This set limits to the extent to which they could accommodate the doctrinal and liturgical expectations of the lay vanguard. Defiance of episcopal authority entailed suspension and deprivation of the resources of a state church for promoting reform. Frustration of lay expectations precipitated schism and loss of control over the popular Reformation.

This organizational dilemma remained unresolved in the pre-Revolutionary era. Indeed, it became more acute when a conservative reaction in the church gathered momentum under the rule of Archbishop Laud during the reign of Charles I. At this point, Puritan clerics could no longer bridge the gulf between the church, with its official doctrines and liturgy, and an ongoing process of popular Reformation. Prior to this time they had managed to maintain a tenuous balance between the conflicting demands of their ecclesiastical superiors and their restive lay followers. This was no mean feat, given the independence and assertiveness of many lay dissenters.

DIRECT AND INDIRECT EVIDENCE SHOWS THAT LAY DISSENTERS POS-sessed strong views on what constituted proper worship and that they readily communicated these views to their pastors. An amusing example occurred in a letter to a cleric addressed, in part, to "the most deutero-nomicall polidoxologist and pantifilogicall linguist" from his seventeenth-century "semipagan auditors," who complained: "We lose the gravity and system of your doctrine, and our commonsense is admiring at the words we understand not."[1]

This lay activity produced a shifting balance between clerical and lay roles in religious life that increasingly favored lay intellectual initiatives at the expense of clerical authority. This development was in evidence at the beginning of the Reformation, for, even then, popular dissent compli-cated official efforts to create a new faith. In 1538 orders were given re-quiring all churches to purchase and make available English Bibles. Im-mediately, further orders had to be given to prevent lay Bible-reading from competing with divine services. The futility of such orders appears in the fact that they had to be reissued in a royal proclamation of 1541 and in admonitions by the bishop of London in 1542. Not only did zealous parishioners read the Bible during services; some also undertook to pub-licly read and comment on it, usurping a clerical prerogative. In response to reports from Calais about these practices, Archbishop Cranmer wrote to the lord deputy of Calais in 1539, complaining about laypersons who "do much abuse the King's Grace's intent" in ordering the provision of Bibles. He ordered that it was to be read "not in contempt or hindrance of any divine service . . . nor that any such reading should be used in the church as in a common school, expounding & interpreting scriptures, un-less it be by such as have authority to preach and read."[2]

From the Elizabethan Settlement in 1559 to the meeting of the Long Parliament in 1640, lay intellectual initiatives shaped both the Puritan movement and its opposition. The "formal priest" ridiculed in a dialogue composed by a Puritan cleric in the 1560s lamented the consequences of clerical efforts to promote literate religion: "It was never good with us priests since every soldier and servingman could talk so much of the scriptures. And these foolish ministers are the cause thereof, which would make all men as wise as themselves." Fifty years later another cleric

1. BoL, *MSS. Rawls.* D399, f. 184ʳ.
2. Cranmer, *Works*, in *PS*, XVI. 391–92; *LL*, V. 586.

caustically observed, "Many nowadays of the laity will challenge to themselves great knowledge, yea and think themselves . . . wiser than their leaders."[3] At the end of the pre-Revolutionary era, Puritan clerics echoed these remarks in complaints to the Long Parliament about strife between ministers and their parishioners: "Ministers complain of their people, that they are factious, seditious, covetous, disrespectful of the ministry . . . The people complain of their ministers, that they are dumb dogs . . . & both blame each other for God's anger."[4]

Clerics hostile to Puritanism regarded intellectual initiatives among its lay adherents as a threat to hierarchical principles, which they took for granted in religious and civil life. They denounced such initiatives, desiring instead

> that all would not preach which can speak; because St. Paul calls every family a church, would not turn every table's end into a pulpit; that the feet in this body should not presume to see nor the hands to speak; that the clue of predestination might not be reeled up at the spindle nor the decrees of God unravelled at the loom; that our lay-divines would see themselves as well as the clergy leaving . . . the disputes of religion to the decision of the church.[5]

In the 1630s Archbishop Laud sought not only to discipline Puritan clerics but also to reestablish the principle of lay subordination to clerics. Sermons delivered by local priests during Laud's official visits defended this battered principle and declared that "lay persons with all readiness should be ruled by the priests in matters of religion." The problem was lack of a *via media* between lay initiative in popular dissent and papal infallibility in Catholicism, for "The Romanist will yield to his prelate absolute submission of conscience . . . the anti-Romanist will obey his pastor no further than he speaks apparent word of God. Thus too servile or [too] saucy." Cultivated sensibility offended by lack of lay servility pervaded these visitation sermons. "'Tis a common delusion of the deceiving serpent to whisper into the laity a contempt of the clergy. Alas, alas, 'tis too frequent . . . The rude sort sit in judgement upon their pastors."[6]

3. Anthony Gilby, *A Pleasant Dialogue, Betweene a Souldier of Barwicke, and an English Chaplaine* (n.p., 1581), Sig. C3ᵛ; Willaim Est, *The Right Rule of a Religious Life* (1616), p. 168. See also above, pp. 26–27.

4. Edward Calamy, *Englands Looking-Glasse* (1642), in *FS*, II. 77. See also Robert Harris, *A Sermon Preached To The Honorable House Of Commons* (1642), in *FS*, III. 14; Obadiah Sedgwicke, *Englands Preservation* (1642), in *FS*, III. 108.

5. Thomas Laurence, *Two Sermons* (Oxford, 1635), pp. 22–23. See also Samuel Gardiner, *A Dialogue Or Conference* (1605), Sig. H4ᵛ.

6. Jasper Fisher, *The Priests Duty & Dignity: Preached at the Triennial Visitation in Ampthill* (1636), pp. 28, 31; John Fealty, *Obedience And Submission* (1636), p. 19. See

Concern with lay Puritanism is a well-known feature of the Laudian reaction. Less well known are the problems encountered by Puritan clerics when they were confronted with lay intellectual initiatives. Though this was generally troublesome to the church, it was especially threatening to Puritan clerics, who intimately experienced the adverse consequences of lay initiative. Their proselytizing efforts encouraged this initiative because of their commitment to edification. One Puritan cleric urged godly pastors to "preach [so] that we may rather make our people scholars than show ourselves scholars to our people." But godly pastors did not hesitate to attack the fruits of such scholarship when it undermined their authority over their parish, created difficulties with their ecclesiastical superiors, and led godly laypersons to tell their less-zealous pastors what God expected of them in their ministry. Cornelius Burges denounced this last activity because it "is no layman's work, but a bishop's office." Yet he feared that "upstarting mushrooms" among the laity might dare even to instruct bishops in their religious duties:

> if bishops must once be taught of them, what must follow next? Why the layman must dispute, and the bishop sit by and hear; the layman should be the master, and the bishop the boy to go to school.[7]

This was only a short step away from Archbishop Laud's warning to King Charles, "No bishop, no king."

In the pre-Revolutionary era, however, lay initiatives gathered momentum but, in lay Puritanism, did not openly assert the congregational principle of subordination of clerics to parishioners. That development awaited the collapse of church controls during the Civil War. Excepting its radical fringes, popular dissent presented a latent rather than an open challenge to the leadership of Puritan preachers. But this alone was sufficient to generate widespread alarm in a society where subordination of laity to clerics was part of the general principle of social and political hierarchy.

LAY INITIATIVES, AND THEIR IMPACT ON RELATIONS BETWEEN PURITAN clerics and popular dissent, were different for heretics, Separatists, and lay Puritans. In each case, Puritan clerics sought to maintain their authority by channeling lay initiatives in directions that were compatible

---

also Samuel Hoard, *The Churches Authority Asserted* (1637), pp. 66–70; William Quelch, *Church-Customes Vindicated* (1636), p. 42; Alexander Read, *A Sermon Preached . . . At A Visitation At Brentwood* (1636), p. 17; Edward Reynolds, *A Sermon Touching The Peace & Edification Of The Church* (1638), p. 11.

7. Cornelius Burges, *The Fire Of The Sanctuarie* (1625), pp. 334–35. See also Robert Allen, *The Doctrine Of The Gospel* (1606), II. 457; Elnathan Parr, *A plain exposition upon chapters 13. 14. 15 and 16 . . . [of] the Romanes* (1622), in *Workes* (1632), p. 83.

with their pastoral supervision from within the church. Against heretical claims to spiritual perfection, Puritan preachers held out the possibility of certitude of salvation; against separation from an allegedly corrupt church, they advised separation from sin. Relations with lay Puritans were, of course, less strained, but as we shall see, they were not unproblematic.

Lay Puritans accepted, in principle, a state church, while heretics and Separatists rejected its compulsory and parochial format. Heresy in turn must be distinguished from Separatism, for Separatists, unlike heretics, followed the same Calvinist doctrine of grace and salvation as was held by Puritans. Criticism of Separatists by Puritan clerics was more moderate than that meted out to heretics, in part because a thin line divided outright separation from Puritan nonconformity. Ceremonial and liturgical practices disliked by Separatists were often abandoned, informally and illegally, by Puritan clerics, who regarded the impatience of Separatists with some sympathy.[8] Heretics they condemned without reservation. William Perkins voiced a widely held view when he distinguished between heretics and Separatists, arguing that "every false teacher is a schismatic, but every schismatic is not a false teacher." The distinction was important because, unlike schismatics, "a heretic may be put to death for his damnable opinions."[9] But if Puritans and Separatists were often not too far apart, there were also times when Separatist beliefs and practices converged with radical heresy. Puritan clerics routinely warned that separation led to heresy, and some Separatist groups did turn eventually to heterodox beliefs. Most Separatists, however, regarded Puritan accusations of heresy as slander.[10] With these caveats in mind, I use this tripartite division of popular dissent as a guide for my analysis of its relations to the Puritan clergy.

Heresy: The Apocalypse and Antinomianism

Two rather different types of heresy circulated on the fringes of popular dissent in pre-Revolutionary England. One type assumed the form of

---

8. One Puritan preacher gently criticized Separatists, "whom I much pity because I am persuaded there are some among them that are conscionable" (Elnathan Parr, *A plain exposition upon the whole 8th-12th chapters of . . . the Romanes* [1620], in *Workes*, p. 117). See also John Brinsley (the elder), *The Third Part Of The True Watch* (1622), p. 47; John Browne, *The History of Congregationalism in Norfolk and Suffolk* (London, 1876), p. 31; John Haweis, *Sketches of the Reformation and Elizabethan Age Taken from the Pulpit* (London, 1844), p. 204.

9. William Perkins, *Workes* (Cambridge, 1608–9), III. 234, 295.

10. See BoL, *MSS. Jones* 30, ff. 24ᵛ-26ᵛ; Henoch Clapham, *Errour On The Right Hand* (1608), p. 18; Henry Jacob, *A Defense Of The Churches And Ministry of England*

millenarian prophecy and predicted the imminence of chiliastic upheaval. The other pursued a markedly different course, one that retreated from the world into quiet contemplation and Antinomianism. Contemporaries identified the former type of heresy with Anabaptism and the 1535 revolt in Münster. Its contours followed the same millenarian eschatology that earlier had animated popular outbursts throughout the Middle Ages, along with prophetic traditions native to England. Antinomianism in England at this time was probably most widely represented by the Family of Love. Heterodox features of both heresies resulted from their radical resolution of the tension in Christian thought between spiritual and temporal realities, between the Gospel promise of freedom from sin and subordination to worldly authority. The immediacy with which millenarians and Antinomians resolved this tension was largely responsible for the subversive qualities attributed to them by hostile observers.

These two types of heresy, though they followed different paths, led toward the same goal: abolition of all temporal and spiritual limitations imposed by sharp divisions between heaven and earth, such as those maintained by Calvinism. The millenarian prophets foresaw the imminent end of the world and consequently promoted, more in word than in deed, the apocalyptic rising of the saints in order to inaugurate the Second Coming of Christ. In contrast, the members of the Family of Love held a subdued, introspective doctrine of the possibility, in this life, of a direct union with God, which they called being "godded with God." Unlike the chiliasts, the Familists quietly dissolved earthly limitations through inner experience.

Differences in organization and individual temperament also characterized these two heresies. Some millenarian prophets were reputed to be violent characters; all of them set out to wage a final war against Antichrist. By contrast, members of the Family of Love were doctrinal pacifists.[11] Millenarian prophets emerged in isolated incidents which represented extreme expressions of rather widespread views about Antichrist that, in moderate form, were heard in respectable circles. Familists formed a self-contained sect that was sufficiently organized to provide support for imprisoned members and to collect tithes.

(Middleburgh, 1599), p. 4; B.R. White, *The English Separatist Tradition* (Oxford, 1971), pp. 161–64.

11. Temperamental differences appear in a dialogue composed by a cleric on familiar terms with radical trends in popular dissent. In the course of a debate, a millenarian becomes enraged and strikes the Familist; see Clapham, *Errour On The Right Hand*, pp. 50–51. See also Keith Thomas, *Religion and the Decline of Magic* (Harmondsworth, Eng., 1973), p. 158, and A.G. Dickens, *The English Reformation* (London, 1964), p. 238, who describes Familism as "a subdued and Anglicised type of Anabaptism."

As a form of prophecy, the millenarian heresy had links to a more widespread feature of popular culture in early modern England. Prophecy was not an especially troublesome activity when it attempted to explain or forecast daily events and mishaps, but it took on ominous overtones when prophetic legends and traditions, native to England, were used to predict the reversal of the Reformation and the revival of the old religion. More ominous still was the specter of an Anabaptist revolt raised by the merger of native prophecy with continental Anabaptism. Often the same native prophecies appeared in popular Catholicism and in Anabaptism. In both cases, prophecy became a vehicle for generalizing chronic economic and religious discontent among the lower classes.[12] Amidst rural unrest of the sixteenth century there were predictions of the return of the "golden days" of the old religion. Elements of popular radicalism are evident in predictions by "lookers for a golden day," who claimed "it was merry in England before the Bible and the English service came abroad. Men lived quietly when they had less preaching. When the mass was up we had all things pleasant and peaceful."[13]

Popular radicalism was just as evident in millenarian prophecy, although its utopia derived not from the return of Catholicism but from the chiliastic eschatology based on the books of Daniel and the Revelation. Essential elements of this eschatology consisted of predictions about the gathering of Jews in Jerusalem, claims on behalf of the messianic role of the prophet, and intimations of bloody revolts, to be followed by the millennial reign of the gospel. Almost all of the millenarian prophets were laymen.[14] The existence of this prophetic tradition came to light periodically as prophets intermittently appeared and made use of rather well-worn predictions. For example, two prophets described by Thomas Heywood in 1636 claimed to know "all secrets whatsoever" and to possess "power over the elements." One of them would be slain and rise up again to reign as high priest over Jerusalem—all this derived from the classic biblical source for the eschatology (Rev. 11:6–11).[15]

These prophecies reveal popular efforts to come to terms with the mo-

---

12. Thomas, *Religion and the Decline of Magic*, pp. 471–83. See also Christopher Hill, *The World Turned Upside Down: Radical Ideas during the English Revolution* (New York, 1972), p. 72, on millenarianism during the Civil War and Interregnum.

13. William Fisher, *A Sermon preached at Paules crosse* (1580), Sig. A7; Richard Porter, *A Sermon . . . Preached in Paules Churche* (1570), f. 12ᵛ. See above, p. 69, and also John Bradford, *A Sermon of repentance* (1553), in *PS*, V. 39.

14. But cf. John Strype, *Annals of the Reformation* (Oxford, 1824), III. 480.

15. Thomas Heywood, *A True Discourse of the Two Infamous Upstart Prophets* (1636), pp. 9–11. See also Clapham, *Errour On The Right Hand*, pp. 31–32, *Antidoton* (1600), p. 33; Edmund Jessop, *A Discourse Of The Errours Of The English Anabaptists* (1623), p. 77; John Waddington, *Congregational History* (London, 1874), I. 62–63.

mentous expectations and uncertainties created by the Reformation. Native prophetic traditions and vernacular Bibles provided resources for this task of understanding a world whose end appeared imminent. Formulated without clerical supervision, prophecies by self-appointed messiahs neglected the fine distinctions of Calvinism, which separated spiritual promise from worldly fulfillment. Messianic insistence on establishing a kingdom of the godly, following a destruction of sinners, pushed prophetic activity in the direction of expressing secular discontents and resentments. The potential of this type of prophecy for mobilizing grievances among the lower classes was a pressing concern of the government, which was well aware of the role native prophecy played in the revolts of 1536–37, 1549, and 1569. This concern was also heightened by fears that continental Anabaptism was infesting England. In this context the government acted firmly to check millenarian prophecy among the laity. Specific doctrines were proscribed and *vernacular* versions of important commentaries on the eschatology were prohibited.[16]

This last problem was compounded by the success of the Reformation in England, for publication of vernacular Bibles made the classic sources of millenarian prophecy available to all who possessed even a rudimentary reading ability. Heywood's description of two millenarian prophets stated that they "are simple tradesmen, who never looked upon any university, or scarcely have been acquainted with a grammar school; who can only read English, though they know not how to speak it truly."[17] But these prophets depended neither on writing nor on the ability to affect proper speech. Their prophetic interpretation required only an ability to read vernacular Bibles.

Popular misinterpretation of scriptures, according to clerics, was the basis of messianic prophecy. Properly understood, these passages of the Bible revealed the errors of Rome, not the impending apocalypse forecast by the millenarians. In 1560, the bishop of Exeter publicly lectured against the messianic view "that Antichrist shall be born of the Jews," and he warned that allegories in the books of Daniel and Revelation could not be understood by laypersons: the "entreating of allegories pertains not to every common sort of people."[18] Puritan clerics blamed millenarian prophecy on lay Bible-reading that was not guided by clerics. Perkins criticized the chiliastic arguments of lay interpreters that "the end of the

16. Christopher Hill, *Antichrist in Seventeenth-Century England* (Oxford, 1971), p. 37, and *Puritanism and Revolution* (New York, 1964), p. 312.

17. Heywood, *A True Discourse*, pp. 11–12. The millenarian in Clapham's dialogue scornfully remarked: "Thanks to his divine majesty, I was never a university man, much less an academical divine, or theologue" (Clapham, *Errour On The Right Hand*, p. 32).

18. William Alley, *The poore mans librarie* (1574), ff. 45ᵛ-46ʳ, 56ʳ.

world shall be three years & a half after the revealing of Antichrist . . . [which] is gathered out of places in Daniel and the Revelation, abused."[19]

The Family of Love presented a greater challenge to Puritan clerics than that posed by messianic prophecy. Familism was more directly linked than Anabaptism to the widespread emergence of heretical sects during the Civil War, after the collapse of ecclesiastical controls. Like Anabaptism, the Family of Love originated on the Continent. Led by a Westphalian known in England as Henry Nicholas, Familists may have immigrated to England in the early 1550s. Evidence suggests that, in the Marian prisons, the Melchiorite beliefs of Anabaptists who had earlier immigrated to England coexisted with the distinctive beliefs of the Familists.[20] In England, these beliefs focused on spiritual introspection that was thought to express a direct union with God. The mystical writings of H.N., as Nicholas was called, provided a doctrinal basis for this Antinomian faith. Emphasis on religious experience as a realm of spiritual perfection led to a radical devaluation of worldly commitments, such as loyalty to any specific government. Familists were not actively subversive but appear to have held that submission to government was merely a matter of expediency.

By the latter part of the sixteenth century, Familism had gained native proselytes and spread throughout the south of England. It appeared in the southwest, where the bishop of Exeter reported the appearance of "that hurtful sect . . . of the which company I have brought twenty to open recantation in this Cathedral church." The bishop of Lincoln complained in 1575 about "the Familiars of Love." They may have arrived in Surrey as early as 1570; by the decade's end, Familists appeared before justices of that county. A tract in 1606 added Sussex, Middlesex, Berkshire, and Hampshire to the above counties as places where Familists existed "twenty years ago."[21] Hints of internal divisions in Familism appear in 1637 in testimony by a cutler, who reported the existence of two types of Familism in London: the Family of the Mount and the Family of the Valley. The

---

19. Perkins, *Workes*, I. 265. See also William Gouge, *The Whole Armour of God* (1627), pp. 160–61.

20. Melchiorite Anabaptism denied Christ's humanity, while Familism denied the divinity of Christ. Both beliefs were attributed to heretics in Marian prisons. See John Standish, *A discourse wherein is debated whether it be expedient that the scripture should be in English* (1555), Sig. D8; *ZL*, 2d ser. II. 213.

21. BrL, *MSS. Lands.* 33, f. 29ʳ; John Strype, *The Life and Acts of Archbishop Whitgift* (Oxford, 1822), I. 421–22, III. 158–59; *APC* 1578–80, pp. 444–45; Anon., *A Supplication Of The Family Of Love* (1606), p. 57; Thomas Cooper, *The true and perfect copie of a godly sermon* (1575), Sig. D6ᵛ; Peter Heylyn, *Aerius Redivivus* (1672), p. 229; John Rogers, *The Displaying of an horrible secte of grosse and wicked Heretiques* (1578), p. 98; *VCH* Surrey, II. 28.

beliefs of these groups bear a strong resemblance to those of the Yorkshire Grindletonians, who, according to Christopher Hill, may link the Familists to the early Quakers.[22]

A rare glimpse into the way Familism spread occurs in a polemical tract against the Familists. Its author questioned a Cambridgeshire husbandman who testified that, in 1555, he had traveled to an inn in Colchester, Essex, to witness a conference between a Familist organizer, a joiner named Vitels, and a servingman, John Barry:

> One John Barry, servant to Mr. Laurence of Barnhall in Essex came to the same inn, to reason with the joiner about the divinity of Christ, whom Vitels denied to be God . . . Yea, quoth Vitels, the same mind must be in you which was in Christ, the same mind must be in you which was in Christ . . . Which words so often he repeated that thereby he put Barry to silence . . . so that he had not a word to say, to the great offense of divers, but especially of 2 women gospellers, which came with Barry to hear him and Vitels confer about the matter.[23]

This testimony vividly illustrates several aspects of Familist heresy that reveal a high degree of lay initiative: it shows the popular milieu of this heresy, the intense doctrinal involvements of a religious vanguard drawn from this milieu, and the fact that heretical contacts transcended local boundaries.

Contemporary opinion and modern research describe Familists as small farmers and artisans in the rural areas, and as scriveners, weavers, tailors, and servants, many of them women, in the towns.[24] Puritan clerics, who played a leading role in the effort to detect and suppress Familism, stated that this "new doctrine" originated "not among us but among the simple sort and ignorant men of the country."[25] However, the humble social origins of the Familists did not prevent them from traveling long distances in order to attend conferences, gain converts, and find suitable spouses. Disdainful charges that Familists were heretical basketmakers had a strong

---

22. BoL, *MSS. Tanner* 70, f. 181; Hill, *World Turned Upside Down*, pp. 62, 65–68. Lists of Grindletonian beliefs are recorded in BoL, *MSS. Rawls.* D399, f. 196, D1347, f. 317.

23. William Wilkinson, *A Confutation of Certaine Articles delivered unto the Familye of Love* (1579), pp. 4–6.

24. Felicity Heal, "The Family of Love and the Diocese of Ely," *Studies in Church History* 9 (1972), pp. 220–21; Rogers, *Displaying of an horrible secte*, p. 55; Hill, *World Turned Upside Down*, pp. 21–23, 29. BoL, *MSS. Tanner* 70, ff. 181–82.

25. Richard Greenham, *Workes* (1612), p. 17. See also Richard Sibbes, *Works* (Edinburgh, 1862–63), II. 316; Thomas Taylor, *The Rule Of The Law Under The Gospel* (1631), Sig. A6ᵛ-7ʳ.

element of social reality to them, the same reality underlying the earlier Lollard heresy: both found their strongest supporters among the "mobile elements in the lower and middle reaches of society."[26]

Lay initiative in Familism is also reflected in its reliance on books and in the secretive manner in which these heretics circulated their writings. The popular social milieu of Familism was clearly not incompatible with literate religion. Familists in Elizabethan Cambridgeshire were at least semiliterate, and their leader, a glover, possessed more than a half-dozen heretical tracts. In 1576, a Sussex clergyman who sought to remove suspicion of his Familist sympathies promised to report "all such their books that shall come into my hands." Books and manuscripts circulated among London Familists in the 1630s.[27]

Further evidence of the semiliterate achievements of the Familists exists in hostile proceedings instituted against them. A heretical pacifist confessed in 1575 to his Puritan interrogator, "I cannot frame my style with such excellency of speech . . . for I have not been at university." But his lack of style did not prevent him from ably citing numerous scriptural passages in defense of his beliefs. A few years later, an author of anti-Familist tracts declared that these heretics "are all unlearned, save some who can read English."[28]

Puritan clerics thought that the Antinomian heresy too, like the messianic prophecies, was the product of lay access to vernacular Bibles. They argued that, in the absence of clerical supervision, scriptural writ was being misinterpreted by commoners, who turned its lessons into perverse allegories to suit their deformed intellects. This, said the Puritan clerics, was "the practice of the Family of Love . . . who turn the natural sense of scriptures into allegories."[29] These attacks on Familism had secular as well as religious motivations: allegorical abuse of scriptural writ was associated with the irrational mental habits of the lower classes. According to Puritan clerics, Familists allegorically interpreted the Bible in order to

26. Hill, *World Turned Upside Down*, pp. 36–37. See also Margaret Spufford, *Contrasting Communities: English Villagers in the Sixteenth and Seventeenth Centuries* (Cambridge, 1974), p. 257; A.G. Dickens, *Lollards and Protestants in the Diocese of York, 1509–1558* (Oxford, 1959), p. 246.

27. PRO, *SPD* SP 12/133/f. 98ʳ; Anon., *A Discovery Of . . . the Family of Love* (n.p., 1622), p. 86; Spufford, *Contrasting Communities*, p. 208; *Sussex Archaeological Society* 29 (1874), p. 192; BoL, *MSS. Tanner* 70, f. 181.

28. Albert Peel, "A Conscientious Objector of 1575," *Transactions of the Baptist Historical Society* 7 (1920), pp. 89–90; George Williams, *The Radical Reformation* (Philadelphia, 1962), p. 789.

29. Perkins, *Workes*, III. 237. See also John Knewstubs, *A Confutation of monstrous and horrible heresies* (1579), f. 84ᵛ; George Gifford, *Foure Sermons* (1582), Sig. A8ᵛ; Greenham, *Workes*, p. 228; Richard Rogers, *Seven Treatises* (1610), p. 369.

appeal to "the common sort of people." Thomas Wilcox observed that "it has most commonly been the practice of heretics to allegorise upon scriptures, that thereby they might feed the humours of the poor and simple people, who through their corruption wonderfully delight in such a deformed handling of the word." He noted specifically that "this allegorical handling of the scripture . . . has been the mother to bear and bring forth . . . the opinions of the detestable Family."[30] In this view, the Antinomian heresy was the product of lower-class access to vernacular Bibles.

Despite its quietist nature, secular officials regarded Familism as tantamount to treason. Twice in 1580 a bill was read in Parliament that declared "the doctrine was not only heresy, but also tending to sedition and disturbance of the state."[31] The link between the Antinomian heresy and sedition lay in its belief that the spiritual freedom promised in the Gospels superseded and abolished all outward ordinances justified by the Old Testament. These ordinances allegedly included temporal authority, private property, and an ordained ministry. An Elizabethan Familist confessed that he had been told that "there should come a time when there should be no magistrates . . . upon earth, but all should be governed by the spirit of love." Other Familists and informants claimed that each member "was to have all of his goods in common with the rest of his brethren."[32]

However, these remarks should be viewed with caution. Remarks on authority and private property probably say more about official fears than about Familist doctrine. Its Antinomian disregard for the Law was, in fact, largely confined to spiritual matters. With regard to secular matters, Familist doctrine seems to have been guided, at worst, by principles of passive indifference. Some Familist writings pledged loyalty to all rulers, be they Protestant king or pope![33] Nonetheless, Puritan clerics firmly associated Antinomian denial of Old Testament Law with secular sedition. Preachers like Perkins arraigned Familism for distorting the meaning of Christ's sacrifice, by thinking "that by the death of Christ they have a liberty to live as they list," a liberty that included "freedom from all au-

30. Thomas Wilcox, *The Unfouldyng of sundry untruths* (1581), Sig. A5ᵛ, A6ᵛ. See also Samuel Otes, *An Explanation Of The Generall Epistle of St. Jude* (1633), p. 398; Rogers, *Displaying Of An Horrible Secte*, p. 55.

31. *Archaeologia* 36 (1855), p. 114; *CJ*, I. 127, 130.

32. PRO, *SPD* SP 12/133/f. 98ᵛ; Alfred John Kempe, ed., *The Losely Manuscripts* (London, 1836), p. 228n. See also Greenham, *Workes*, p. 684; John Udall, *Obedience To The Gospel* (1588), Sig. F2.

33. At least one opponent conceded that Familists did not advocate insubordination; see Anon., *A Discovery Of The Abominable Delusions of those, who call themselves the Family of Love* (n.p., 1622), pp. 37, 79. For Familist arguments, see BoL, *MSS. Rawls.* A382, pp. 10–11, 161–62; C554, ff. 26–27.

thority of magistrates."[34] More probable casualties of this heretical denial of the Law consisted of the right to wear weapons and wage war.[35]

Anxiety over its potential for revolt rather than an accurate assessment of its doctrines accounts for the vehemence of anti-Familist attacks. It was the specter of insubordination among the lower classes that most alarmed clerics and government officials. This is apparent in remarks by a Puritan preacher from Essex who in the 1630s summed up the thinking of several generations of reformers who associated the Antinomian heresy with popular insubordination. He bitterly attacked Antinomian heretics, who argued "that Christ died for them, and that they shall be saved, but how they came by this persuasion they cannot tell. But it is suspicious to have goods, and know not how one came by them."[36]

These remarks are doubly revealing, for they show that clerical prerogatives as well as property rights seemed threatened by Antinomians. The "suspicious" goods of Antinomians referred not only to stolen property but to spiritual benefits that accrued to laypersons without clerical aid. Thus, in addition to their distaste for its secular implications, Puritan preachers opposed Antinomian trends because the emphasis on the primacy of inner experience occurred at the expense of clerical authority.

The Antinomian heresy upheld the possibility of a spiritual perfection in this life that accompanied the inner experience of a direct union with God. Puritan preachers opposed this doctrine, pointing out that perfection resided in heaven and contrasting the Calvinist search for evidences of election to Antinomian revelation. In place of Antinomian visions and revelations of spiritual perfection, they offered certainty in this life of subsequent release from spiritual imperfection.

Claims to spiritual perfection in this life violated the fundamental axioms of Calvinism. In accord with these axioms Puritan clerics argued that religious knowledge is "imperfect in this life, perfect in the life to come." Knowledge in this life is "by faith and hope"; in the next, "it is by vision." John Rogers, cited above, instructed his readers that "though we cannot perfectly know our hearts, yet we may . . . discern enough to assure us of our sanctification."[37] In this way Puritan clerics competed with

34. Perkins, *Workes*, I. 532. See also Joseph Bentham, *The Societie of The Saints* (1630), p. 193; William Sclater, *A Sermon Preached At the last generall Assise* (1616), p. 5; John Stockwood, *A verie godlie and profitable Sermon* (1587), Sig. B8.

35. See Henry Ainsworth, *An Epistle Sent Unto Two Daughters of Warwick from H.N.* (Amsterdam, 1608), p. 53; John Stockwood, *A Sermon Preached at Paules Crosse* (1579), p. 41; Thomas White, *A Sermon Preached at Pawles Crosse* (1589), p. 45.

36. John Rogers, *The Doctrine Of Faith* (1633), p. 32. (This is a different John Rogers from the one cited earlier in this chapter.)

37. Nathaniel Cole, *The Godly Mans Assurance* (1633), p. 106; Richard Sibbes, *Yea*

Familism to establish the grounds on which zealous laypersons would evaluate religious experience. Not only did they uphold Calvinist orthodoxy, emphasizing the gulf between religious practice in a sinful world and the saints' perfection in heaven; they also retained a prominent role for clerics in the evaluation of religious experience. This role was an adjunct to individual introspection, prayer, and Bible-reading, for which the Puritan clergy was prepared to provide guidance.

The existence of vernacular Bibles and a preaching ministry, according to Puritan clerics, had abolished the need for Antinomian revelation. Perkins and other Puritan clerics taught that "a man by faith may be certainly persuaded of his own election and salvation in this life without any extraordinary revelation." "We must not now look for trances and visions," he argued, "but we must use continual study [of] the word." Certitude of election could be found only through faith *and* diligent satisfaction of those religious duties which were amenable to clerical supervision. "By this it is easy to discern the illumination of Anabaptists and Familists," remarked Perkins, for these heretics "look for the spirit by revelation, and not in the exercise of the word and prayer." [38]

These remarks further indicate that the most immediate threat posed by Antinomianism was not its putative denial of secular authority and property rights but its rejection of an ordained ministry and those aspects of worship in which clerics asserted their pastoral leadership. Puritan clerics subjected Familists to relentless attack because, in the final analysis, they "despised the ordinary course of the ministry of men, and of attaining to the knowledge of salvation by the written word, and stand upon private revelations." [39] In opposition to this, the variety of religious experience commended by Puritan preachers maintained a more even balance between clerical authority and lay participation in religion.

The threat posed by Familism to clerical control of popular dissent thus led to extended efforts by Puritan preachers to detect and repress it. As indicated by the writings of Greenham, Knewstubs, Rogers, and Wilcox, cited above, Puritan preachers took a leading part in the campaign, spon-

---

And Amen (1638), in *Works*, IV. 118; Rogers, *The Doctrine Of Faith*, p. 39. See also John Randall, *Three and Twentie Sermons* (1630), II. 269.

38. Perkins, *Workes*, I. 363, 518; III. 219, 239. See Edward Elton, *The Triumph Of A True Christian* (1623), p. 195, who says it is not "illumination . . . that will prove you are regenerate." See also Greenham, *Workes*, p. 674; Sibbes, *The Witness Of Salvation* (1629), in *Works*, VII. 382.

39. Samuel Hieron, *The Dignity Of The Scripture* (1613), in *All The Sermons of Samuel Hieron* (1614), p. 82. See also Edward Elton, *An Exposition of the Epistle . . . to the Colossians* (1615), p. 1263; Robert Jenison, *The Christians Apparelling By Christ* (1625), p. 339; Thomas Taylor, *Three Treatises* (1633), p. 68.

sored by church and state, to repress Familism. Not only did Greenham—after Perkins the most prominent Puritan of his era—assist the bishop of Ely in examining and conferring with Cambridgeshire Familists, he also earned the thanks of the Privy Council. In fact, the Council *required* the bishop to use Greenham's services. The Council also ordered justices of the peace in Surrey to proceed against the Family of Love "with the aid of godly preachers," and it commended the aid of a notorious Puritan preacher, John Knewstubs, to six bishops who were ordered to repress Familism.[40]

For their part, Puritan preachers and their lay patrons seldom failed to mention these activities when ecclesiastical and secular authorities reprimanded or suspended the preachers for nonconformity. Official toleration of clerical nonconformity, they argued, allowed preachers who had good credit with popular dissent to dissuade it from heretical pursuits. Some Puritan preachers may have cited the spread of Antinomian heresy to discredit their adversaries within the ecclesiastical hierarchy. In 1579 the anti-Puritan bishop of Norwich received orders from the Privy Council to take action against Familists. He replied that reports of Familism in his diocese had been circulated "cunningly to accuse me of negligence."[41]

For the most part, however, Puritan clerics and their lay supporters cited the positive role played by godly preachers in containing heretical trends among the laity. As we saw in the previous chapter, this argument had an undeniable appeal: efforts to combat heresy more than compensated for the nonconformity of Puritan clerics.[42] Now we can better see why this argument was not disingenuous. Heterodox developments in popular dissent threatened not only secular institutions and values but also the religious rationale upon which Puritan clerics exercised their pastoral authority over the godly.

Separatists and the State Church

Though Separatists generally did not challenge the core tenets of Calvinism, their rejection of the Church of England made them as threatening to Puritan clerics as the heretics were. Separation generally followed

40. *APC* 1580–81, pp. 232–33, 317; *VCH* Surrey, II. 28.
41. BrL, *MSS. Lands.* 29, f. 94.
42. Gilby, *A Pleasant Dialogue*, Sig. C8. See also Francis Bacon, *A Wise and Modest Discourse* (1641), p. 34; John Davenport, quoted in Champlin Burrage, *Early English Dissenters* (Cambridge, 1912), II. 283; Josiah Nichols, *The Plea Of The Innocent* (1608), pp. 118–19; Albert Peel, ed., *The Seconde Parte of a Register* (Cambridge, 1915), I. 229–30, II. 188–90; *CSPD* 1591–94, pp. 275–76; *An Humble Motion With Submission Unto*

on the sectarian impulse to gather a congregation of visible saints. The formation of such groups occurred when official enforcement of conformity frustrated the religious priorities of the zealous laity. Separatist withdrawal from the church was, however, unacceptable to Puritan preachers. For them this meant renunciation of the resources of a state church, which offered them potential control over all laypersons, enabling them to cultivate piety throughout society and not just among small groups. Diametrically opposed priorities on organization thus animated conflicts between Puritan clerics and the Separatists.

Like radical heresy, Separatism emerged from lay initiatives in popular dissent. Both developments were, in part, unanticipated consequences of activities by Puritan clerics. The first incidence of separation from the Church of England occurred in the 1560s. Suspension of popular preachers in London who refused to wear prescribed attire—notably, the surplice and cap—led groups of London parishioners to worship outside the church under the direction of the suspended preachers.

However, more than lay subservience to popular preachers characterized this episode. When membership in the church was not only compulsory but parochial (that is to say, one had to attend the church in one's parish, or neighborhood), a preference for a specific minister was a bold expression of lay sentiment. Though such preferences were certainly fed by Puritan preaching, once acquired they were expressed by laypersons in ways that were not anticipated by Puritan preachers. There was not a more venerable reformer than the elderly Miles Coverdale, who had produced the first official version of a vernacular Bible during the reign of Henry VIII, but some dissident laypersons expressed dissatisfaction with his reluctance to provide them with godly services. One observed: "Father Coverdale, of whom we have a good opinion, and yet (God knoweth) the man was so fearful that he dared not be known unto us where he preached, though we sought it at his house." Clerics complained that those among them who stopped short of separation, despite their disavowal of surplice and cap, were attacked by their former followers, "who now regard them as semi-papists." Bishops and Puritan preachers both denounced this consequence of Puritan teaching, in the early Elizabethan church, for it made laypersons less amenable to clerical guidance and more willing to judge critically their doctrine and practice.[43]

The . . . *Privie Counsell* (n.p., 1590), p. 84; *The Unlawful Practices Of Prelates Against Godly Ministers* (1584), Sig. D2ᵛ.

43. Patrick Collinson, *Archbishop Grindal, 1519–1583: The Struggle for a Reformed Church* (Berkeley and Los Angeles, 1979), p. 170; *ZL*, pp. 201–2, 237. And see Anon., *An answere for the tyme* (1566), pp. 138–39; Gilby, *A Pleasant Dialogue*, Sig. K3ᵛ; Robert Crowley, *A Briefe discourse against the outwarde apparell* (n.p., 1566), Sig. C1ʳ.

In subsequent episodes of Separatism in pre-Revolutionary England, lay initiative was equally in evidence, separation being precipitated by episcopal interference with the ceremonial and liturgical expectations of the godly laity.[44] When popular ministers were suspended, household worship, often in the company of neighbors and the suspended cleric, replaced church attendance. This path, leading from episcopal persecution to separation, is nicely illustrated in the following description of a godly household:

> While they had a minister, the whole household met at the church twice every Sabbath, and once every weekday. But since the restraint of their minister,. they meet every morning in the weekday in the parlour.[45]

Here becomes evident the thin line separating Puritan worship and Separatism. Puritan clerics ordinarily encouraged Bible-reading and household worship as necessary adjuncts to public worship. They also stressed the necessity of household religion in place of church worship when no pastor was available. What they were not prepared to support, however, was this withdrawal from the church as a response to its ceremonial and liturgical corruptions, which they themselves often denounced.

These corruptions included certain ceremonies—notably, bowing and kneeling, signing infants with the cross in baptism, and the use of clerical vestments. Also important was the problem of lax church discipline—for example, admission of all parishioners, profane or godly, to communion. The Separatist remedy for this was to leave the church and allow each congregation to select its ministers and to control admission to communion.

Reforms desired by Separatists thus pointed to a far more democratic

44. Patrick Collinson, *The Elizabethan Puritan Movement* (London, 1967), pp. 204, 380–81. For the same explanation of Separatism by a contemporary Puritan, see Anon., *Sophronistes* (1589), Sig. D2ʳ. Some church historians deny that episcopal persecution precipitated separation; see White, *English Separatist Tradition*, p. 125, who cites Roland A. Marchant, *The Puritans and the Church Courts in the Diocese of York, 1560–1642* (London, 1960), pp. 160–66. Marchant argues that episcopal persecution of the Scrooby Separatists was not severe, but his work mainly traces actions taken after the rise of these Separatists and does not examine in comparable detail the events leading up to their separation from the church in 1606 (the act books of the High Commission are missing for the critical years 1604–6).

45. Anon., *Short Questions, and answeares* (1635), Sig. A5ᵛ. See Christopher Haigh, *Reformation and Resistance in Tudor Lancashire* (Cambridge, 1975), p. 311, for a will that bequeathed "one little Bible to my son Richard and . . . my wife, and they to see the same occupied every Sabbath day when there is no sermon nor sacraments in ministering." See also Stuart Barton Babbage, *Puritanism and Richard Bancroft* (London, 1962), p. 376; Christopher Hill, *Society and Puritanism in Pre-Revolutionary England* (New York, 1967), pp. 454, 468.

organization of church life than was possible in the Church of England. Early Separatist leaders such as Henry Barrow and Robert Harrison declared, in the same words, "We deny that a parson or vicar placed by a patron or a lord bishop can be a pastor."[46] This alternative to episcopal ordination, which would have clerics depend "upon the flock unto which they administer," threatened episcopal authority and the right of aristocratic patrons to present clerics to benefices in their control. It also undermined the principle of subservience of laity to clerics, because congregational control of clerics made the priesthood of all believers more of a reality than an ideal. Lay choice of ministers required doctrinal competency among laypersons, and Separatists accordingly encouraged all (male) believers to exercise their talents in interpreting the Bible. Although this liberty was somewhat circumscribed by a distinction between public and private preaching, Separatists argued that this lay activity was necessary if congregations were intelligently to choose their own pastors.[47]

Separatists readily acknowledged the lay initiative underlying schismatic developments. Early leaders such as Robert Browne, Robert Harrison, and Henry Barrow criticized Puritan clerics for resisting this initiative and trying to restrain zealous laypersons. They taunted the Puritan ministry with the fact that these laypersons "whom you challenge to yourself the honor of parentage" were actually "more forwarder than their father"; "if they wax more forward than yourselves, they find heavy friends of you." Harrison noted the Puritan preachers' fear that they might lose control over popular dissent: "I think you fear that all the best will away."[48] Their polemical writings addressed not only Puritan clerics but also ordinary laypersons. To various arguments by Puritan preachers, Separatist writers replied, "How unsound and corrupt this interpretation of yours is, let the godly consider."[49] Their opponents complained that Separatists "fill the margins of their books with such store of scripture that the simple might think they have even a cloud of witnessses against us."[50]

46. Henry Barrow, *A Brief Discoverie of the False Church* (1590), in *ENT*, III. 436, *Profes of Aparant Church* (1587), in *ENT*, III. 76; Robert Harrison, *A Treatise of the Church* (1580/81), in *ENT*, II. 36. See also John Canne, *A Necessitie Of Separation* (1634), pp. 8–9.

47. Robert Browne, *A True and Short Confession* (1584), in *ENT*, II. 410; Henry Ainsworth and Francis Johnson, *An Apologie Or defense Of Such True Christians* (1604), p. 46; Barrow, *Brief Discoverie*, p. 533.

48. Harrison, *Treatise of the Church*, pp. 52, 55. See also Henry Barrow, *Four Causes of Separation* (1587), in *ENT*, III. 59–60, *A Plaine Refutation* (1591), in *ENT*, V. 254; Browne, *A True and Short Confession*, p. 411.

49. Henry Barrow, *Barrow's Final Answer to Gifford* (1591/92), in *ENT*, VI. 194. See also Barrow, *A Plaine Refutation*, p. 184; John Greenwood, *A Brief Refutation* (1591), in *ENT*, VI. 29.

50. Anon., *The Church of England is a true Church of Christ* (1592), p. 56.

The Puritan clerics, in response, acknowledged that the church had deficiencies, but they nonetheless defended its validity as a true church. Though they wanted a presbyterian polity in place of the episcopal structure, which impeded rigorous church discipline, they argued that where the minister was a Puritan, there existed a *de facto* discipline, due to a prayer-book rubric that allowed him to exclude the uncatechized from communion. In addition, they argued that cultivation of piety through preaching was more important than seemingly intractable issues of church polity. Puritan preachers taught that "discipline [is] necessary for the beauty and well-being of the church, but not essentially or inseparably necessary." The "necessity of preaching" meant that it was wrong to separate even from a church that lacked a desirable disciplinary and liturgical order. Even those Puritan clerics who led the agitation for a presbyterian reform of the church, such as John Field and Thomas Wilcox, expressed this view: "We think it utterly unlawful for any to withdraw themselves from that congregation where the word of God is truly preached." To Separatist charges that the Church of England was improperly gathered, Puritan preachers replied disarmingly, "Our church was gathered by the preaching of the word."[51] In effect, Puritan preachers sidestepped Separatist attacks by emphasizing preaching and moral reform over ecclesiological issues.

Like their reaction to radical heresy, the hostility of ecclesiastical officials and Puritan preachers to Separatism is partly explained by its lower-class milieu. Episcopal officials referred to Separatism as a lower-class usurpation of ecclesiastical authority.[52] Hostility to Separatists among Puritan clerics was also motivated by their fear of losing their credibility as leaders of popular dissent. They were acutely sensitive to Separatist efforts to lead popular dissent out of the church, as is evident in the attention paid to this problem by members of the presbyterian classis movement at Dedham and Braintree.[53]

The central feature of the Puritan ministry, preaching, was called into

51. Randall, *Three And Twentie Sermons*, p. 315; *The Church of England is a true Church*, pp. 9–10; Peel, *Seconde Parte*, I. 86. See also Anon., *A parte of a register* (n.p., 1593), p. 401; John Ball, *A Friendly Triall Of The Grounds Tending To Separation* (Cambridge, 1640), p. 287.

52. Occupations of Separatists are listed in *ENT*, VI. 293–94; T.P. Crippen, "The Brownists in Amsterdam," *Transactions of the Congregational Historical Society* 2 (1905), pp. 160–72. For views of the church hierarchy, see Richard Gardiner, *A Sermon* (Oxford, 1622), pp. 23–24; Richard Hooker, *Of The Law of Ecclesiastical Polity*, in *Works* (Oxford, 1845), I. 128.

53. Roland G. Usher, ed., "The Presbyterian Movement in the Reign of Queen Elizabeth, As Illustrated by the Minute Book of the Dedham Classis, 1582–1589," *CS* 3d ser. 8 (1905), pp. 55–56. For members of the Braintree classis, see George Gifford, *A Short Reply unto . . . Henry Barrow and John Greenwood* (1591), Sig. A3ᵛ; M.M.

question by the Separatists, who regarded its practice as a way of diverting attention away from corruptions in the church. For laypersons who regarded clerics as dissemblers or hypocrites, Separatist polemics could strike a resonant chord. Indeed, skepticism about clerics forms an integral part of the early Separatist tradition, and it later appears in John Lilburne's writings, where godly preachers are denounced along with lordly bishops: "The more godly and able the minister is that still preaches by virtue of his episcopal call, the more hurt he does, for the people that have such a minister will not be persuaded of the truth of things . . . the holiness of the minister is a cloak to cover the unlawfulness of his calling."[54]

One response of Puritan clerics was to plead for reform of the more visible and objectionable "corruptions" of the church. This would, they hoped, make it easier to repress the Separatists, for "how justly might they be punished that after such a reformation . . . should still remain obstinate."[55] The notion that to punish zealous laypersons for separation was not entirely just under present circumstances reveals the dilemma confronting Puritan preachers, whose credibility as leaders of popular dissent was being threatened. Pleading for ceremonial and liturgical reform was, however, probably the least efficacious response to this threat, for the church hierarchy made it increasingly evident that no such reform would be forthcoming.

Efforts by Puritan clerics to contain Separatist trends met with more success when they conferred privately with Separatist leaders and sought to dissuade them from more extreme courses of action. The credibility of these preachers with popular dissent made them especially useful to ecclesiastical officials who otherwise were hostile to Puritanism. For example, Whitgift used Puritan preachers to confer with Separatist ringleaders. Other preachers conferred with Harrison and Browne, of course not failing to inform Lord Burghley of their efforts. In New England, John Cotton recalled how John Dod and Arthur Hildersham, two prominent

---

Knappen, ed., *Two Elizabethan Puritan Diaries* (Chicago, 1933), p. 76. I discuss the classis movement later in this chapter.

54. John Lilburne, *A Worke Of The Beast* (1638), in William Haller, ed., *Tracts on Liberty in the Puritan Revolution* (New York, 1933), II. 19. For early Separatists, see Barrow, *Brief Discoverie*, pp. 483, 491, 500; Browne, *A True and Short Confession*, pp. 417–19; Albert Peel, ed., "The Notebook of John Penry, 1593," *CS* 3d ser. 67 (1944), p. 7.
    In 1606, Sir John Coke, secretary of state, wished that his cousin "and all who prefer conventicles before the public and ordinary service of the Church" could hear sermons "by a zealous minister." Presumably this would dissuade them from Separatism (HMC, *MSS. Cowper*, p. 62).

55. *Certaine Advertisements For The Good Of The Church*, p. 15. See also William Jackson, *The Celestiall Husbandry* (1616), Sig. A3ᵛ.

Puritan preachers, nearly dissuaded John Smyth from following the Separatist path to Amsterdam. Conferences of this kind were probably responsible for moderating the views of some Separatist leaders, such as the semi-Separatists, who allowed some communion with Puritan congregations in the Church of England.[56]

Opportunities to contain Separatism also existed in the ordinary pastoral activities of Puritan clerics. In their public sermons and private conferences with parishioners they worked to keep the lay vanguard within the church. It was the Puritan clergy who bridged an increasingly wider gulf between an ongoing process of popular reformation and the official version of it that was enshrined in the canons of the church established by the Elizabethan Settlement. When arraigned for fostering schism by the example of their own nonconformity, Puritan preachers typically pleaded that they, "more than any of those who lay this blame upon them, have labored with many and with God's blessing prevailed with a number to the keeping in the unity of [the church] such as otherwise would have departed from it."[57] In view of these efforts, the preachers and their lay patrons advised church leaders against suspensions for nonconformity. The arguments made by the Norfolk preachers who were threatened by Archbishop Whitgift show the tenor of many pamphlets and petitions against episcopal persecution of Puritan preachers: their preaching had helped to convince zealous laypersons of the error of separation, and to suspend them would undo this work among these laypersons, "whose danger is now more than in times past by means of the late schism of Browne, from which we had much ado to keep them even when by our ministry there was reasonable plenty of preaching."[58] Powerful lay patrons of the Puritan ministry made the same point in petitions from the Norfolk gentry in 1584, from Suffolk gentry and justices of the peace in 1582 and again in 1592, and in two petitions from Northampton gentry and justices of the peace in 1605.[59]

---

56. John Browne, *Congregationalism in Norfolk and Suffolk*, pp. 60, 64, 70; Robert Browne, *A True and Short Confession*, pp. 406–8; Burrage, *Early English Dissenters*, II. 293; Henry Martyn Dexter, *The Congregationalism of the Last Three Hundred Years* (London, 1880), pp. 86, 92; Waddington, *Congregational History*, I. 22–75; White, *English Separatist Tradition*, pp. 122, 158.

57. Peel, *Seconde Parte*, II. 81. See also William Ames, *A Reply To Dr. Mortons Generall Defense* (1622), p. 33.

58. Peel, *Seconde Parte*, I. 224. See also BrL, *MSS. Add.* 38,492, f.10ᵛ; Anon., *A Short Dialogue* (1605), p. 63; Anon., *A Triall of Subscription* (1590), p. 25; Strype, *Whitgift*, III. 285–86.

59. *A parte of a register*, pp. 128–29; BrL, *MSS. Sloan* 271, f. 33ᵛ; *CSPD* 1591–94, pp. 275–76; Peel, *Seconde Parte*, I. 225; PRO, *SPD* SP 14/12/f. 287ᵛ.

The Puritan Laity

The fundamental dilemma confronting Puritan clerics in their relations with the Puritan laity was broadly similar to the one they faced in relation to Separatism. They had to channel lay initiatives in directions that were compatible with the pastoral authority of a parochial clergy. But this development was blocked by the unwillingness of Anglican officials to countenance lay initiatives in popular dissent. Lay Puritanism had the same unyielding convictions that had characterized popular dissent since the inception of the Reformation: an attachment to an edifying, literate religion whose high degree of rationality produced strongly dualistic and iconoclastic world views. When Puritan clerics supported these convictions, lay Puritans readily followed their pastoral leadership. When they were opposed or indifferent to them, Puritan clerics discovered their lay followers to be unresponsive to their leadership.

The failures and successes of pre-Revolutionary Puritanism critically depended on whether the activities of its clerical leaders supported, opposed, or were irrelevant to the focal concerns of lay Puritans. An example of irrelevance is the failure of the classis movement, a wholly clerical extension of Puritanism that attempted to reform church polity along presbyterian lines in order to create an effective disciplinary apparatus. This movement gathered momentum in the 1570s and 1580s only to be abruptly terminated by government prosecution, initiated in 1590. Lack of lay involvement was the principal reason for the government's ability to isolate and repress these clerical activities. This lack of involvement did not stem from explicit opposition but from the absence of any link between the classis movement and lay Puritanism.

The reform desired by the classis movement would have established in England a Calvinist system of discipline that was used in continental churches. The lay *seniores* and *presbyteri* of Calvin and Beza were known in England as ancients, elders, governors, and overseers. They were to assist ministers by bringing the resources of the secular community to the enforcement of godliness. Clerics who lobbied on behalf of a presbyterian reform of the English church met secretly and illegally to implement this goal, jointly administering religious affairs at the parish level. Laymen, however, were not involved in these classis meetings, and Puritan clerics tended increasingly to view the office of elder as a ministerial, not a lay, office.

Separatists, who also desired ecclesiological reform along presbyterian lines, rebuked Puritan clerics for proposing a new church polity that was no more amenable to lay initiative than the existing episcopal structure.

Foreshadowing John Milton's caustic remark that "new presbyter is but old priest writ large," Separatist writers observed that "both sides, both bishops and this new classis, take upon them to make ministers without the people." They denounced secret meetings of the classis because it "only consists of priests . . . People of the churches be shut out, and neither be made acquainted with the matters debated there, [nor] have free voice in those synods and councils."[60]

Lack of lay involvement in the classis movement also appeared in its inability to attract support from powerful lay patrons. Although it offered greater control to local elites over religious matters, a presbyterian polity would also have subjected them to its discipline. Referring to this latter possibility, Bishop Cox in 1574 observed that, "should anyone seek to compel our great men to submit their necks to it, it would be much the same as shaving a lion's beard." The enthusiasm of aristocratic supporters for the preaching program of the Puritan ministry clearly did not extend to its plans for ecclesiological reform. Thus the classis movement failed to gain lay Puritan support in elite as well as popular circles. Consequently, the attack led by Bishop Bancroft left it completely isolated. Its repression showed how utterly it failed "to secure either widespread popular support or effective patronage of the influential."[61] Not until the collapse of the episcopal hierarchy during the Civil War did Puritan ministers again attempt, once more unsuccessfully, a presbyterian reform of the church.

Puritan clerics met with far more success when they sought to promote moral rather than ecclesiological reform, for they directly addressed the focal concerns of lay Puritanism. After the collapse of the classis movement in 1590–91, the clerics, in the remaining half-century of pre-Revolutionary Puritanism, concerned themselves almost exclusively with spiritual regeneration, to the neglect of institutional reform. This is the era in which Puritan preachers perfected their pastoral talents and a style of pulpit oratory that chronicled the inner experience of regeneration. It is this aspect of Puritanism that forms the subject matter of William

60. Collinson, *Elizabethan Puritan Movement*, pp. 229, 355; Barrow, *Brief Discoverie*, pp. 534, 559, and see also pp. 519, 556, 560–62; Robert Browne, *An Answere to Mr. Fowler's letter* (n.d.), in *ENT*, II. 520–22; J.M. Ross, "The Elizabethan Elder," *Journal of the Presbyterian Historical Society* 10 (1953); White, *English Separatist Tradition*, pp. 142–49.

61. *ZL*, p. 307; J.M. Ross, "Some Aspects of the Development of Presbyterian Polity in England," *Journal of the Presbyterian Historical Society* 13 (1955), p. 8.

For opposition to the classis movement from aristocratic supporters of Puritanism, see Collinson, "Letters of Thomas Wood," p. xxxii, n. 1; Conyers Read, *Lord Burghley and Queen Elizabeth* (London, 1960), p. 294; Carson I.A. Ritchie, "Sir Richard Grenville and the Puritans," *EHR* 77 (1962), pp. 518–23.

Haller's classic work, *The Rise of Puritanism*. Sabbatarian obligations, the conduct of household worship, introspective applications of the doctrine of faith—these were the chief concerns of this period of Puritanism.

To be sure, this development was an extension of well-established trends initiated by the Reformation. Clerical reformers had always been concerned with these pastoral activities. But organizational problems confronting the Puritan ministry greatly aided this development. Pressed from above by an episcopal hierarchy that forbade criticism of church polity, and from below by Separatist attacks on church corruptions, Puritan clerics found a solution in a program of moral reform based on the initiative of individual laypersons.[62]

At the end of the pre-Revolutionary era, the reflections of one cleric explicitly associated lack of an effective church discipline with pastoral developments in Puritanism:

> Putting a difference between men and men . . . has been the chief work of the godly ministers in England in this last age, who though they wanted the ordinance of excommunication in their churches, yet in lieu of it they had excommunicating gifts, and were forced, because of that profane mixture in churches, to spend most of their ministry in distinguishing men, by giving signs and marks of a man's natural and regenerate estate, and convincing and discovering carnal men to themselves and others.[63]

Providing "signs and marks" of reprobation and election required that clerics impart to the laity a knowledge of the Calvinist economy of grace and salvation. Thus the organizational constraints and opportunities that confronted Puritan preachers accentuated a general tendency in the Reformation to make the logic of religion intelligible to the laity. According to Francis Bacon, Puritan ministers "intice the people to hear controversies, and all manner of doctrine; they say no part of the counsel of God is to be suppressed, nor the people defrauded."[64]

A formal disciplinary apparatus, such as the presbyterian eldership, would indeed be superfluous if individual laypersons were able to monitor their own spiritual progress and that of others. Puritan preachers devoted themselves to this goal, providing a guide to laypersons who would indi-

---

62. See Collinson, *Elizabethan Puritan Movement*, p. 433; Hill, *Society and Puritanism*, pp. 501–6.

63. Thomas Goodwin, *Exposition Of The Revelation* (1639), in *Works* (Edinburgh, 1861), III. 130–31. For Greenham and Perkins, see I. Breward, "The Significance of William Perkins," *Journal of Religious History* 4 (1966); M.M. Knappen, *Tudor Puritanism* (Chicago, 1966), p. 382.

64. Bacon, *A Wise and Modest Discourse*, p. 43.

vidually accomplish the tasks, formerly associated with a disciplinary apparatus, of identifying saints, rewarding godliness, and punishing sinners. The net result was a realignment of the activities of Puritan clerics with the focal concerns of lay Puritanism. A program of spiritual reform, guided by preaching, allowed the clerics to lead reform from within the church while, at the same time, it enabled them to encourage lay initiatives in religious matters.

Puritan clerics maintained their command over the main body of popular dissent by cultivating a simple, expository style of preaching that provided hearers with casuistical guides for spiritual evaluation. They collected their sermons in books such as *The plaine mans path way to Heaven,* by Arthur Dent (twenty-one editions of which appeared between 1601 an 1640), *A treatise of exposition upon the ten commandments,* by John Dod and Robert Cleaver (nineteen editions between 1603 and 1635), and *A garden of spirituall flowers,* by Greenham, Perkins, and others (twenty editions between 1609 and 1640).

By far the most popular Puritan author was William Perkins, who was, according to John Cosin, "their great Rabbi." [65] More than two hundred editions and reprints of his writings appeared between 1590 and 1640. Other popular authors of this period include Henry Smith, whose individual, collected, abridged, and pirated writings number over one hundred fifty items; John Preston, with ninety editions and reprints to his credit; Richard Sibbes with sixty editions and reprints to his; and many lesser-known Puritan divines, such as Samuel Smith, the author of three works that were reprinted ten or more times. Aside from folio editions of collected works, most of these writings appeared in inexpensive quarto editions destined for lay readers. These were manuals of practical divinity, written in a simple and compact style to relate highly technical points of divinity to the inner experience of regeneration.

THERE EXIST SEVERAL TYPES OF EVIDENCE REGARDING THE PURITAN laity's receptivity to this edifying style of religion and the impact of this on Puritan clerics. For example, lay knowledge of doctrine, gained from reading the Bible and from listening to sermons, promoted one especially troublesome type of intellectual initiative: lay judgment of clerics. Some Puritan clerics justified this initiative, arguing in simple tracts, intended for popular consumption, that "he which knows not when pure doctrine and wholesome is uttered, is not as yet among the number of the sheep of

---

65. G. Ornsby, ed., "The Correspondence of John Cosin," *Surtees Society* 52 (1869), p. 54. Publication figures are taken from A.W. Pollard and G.R. Redgrave, eds., *A Short-Title Catalogue of Books Printed in England, Scotland, & Ireland and of English Books Printed Abroad, 1475–1640* (London, 1946).

Christ."[66] Contemporaries, however, observed that, during preaching, each Puritan layperson "had his own Bible, and sedulously turned the pages and looked up the texts cited by the preachers . . . to see whether they had quoted them to the point, and accurately, and in harmony with their tenets." Several Puritan preachers sought to dissuade their parishioners from this practice.[67]

Lay Puritan judgment of clerics manifested itself most visibly in the practice of "gadding": leaving one's own parish for another, where a more godly form of worship was available. Frequently this practice arose where Puritan parishioners were saddled with a nonpreaching incumbent or where the preacher used various ceremonies that grated on Puritan sensibilities. Yet it also occurred despite the presence of a "sincere" and godly minister, when zealous laypersons thought that another preacher had more powerful gifts to offer.

Gadding abroad to sermons was so widespread a practice of lay Puritanism that it was taken for granted by its supporters as an expression of godly life. A tract eulogizing a Lancaster woman noted that "She would not be without the word preached, though many times she went far for it." But opponents expressed dismay that ordinary laypersons would presume to decide which clerics were sound in doctrine and practice: "That parishioners should throng by the thirties and by forties to other churches . . . what is this but for the people to usurp episcopal authority?" Another cleric, addressing himself not to "Brownists and Barrowists" but to "those who are nearer friends to our church," requested lay Puritans

> not [to] gad . . . but rather think that God in his wisdom has placed your ministers over your own parishes. Hear their voices: if you will not hear them but rather choose unto yourselves other places and hunt after other men, you go about preposterously and saucily to break that order which the God of wisdom has set.[68]

The level of lay intellectual initiative in this practice can be gauged by the forces arrayed against it. Not only was this practice illegal in a compulsory church, which fined parishioners for nonattendance at parish ser-

---

66. George Gifford, *A Briefe discourse of certaine points of the religion, which is among the common sort of Christians* (1598), p. 16. See also Arthur Dent, *Plaine Mans Path-way to Heaven* (1603), pp. 269–70.

67. Spufford, *Contrasting Communities*, p. 263. Some preachers told their auditors that this practice was a sin; see Cole, *The Godly Mans Assurance*, p. 341; Stephen Denison, *The New Creature* (1622), p. 112; Arthur Hildersham, *CVIII Lectures Upon The Fourth Of John* (1632), p. 134.

68. Anon., *A Briefe Discourse Of The Christian Life and death, of Mistris Katherin Brettergh* (1617), p. 2; Read, *Sermon At Brentwood*, pp. 18–19; George Benson, *A Sermon Preached At Paules Crosse* (1609), pp. 17, 29.

vices; it also abrogated local custom, which united religious and residential life. Of course, not all instances of laypersons leaving their parish for services elsewhere indicate Puritan attitudes, but in all of the examples cited here the importance attached to an edifying style of worship based on preaching is explicit.

Lay Puritans subordinated the sacramental aspects of worship to preaching, arguing that "the sacraments are no sacraments being administered without a sermon," and they crossed parish boundaries in search of a communion service that included a sermon.[69] A related reason for gadding was to find a ministry that did not use disliked rituals, even though preaching might be available at home. According to one hostile observer, lay Puritans boasted that they "would hear none that is conformable, or if we do . . . we say his gifts be decayed & his preaching be without power."[70]

Through gadding, the ceremonial and doctrinal components of a ministry were subjected to a remarkably popular tribunal: one that recorded a negative verdict by moving elsewhere. Small groups of laypersons, sometimes drawn from several parishes, might travel together to hear a sermon and afterwards adjourn to a nearby home for supper, where they would discuss the sermon and repeat it from notes taken during the service. This symbiosis of gadding and household religion is recorded in church records and has been described by historians.[71] Evidence used in the prosecution of one gadding layperson shows how gadding and household religion combined to produce lay Puritanism's distinctive style of worship. In 1636 persistent rumors linked the Yarmouth preacher John Brinsley to illegal conventicles. One anonymous informant reported that "the people's running to his sermons on Sunday caused much disorder." Subsequently, a Yarmouth grocer appeared before the High Commission, whose records

---

69. *Archaeologia Cantiana* 25 (1902), p. 22. See also Bacon, *A Wise and Modest Discourse*, p. 44; Collinson, *Elizabethan Puritan Movement*, p. 374; Hill, *Society and Puritanism*, pp. 62–63; Marchant, *Puritans and the Church Courts*, p. 42; George Roberts, ed., "The Diary of Walter Yonge, Esq.," *CS* 41 (1848), p. 94n; William Urwick, *Nonconformity in Herts.: Being Lectures upon the Nonconforming Worthies of . . . the County of Hertford* (London, 1884), pp. 290–91; Usher, "Dedham Classis," p. 48.

70. George Downame, *A Sermon defending the honourable function of Bishops* (1608), Sig. A2. See also John Burges, *An Answer Rejoyned To That Much Applauded Pamphlet* (1631), I. 5; Claire Cross, *The Puritan Earl: The Life of Henry Hastings, Third Earl of Huntingdon* (New York, 1966), pp. 138–39; Jackson, *Celestiall Husbandry*, pp. 45–46; Symon Press, *A Sermon Preached at Eggington, in the county of Darby* (Oxford, 1597), p. 9.

71. For church records, see [Richard Montagu], *Articles of enquiry and direction for the dioces of Norwich* (1638), Sig. B3; PRO, *SPD* SP 16/280/ff. 49ᵛ-51ᵛ. For secondary accounts, see C.D. Chalmers, "Puritanism in Leicestershire, 1558–1633" (M.A. thesis, Leeds University, 1962), p. 158; Collinson, *Elizabethan Puritan Movement*, p. 375.

show that he admitted that, with his servant and apprentice, he had traveled six miles from his home

> into the church of Sommerleyton town and heard . . . a sermon
> preached by Mr. Brinsley . . . [Then] the examinate and his said
> family went to the private dwelling house of one Taylor in Somerleyton where he had dinner.

He shared this meal with some shoemakers, a chapman, and others, all of whom paid "a pence apiece" for the meal. Then, according to the Commission's report,

> [they went] and heard Mr. Brinsley preach in the afternoon . . .
> and the sermon ended, a motion was made . . . that so many of the
> company there assembled as would go along with the said Knight
> should hear the said Knight preach again at the house they came
> from.

It is unclear whether Knight was a minister or not. The company then went to Taylor's barn,

> and the said Knight began with a prayer of his own . . . and then the
> said Knight in the said barn took a text out of the prophet Isaiah . . .
> which he handled in exhorting the people to examine themselves
> whether they had the Son in them by faith or no . . . and told them
> that those that had found faith should find it working in them by the
> operation of the Spirit.[72]

Only a very thin line separated this activity, with its collection of funds for food and worship held in a barn, from outright separation from the church. Composed of godly laypersons drawn from several parishes, the gadding society of lay Puritanism existed in the interstices of the church. Opposed by increasingly hostile ecclesiastical forces, its elusive and resilient nature owed much to its diffuse, nonparochial structure, organized as it was around attendance at sermons, informal conferences, and household religion.

At the same time, however, these groups of the godly firmly regarded themselves as members of the church. In effect, gadding enabled them to remain a pious vanguard within the church, unlike the Separatists, who were renegades against its order. According to a cleric who was familiar with the nuances of lay Puritanism, gadding parishioners "do commonly

---

72. BoL, *MSS. Tanner* 68, f. 98ʳ, *MSS. Tanner* 80, f. 130. For a similar but earlier report on another Yarmouth grocer see Nicholas Fuller, *The Argument of Master Nicholas Fuller* (n.p., 1607), p. 1.

call any small company of their own party the church and the Christians of such a town."[73]

Gadding to sermons was a regular feature of Sunday worship among lay Puritans in Elizabethan Essex and Stuart Cheshire, Lancashire, and York. It also occurred in the southwest and the dioceses of Lincoln, Norwich, and Peterborough.[74] Unlike clerical nonconformity, this lay practice proved difficult to control. In 1634 the chancellor of the Lincoln diocese reported to Archbishop Laud that gadding laypersons "are the most troublesome part of the ecclesiastical inquisition." At about the same time, Bishop Wren's attempt to enforce Laud's injunctions against Puritanism in the Norwich diocese was thwarted by the gadding laity. One parish had its Puritan minister suspended; but then, when a rural dean "came to officiate, there ran 200 at once to other churches." At the beginning of divine service in another church the pews were empty, "for during the time of prayers none of them appear"; but then, "at the sermon," parishioners fill the pews, and, "the sermon ended, they all presently vanish and depart." Emphasis on edification led lay Puritans to neglect formal prayers in favor of preaching, and gadding facilitated this neglect, for Puritans attended whichever nearby parish had sermons on Sunday. Patterns of bell-ringing announced which church had sermons, a practice ended by Wren, who defended his action by noting that "many of the ministers had of themselves taken the very same order for ringing to keep their people from gadding."[75]

The staunchly Puritan town of Northampton had a long history of gadding laypersons, who were the object of official concern in 1573, 1579, 1611, and 1614. A crisis arose in 1621 when a town resident promoted charges in Parliament against the chancellor of the diocese for "troubling

---

73. Burges, *An Answere Rejoyned*, I. 5. Cf. Strype, *Whitgift*, II. 337–38.

74. For Essex, Cheshire, Lancashire, and York, see *CSPD* 1639–40, p. 519; Collinson, *Elizabethan Puritan Movement*, pp. 373–74; Marchant, *Puritans and the Church Courts*, pp. 42, 86, 99, 171–97; R.C. Richardson, *Puritanism in North-West England: A Regional Study of the Diocese of Chester to 1642* (Manchester, 1972), p. 84.

For the southwest, see Mary Bateson, ed., "A Collection of Original Letters from the Bishops to the Privy Council, 1564," *CS* n.s. 9 (1895), p. 52; BoL, *MSS. Tanner* 140, f. 169ʳ; Ian W. Gowers, "Puritanism in the Country of Devon between 1570 and 1641" (M.A. thesis, University of Exeter, 1971), pp. 39–40, 175–87; HMC, *MSS. Exeter*, p. 95; Peel, *Seconde Parte*, II. 76; Roberts, "Diary of Walter Yonge," p. 24; *VCH*, Wiltshire, III. 37.

75. BoL, *MSS. Tanner* 68, ff. 2110f. 10ᵛ, 210ᵛ, *MSS. Tanner* 220, f. 83ʳ; *CSPD* 1634–35, p. 149. For additional records relating to Lincoln and Norwich dioceses, see BoL, *MSS. Tanner* 68, ff. 209ᵛ–213ᵛ; *CSPD* 1634–35, p. 64; PRO, *SPD* SP 16/274/f. 24ᵛ; Richard Tedder, *A Sermon Preached At Wimondham* (1637), p. 12.

men for going from their own parish church to hear sermons." In reply, the chancellor informed King James that "I trouble none but where I find either manifest contempt of the liturgy of the church or of their own minister. The fault is now too common. The Puritans go by troops from their own parish church (although there be a sermon) to hear others whom their humor better affects."[76]

By the end of this era, gadding to sermons had become a prominent feature of lay Puritanism throughout England, and it raised far-reaching questions about lay subserviency to clerics. "'Tis well known," complains one writer in 1642, how many "be now well fed to the full, and may go from one church to another to please their palate, and taste of what pleases them best."[77] This and other observations, cited above, indicate that lay initiative in gadding often involved more than leaving a parish merely because it had a minister who did not preach. It also could express lay preference for one preacher over another. This latter possibility was certainly not what Puritan clerics had hoped for when they encouraged gadding laypersons.

Originally, gadding was encouraged by Puritan clerics as a temporary remedy for the lack of preachers in the Church of England. In 1586 these clerics justified this activity for laypersons who, "being pestered with an ignorant or blind or idle minister, . . . do seek to other places where they may be taught their duty and obedience, considering that the want of such godly instruction is the special cause of many heretical and traitorous practices."[78] And until the ascendancy of Archbishop Laud, a certain amount of gadding had been officially tolerated by the church.[79] Not only did this toleration attempt to compensate for the lack of preachers among the English clergy; it also sought to accommodate the initiative of laypersons who would not remain within the church unless granted relief from their unpopular pastors. As bishop of London, Edmund Grindal urged lay Separatists, in 1567, to attend services in nearby parishes as an alternative to leaving the church because of their dislike of their own pastors. In 1621 a Puritan preacher responded in the same manner to laypersons who challenged the legitimacy of a church that included "dumb

76. *APC*, 1570–80, pp. 133, 219; Babbage, *Puritanism and Richard Bancroft*, p. 11; PRO, *SPD* SP 14/67/#58, 14/77/f. 153, 14/122/f. 241ʳ.

77. Giles Calsine, *A Messe of Pottage* (1642), Sig. A2ʳ.

78. Peel, *Seconde Parte*, II. 195. See also BoL, *MSS. Tanner* 280, f. 135; Anon., *A Defense Of the godlie Ministers* (1587), p. 49; Bownde, *Doctrine Of The Sabbath*, pp. 169–73; *CSPD* 1635, p. 538; Gifford, *A briefe discourse*, ff. 4ʳ-5ᵛ; Taylor, *Three Treatises*, p. 91.

79. BrL, *MSS. Add.* 39,454, ff. 47ʳ, 239ᵛ; Collinson, *Elizabethan Puritan Movement*, p. 374; Marchant, *Puritans and the Church Courts*, p. 186; PRO, *SPD* SP 16/293/f. 264ʳ; W.J. Sheils, "The Puritans in the Diocese of Peterborough," *NRS* 30 (1979), p. 131; *VCH*, Norfolk, II. 262.

dogs" among its clergy: "But what say you to a dumb minister? He is no minister . . . His sacraments are no sacraments?" The preacher's answer was to allow gadding as a permissible lay reaction to such ministers.[80]

But by the late sixteenth century, Puritan clerics began to experience the adverse consequences of gadding. A *de facto* choice of ministers by gadding laypersons did not always work to the advantage of Puritan preachers, who had to compete among themselves for auditors. This problem appeared in deliberations of the Dedham classis in response to complaints by a Colchester preacher who, between 1583 and 1587, reported several times that some of his parishioners left his church during communion in order to hear sermons by another Colchester preacher. He noted how these parishioners "refused to hear him on the Lord's Day when he . . . did preach and told of one woman that professed a desire to come to the communion with him, and yet thought she should not overcome herself to the sacrament because she should lose the exercise of the word." The classis defended the minister and conferred with the other preacher, but in 1587 the offending parishioners still continued their gadding.[81]

In response to this problem the Puritan ministry attempted to set limits to gadding. In 1589 a book appeared devoted entirely, as its full title indicates, to *Perswading the people to . . . attend the ordinance of God, in the ministerie of their own pastors.* The tract is in the form of a dialogue, which begins when the narrator spots a gadding layman "with his wife and family" who

> have been at some sermon this morning, for being the Sabbath of the Lord, he would not for his piety and zeal be otherwise occupied . . . But because he absents himself from his own pastor, and follows a strange ministry, I will assay if I may reform him in this point, wherein, in my opinion, very many, partly of ignorance, and partly of an excess of zeal, do greatly and grievously offend.

As is always the case in such dialogues, the antagonist quickly comes to share the protagonist's viewpoint: only lack of a preaching minister justifies gadding abroad for sermons.[82] This was the limit Puritan preachers attempted to set for gadding, and it would have been greatly to their advantage; for almost all Puritan clerics were preachers, while the vast ma-

---

80. Grindal, *Remains*, p. 204; Richard Preston, *The Doctrine Of The Sacraments* (1621), p. 275.

81. Usher, "Dedham Classis," pp. 28, 48, 64. Usher is mistaken when he claims, p. 62n, that the classis was "congregationalist" because it declared "that a pastor should have his own people." This formulation was meant to limit free lay choice of ministers.

82. Anon., *Sophronistes*, Sig. A2ʳ.

jority of the clergy was not. However, even prominent Puritan preachers like Arthur Hildersham experienced considerable difficulty in trying to get his parishioners to accept this limit to gadding.[83] This unsettled situation prevailed up until the Civil War, when the lay initiative underlying gadding emerged more fully and openly in the form of congregationalism and free lay choice of ministers.

LIKE PREACHING, CEREMONIAL NONCONFORMITY WAS ANOTHER ENduring feature of pre-Revolutionary Puritanism that involved a high degree of intellectual initiative and lay judgment of clerics. As is well known, certain ceremonies—bowing and kneeling, use of the cross in baptism, and clerical attire—were points of contention between Puritan clerics and their ecclesiastical superiors. But much evidence indicates that the clerical "acts of conscience" that have dominated popular and scholarly accounts of Puritanism were frequently extorted from clerics by their parishioners, who found certain ceremonies offensive. Lay opposition to ceremonialism stemmed from various critical and skeptical sentiments inherited from earlier popular dissent. It also affirmed a sense of group identity among a lay vanguard in a church that was increasingly hostile toward it.

In the early years of the Elizabethan period, lay opposition to the ceremonies of the church was prompted by memories of the Marian persecution. During the controversy over clerical vestments in the mid-1560s, wearers of the surplice and cap were informed that these "glorious badges of the enemy" provoke many "who so soon as they see you in these garments, their blood is up, remembering how they burned the books of God . . . that they burned their brethren of late." Archbishop Grindal allowed one cleric to officiate in an Essex parish without the surplice. The parish was hostile to such "popish attire," no doubt because the Marian executions claimed many of its victims in that area. The cleric was advised "to tolerate this situation 'for a time . . . but yet in the mean time privately to exhort the godly so as to frame their judgments that they conceive no offense if it be altered hereafter by authority.'"[84]

In early Stuart England, episcopal efforts to enforce ceremonial conformity seemed like a foreign intrusion in Puritan parishes where an established style of nonconformity had reigned for several decades. When

83. Hildersham, *CVIII Lectures*, pp. 253–54, 268–72, 306, 309, *CLII Lectures Upon Psalme LI* (1635), p. 23. See also, Thomas Adams, *Workes* (1629), p. 974; John Brinsley (the younger), *The Preachers Charge, And Peoples Duty* (1631), p. 29; Parr, *A plaine Exposition*, p. 249; Thomas Stoughton, *Two Profitable Treatises* (1616), pp. 241–42.

84. Gilby, *A Pleasant Dialogue*, Sig. K3ʳ; Collinson, *Archbishop Grindal*, p. 172.

pressed by these efforts in 1604–6, Puritan clerics revealed this local state of affairs, in which

> subscription [of clerics to ceremonial conformity] has not been much urged of late . . . save upon some few men whom the bishops favored not. So the ceremonies have grown to such a disuse in very many churches (in some 10 years, in some 20, in some 30, in some more) that it would be . . . very scandalous to bring them into use again.[85]

At both the beginning and end of this pre-Revolutionary era, then, opposition to the ceremonies of the Church of England expressed in highly visible and symbolic ways the religious commitments of lay Puritans. In contrast, Puritan clerics educated at the universities could and often did take a more aloof view of the "indifferent" things that so excited the Puritan laity; but this intellectual detachment was possible only at the cost of losing control over lay Puritanism.

At the ascension of James I to the throne, a concerted effort was made to enforce clerical conformity in the use of prescribed ceremonies. Puritan clerics were caught between the conflicting demands of their superiors and their lay followers, a conflict which the clerics urgently desired to leave unresolved. A frequent response to demands for conformity was the request for more time, a tactic the bishop of Lincoln blamed on the clerics' unwillingness "to be brought into any disgrace with their people." The bishop noted that one cleric, John Burgess, desired more time to "confer with his own people to induce them, lest if he should change upon the sudden, they would fall away from him." Twenty-five years later Burgess wrote about this conference and its consequences:

> I told some of my parishioners that I must wear the surplice or lose my place . . . requiring to know of them how they would accept my ministry if I wore it . . . They answered that they should never profit by it.

Burgess subsequently resigned from that benefice.[86]

Supporters of the ceremonies, and of conformity in general, were well aware of popular sentiments on this issue, and they attacked nonconforming clerics for "being carried away with the stream of popularity." In a 1608 treatise, dedicated to Archbishop Bancroft, Puritan clerics are urged to resist popular sentiment on this issue, because "it was never well

---

85. BrL, *MSS. Sloan* 271, f. 26ᵛ. In defense of a Northampton preacher, the mayor and Aldermen reported that in his church the ceremonies had "grown out of use for nearly forty years," HMC, *MSS. Salisbury* 17, p. 26. See also *Lincoln Record Society* 23 (1926), pp. lxix, cxxvii.

86. HMC, *MSS. Salisbury* 16, p. 379, 17, p. 133; Burgess, *An Answer Rejoyned*, I. 16.

since either the people durst presume to give aim to their minister . . . or the ministers stooped at the pulpit door to take measure of the people's feet." Other supporters of the episcopal hierarchy offered Puritan clerics the unhelpful advice that, if conformity "consequently bring on some discredit unto their ministry, let them know that these are but human respects."[87]

The constraints imposed on Puritan clerics by their dual role as ordained ministers and as leaders of a popular movement made ceremonial nonconformity an intractable issue. The Puritan clergy attached great importance to its own credibility with the lay vanguard within the church, but it was also committed to a comprehensive church; it therefore faced the unpalatable choice of opposing either its popular following or its episcopal superiors. The former course threatened its pastoral control over the popular reformation; the latter led to suspension from the ministry. Neither course was inevitable so long as a *de facto* style of Puritan worship at the local level was left undisturbed through neglect, tolerance, or strategic considerations with regard to Puritanism as an anti-Catholic weapon.

This was the prevailing state of affairs through most of the pre-Revolutionary era, with the conspicuous exception of four crises: the Vestiarian Controversy of the mid-1560s, Whitgift's subscription campaign of the mid-1580s, the effort to enforce clerical subscription to conformity at the ascension of James I to the throne in 1603, and the Laudian reaction in the 1630s, which helped to precipitate the Civil War. Up to the era of Laud, Puritan divines maintained a precarious balance between the conflicting demands of their lay followers, on the one hand, and their superiors, on the other. Some criticized the unbending convictions of lay Puritanism with regard to the ceremonies, hoping to win zealous laypersons to more detached views. Greenham sourly observed that "some say, if they hear one for the peace of the church tolerating some ceremonials, that he is a time-server and a man-pleaser." In another complaint addressed to the Puritan laity, a cleric noted, "Desire we your good commendations? Yea, we would, but then we must show ourselves refractory to established orders."[88]

Other Puritan clerics sought to resolve the issue by affirming, for the

87. Hoard, *The Churches Authority*, p. 51; Samuel Collins, *A Sermon Preached At Paules-Crosse* (1608), p. 28; Leon Hutton, *An Answere To A Certaine Treatise* (Oxford, 1605), pp. 137–38. A cleric who renounced his Puritanism made the same point; see Thomas Sparke, *A Brotherly Persuasion to Unitie* (1607), p. 44. For evidence that Laud and his officials were aware of these popular pressures, see BoL, *MSS. Tanner* 68, f. 295ʳ; *CSPD* 1631–33, pp. 255, 341; PRO, *SPD* SP 16/293/f. 260ʳ.

88. Greenham, *Workes*, p. 59; Jackson, *The Celestiall Husbandry*, pp. 45–46. See also E.S. Schuckburgh, ed., *Two Biographies of William Bedell* (Cambridge, 1902), p. 208.

benefit of their bishops, rather curious notions of conformity; a certain Leicester cleric, for example, claimed to be conformable except for omitting the cross in baptism and not bowing and kneeling or using the surplice, "which we take liberty in" because "the people had conceived some dislike of them." John Davenport probably had this idea in mind when he reported, "I have persuaded many to conformity," even while, according to one observer, he "draws after him great congregations & assemblies of common & mean people." A Puritan lecturer in Newcastle, Robert Jenison, reported that his bishop "knows of old, and still, that I am every way conformable . . . though I be not so urgent as he expects . . . to force them of Allhallows to a conformity in kneeling . . . the communicants being many and I only a lecturer." In 1630 Bishop Laud's Commissary reported on a Chelmsford preacher who spoke "against the schism of inconformity." A "principal lawyer of the town" told the Commissary, "A few such excellent sermons would bring again the people in love with conformity." This puzzled the Commissary, for he "saw no conformity in hood or surplice." Other clerics sought to modify the liturgy so that the issue of nonconformity became moot. In the face of lay refusal to bow at the mention of the name Jesus during divine service, they substituted, in place of "Jesus," the phrase "he says."[89]

All such actions were, at best, delaying tactics, and they failed whenever the authorities embarked on a resolute course of enforcing clerical conformity to the ceremonies and liturgy of the church. At this point, the ambiguous status of Puritanism as a church within a church no longer could provide a shield for its leaders, who now had to chose between sect and church. Though they assured church leaders that their nonconformity was not intended "to cross your Lordships," but instead expressed "the persuasion of our own consciences and . . . the fear that we have to scandalize our Christian brethren,"[90] such appeals were bound to fail; for they not only exposed the widening fissure that divided the institutional church from a popular movement of religious reform, but they challenged the formal structure of episcopal authority in the church. Outright separation from the church, Puritan clerics warned, would be the response of its lay

89. BoL, *MSS. Tanner* 73, f. 475ʳ; *Lincoln Record Society*, 23, p. lxix; PRO, *SPD* SP 14/173/#42–43, 16/161/f. 107ʳ; and see *VCH*, Herts., IV. 330. For modifications of the liturgy, see Edward Boughen, *Two Sermons* (1635), p. 9; PRO, *SPD* SP 16/280/f. 133ʳ.

90. BrL, *MSS. Add.* 38,492, f. 3ʳ. For arguments by Lincolnshire, Warwickshire, and Worcestershire clerics, see Anon., *An Abridgement Of That Book Which The Ministers Of Lincoln Delivered to his Majestry* (1605), p. 49; Anon., *Certaine Considerations Drawne . . . for no subscription . . . within the Diocese of Worcester* (1605), p. 51; PRO, *SPD* SP 14/12/f. 120.

vanguard to episcopal interference. They argued, in 1604–6, that to enforce conformity would transform the latent sectarianism of lay Puritanism into open rebellion against the church.

> We fear that the holding thereto would breed a schism and distur-
> bance of the peace of the church among the common sort, whereof
> we have had already too much experience.

Referring to just the surplice, a clerical petition against enforced conformity declared, "The use of it breeds jars among the brethren, and
brings contempt upon the ministers . . . and draws many from our
congregations."[91]

The experience of Puritan clerics in combating Separatist trends among
their followers lends credence to these claims. The fears they voiced in
their petitions and tracts against conformity reflect their knowledge of the
ease with which lay initiatives in Puritanism could spawn sectarian movements. The attempts of the episcopal authorities to frustrate the ceremonial and liturgical expectations of the Puritan laity further increased
this danger. Throughout the pre-Revolutionary era, then, clerical leadership over a lay vanguard within the church existed precariously, resisting
opposition from above and below. For the most part it succeeded in hold-
ing its position, until the collapse of church controls at the beginning of
the English Revolution allowed the latent sectarianism of Puritanism to
emerge fully and openly in innumerable sects. Here begins the history of
modern denominations, of Presbyterians, Congregationalists, Baptists,
and Quakers. In the pre-Revolutionary era, however, these denominational identities were largely unknown in Puritanism, for it had not yet
differentiated itself from the Church of England but instead maintained
an ambiguous status within it.

This ambiguous status, as a sect within a church, brought with it certain organizational assets as well as liabilities, for it enabled Puritanism to
survive in the face of official hostility. Puritan ministers commanded important resources as ordained ministers in a comprehensive and compulsory
church. Among the most important of these resources were access to the
pulpit—the primary medium of communication—and the spiritual authority conferred upon them as ordained ministers. The major liability of
their position—their subjection to episcopal authority—must be balanced
against the nonparochial society of lay Puritanism, which was far less
visible to the authorities and so tended to escape their control. This state of
affairs was clearly not the product of conscious desires and goals on the

---

91. BrL, *MSS. Add.* 38,492, ff. 7ᵛ, 27ʳ, and see also ff. 24ʳ, 63ʳ; BrL, *MSS. Sloan*
271, f. 26ᵛ; *An Abridgement Of That Book*, p. 49.

part of Puritan clerics. It emerged instead as the product of two organizational constraints acting upon them: the limits imposed by their ecclesiastical superiors and those imposed by their nominal followers, drawn from the ranks of a lay vanguard. Neither group proved to be overly responsive to the needs of a self-constituted group of clerical reformers.

5
The Heavenly Contract-I

> It is of the utmost importance to the
> peace of the church, to have the cove-
> nant of Christians prescribed by our
> Savior in two particulars that seem
> somewhat contradictory, well and
> clearly explained . . . wherein he
> who differs is to be excluded from
> the covenant; and . . . wherein Chris-
> tians may differ and yet keep terms.
>
> Francis Bacon, *The Dignity and Ad-
> vancement of Learning* (1605)

Puritans were Calvinists, but their theology developed into a distinctive form of Calvinism. Pastoral writings by Puritans on election, faith, and spiritual introspection modified Calvin's treatment of these subjects. Though Puritans maintained Calvin's strict views on the mystery of God's decision to elect some and not others, their God was much less remote and unpredictable. They held to Calvin's doctrine on the utter corruption of humanity and its inability to do good works without God's grace, but they justified lay initiatives in religious life. Central to these modifications was the idea of a heavenly contract, an idea that became the conceptual keystone of Puritan divinity.

These theological developments were intimately associated with organizational developments. Puritan covenant theology reflected specific circumstances surrounding the reception and modification of Calvinist ideas in England by Puritan clerics. This theology was the product of clerics, who used theological precedents—from the Bible and from writings by continental reformers—to formulate it. But the theology was strongly influenced by circumstances that were not immediately theological in nature. Religious and secular activities of lay dissenters provided an organizational context which prompted Puritan clerics to use biblical precedents and continental antecedents to create their covenant theology.

The salience of these intellectual *precedents* for Puritan clerics was determined by organizational *pressures;* that is, they used intellectual precedents to modify Calvinism in ways that resolved specific organizational problems. These problems, examined in chapter 4, were created by the dual role the Puritan clerics occupied as ordained ministers in a comprehensive church and as nominal leaders of a popular religious movement that displayed a high degree of lay initiative. We shall now see how covenant theology emerged in response to important developments in relations between Puritan clerics and different factions of popular dissent. By modifying Calvinism with ideas about a heavenly contract, Puritan clerics provided greater scope to lay initiative in religion, but they channeled this initiative in ways that maintained their authority and gave them a prominent role as pastoral guides.

However, covenant theology reflected not only the spiritual interests of the reformed laity but also its secular activities in everyday life. To formulate a theology that accommodated lay spiritual interests, Puritan clerics had to create one that was intellectually intelligible to ordinary laypersons. Covenant theology met this requirement: Puritan clerics borrowed a contractual idiom from secular life to translate major points of Calvinist doctrine into a relatively simple divinity. That they did this to cater to common knowledge among the laity becomes evident when we examine their rhetoric and imagery.

This analysis of covenant theology thus raises issues of direct interest to the sociology of knowledge, which presupposes the existential conditioning of ideas. First, it demonstrates how a system of beliefs can be altered as intellectual precedents are used to resolve organizational pressures. Internal strains in the relations between clerical leaders and lay members of this social movement were in part responsible for its ideological innovations. Second, it presents a striking example of the economic conditioning of ideas. Ideological innovations in Puritanism cannot be explained solely by references to organizational strains, for contractual relations in practical affairs were reflected in the doctrines of Puritan theologians. However, the salience of these economic matters for Puritan clerics also derived from the organizational context discussed above, and this context cannot be reduced to either economic or theological imperatives. It was determined by the efforts of clerics to maintain their pastoral authority against threats posed by an insurgent laity and by increasingly hostile church officials.

Thus, the analysis presented here shows how the internal organization of a social movement mediates between its beliefs and its socioeconomic environment. While this emphasis on movement organization as a variable, mediating between beliefs and socioeconomic structure, does not resolve all of the problems that are involved in relating ideas to their social context, it does enable us to identify rather precise lines of causal influence while avoiding reductionist assumptions about ideas and their social origins.

In this chapter, in analyzing organizational pressures and the rise of covenant theology, I will follow the outline I used in chapter 4, proceeding from radical heresy to sectarianism and lay Puritanism. I postpone to the next chapter a discussion of economic influences on Puritan covenant theology. The evidence for a causal relation between organizational problems and theological developments is biographical, chronological, and hermeneutic in nature. The biographical evidence associates theological innovators with organizational priorities not shared by all Puritan clerics. The chronological evidence demonstrates a correlation between different organizational problems and stages in the development of covenant theology. The hermeneutic evidence consists of changes undergone by the covenant concept in England. Taken together, these three kinds of evidence provide a strong case for attributing the rise of covenant theology to circumstances that lie outside the realm of divinity.

Continental Antecedents and Heretical Pressures

The idea of a heavenly contract between God and man, in which temporal and spiritual benefits are a reward for fealty to God, is as old as Jewish thought. In Protestant theology this idea appeared on the Continent at the beginning of the Reformation. It was used to refute various beliefs associated with the radical wing of the Reformation, mainly those of the Anabaptists. This was also the origin of speculation on the covenant by English reformers, who faced heretical challenges roughly similar in nature to those that confronted Bucer, Bullinger, Calvin, and Zwingli. Efforts to combat Anabaptist and Antinomian heresies in England invariably led English clerics to the ideological resources developed for this purpose by continental divines.

The idea of a covenant first appeared in Protestantism in Zurich, where the Swiss reformer Zwingli was challenged by Anabaptists to defend infant baptism. Zwingli anticipated many of Calvin's doctrines, including the principle of a state church, a principle that was challenged by Anabaptist attacks on infant baptism. In arguing that baptism should be administered only to persons able to account for their faith, Anabaptists advanced a sectarian model of church polity in which only visible saints would be received into the congregation.

Zwingli defended infant baptism by defining it as a *Bundeszeichen*, an outward sign and seal of the covenant between God and humanity. He described this covenant as a testament which included children because of their parents' inclusion within it. The seal of the covenant, namely baptism, belonged by right to Christian infants as a consequence of their parents' participation in the covenant. Later, Calvin and other clerical leaders of continental Calvinism used this argument about the contractual right of infants to baptism in order to attack Anabaptism.[1]

In Geneva, Strasburg, and Zurich, the appearance of Protestant ideas about the covenant was in the first instance a response to religious radicalism. But denial of infant baptism was only one aspect of a broader attack by heretics on the efficacy of the Law in the Old Testament. As we have already seen, other radical beliefs, such as the rejection of Christian magistracy, also were consequences of heretical interpretations of Christ's intercession as an event that substituted spiritual freedom in the Gospel for all outwardly binding decrees of the Law. Continental Calvinists responded to this interpretation by using the covenant concept to establish the validity of Old Testament Law. According to them, God's covenant with the faithful spanned both Testaments, differing only in the nature of its deliverer (Christ in place of Abraham) and in the manner of its satisfaction (faith in place of works).

By positing this continuity in the history of salvation, early covenant theology enabled Protestant theologians to maintain a distinction between Law and Gospel while at the same time retaining the validity of the Law. There was one essential covenant, not two, as some Anabaptists claimed, of which only the latter was valid. Referring to these heretics, Calvin declared, "In asserting a difference of covenant, with what barbarian audacity do they corrupt and destroy Scripture."[2] This view acknowledged that Christ's intercession mitigated the Old Testament demand for perfect outward obedience; but it also insisted that humanity was still bound to try to uphold the Law and all essential observances that followed from it, such as submission to temporal rulers, compulsory membership in a state church, and deference to its ordained ministry.

These arguments appeared in England during the reign of Edward VI,

1. Ulrich Zwingli, *Antwort über Balthasar Hubmaiers Taufbüchlein* (1525), in *Corpus Reformatorum* 91 (Leipzig, 1915), p. 641, and see also pp. 633, 637–39. See also John Calvin, *The Institutes of the Christian Religion* (London, 1962), II. 546 (4,16,24); Martin Bucer, quoted in George Williams, *The Radical Reformation* (Philadelphia, 1962), p. 300; Henry Bullinger, *Fifty Sermons Divided into Five Decades* (1577), in *PS*, X. 387. The relevance of these continental works for Puritan theology has been discussed by Richard L. Greaves, "The Origin and Early Development of English Covenant Thought," *The Historian* 31 (1968), pp. 23–24; R.T. Kendall, *Calvin and English Calvinism to 1649* (Oxford, 1979), pp. 51–76; Jens G. Møller, "The Beginnings of Puritan Covenant Theology," *JEH* 14 (1963), pp. 47–48. See also J. Wayne Baker, *Heinrich Bullinger and the Covenant* (Athens, Ohio, 1980), pp. 141–42, who notes that covenant theology had a theological context distinct from that of battles between reformers and Anabaptists.

2. Calvin, *Institutes*, II. 535 (4,16,10). For arguments on the continuity of the covenant, see Bullinger, *Decades*, in *PS*, VIII. 283–300; Calvin, *Institutes*, I. 391 (2,11,4), II. 531–32 (4,16,5–6); Casper Olevian, *An Exposition of the Symbole of the Apostles* (London, 1581), pp. 124–26, 233.

when the spread of radical heresy, such as Familism, began to trouble reformers. Among the earliest writings by Bullinger and Calvin to be translated into English were those that used covenant ideas to refute heretical
denials of the validity of infant baptism and, more generally, of the Old
Testament. The translator of two works by Bullinger undertook his work
so "that the ignorant & simple might have a wholesome antidote and
counterpoison" against Anabaptist attacks on infant baptism and magistracy. Both works are dialogues in which the Anabaptist figure dismisses
the validity of infant baptism and magistracy as appurtenances of Old
Testament Law. The faithful Christian who defends these things declares
that "the covenant made with Abraham stands still."[3]

Among the earliest polemics against Anabaptists composed by an English author is a tract by William Turner that appeared in 1551. Turner
was a prominent figure in the early progress of the English Reformation.
His advanced ideas outpaced the slow march of reform during the reign
of Henry VIII, and, after his books were banned, he resided on the Continent during the last years of that reign. Upon Edward's ascension,
which produced a more favorable climate for reform, Turner returned to
England and, encountering native heretics, defended the institution of infant baptism with continental ideas: "Our baptism and the circumcision
are all one spiritually, and in signification, and only do differ in the elements. All they that were received into the covenant made to the fathers of
the Old Testament were circumcised . . . So all they that are received into
the covenant made to us of the New Testament are by baptism received
into our church."[4] Over the next century, Puritan clerics invariably re-
sorted to this argument, as in Robert Cleaver's *The Patrimony of Christian
Children,* whenever they discussed heretical attacks on infant baptism. It
appears in many of their catechisms in passages that explain the perpetual
duty of parents to have their infants baptized.[5]

3. Henry Bullinger, *A most necessary & frutefull Dialogue, betweene ye seditious Liber-
tine . . . & the true obedient christian* (Worcester, 1551), Sigs. C2ʳ, C7ᵛ-8ʳ, and *A moste
sure and strong defense of the baptisme of children* (Worcester, 1551), Sigs. A5ʳ, C5. See also
John Calvin, *A Short Instruction . . . agaynst . . . Anabaptists* (1549), Sigs. D4ᵛ-5ʳ. The
translator of Bullinger's two tracts is John Vernon, whose writings against radical heretics
and papists are cited above in chapter 3, notes 8, 42, and 44.

4. William Turner, *A Preservative, or triacle, agaynst the poison of Peligus* (1551), Sigs.
F5ᵛ-6ᵛ. See also Anon., *A Brife And Faythfull declaration . . . made by certeyne men suspected of heresye* (1547), Sigs. A6ʳ-8ᵛ.

5. Cleaver's work appeared in 1624. See also William Ames, *The Marrow of Sacred
Divinity* (1642), pp. 94, 207; Richard Sibbes, *The Faithful Covenanter* (1639), in *Works*
(Edinburgh, 1862–63), VI. 22; Thomas Wilson, *A Commentarie upon . . . the Romanes*
(1614), pp. 928–30.

For catechisms, see Anon., *A Catechism of Christian Religion* (1617), Sig. C1; H.B.,
Grounds of Christian Religion (1635), p. 19; R.B., *A Briefe Catechisme* (1632), p. 7; John

Puritan clerics were also concerned with the broader heretical attack on the validity of the Old Testament. In this matter, however, they were more original in their discussion of the covenant. When demonstrating the essential continuity of God's covenant, they distinguished between a covenant of works and a covenant of grace. This distinction became a commonplace of Puritan divinity, largely due to William Perkins, who adopted it from writings by Caspar Olevian (1536–87) and Zacharias Ursinus (1534–83), theologians at Heidelberg. Using their distinction between a *foedus legalis* and a *foedus gratiae*, Perkins transformed the history of God's dealings with humanity into a parable of two contracts. His unrivaled authority among Puritan clerics in the pre-Revolutionary era was responsible for the attention given to the covenant of works, its abrogation by the Fall of Adam, and its supersession by the covenant of grace.[6]

According to Perkins, the covenant of works "is God's covenant made with condition of perfect obedience," while the covenant of grace requires that the believer "by faith receive Christ and repent of his sins."[7] Puritan clerics used this distinction to uphold the validity of the Law, of God's original demand for obedience, which humanity was clearly unable to meet after the Fall. In view of this inability, God provided a covenant of grace, which mitigated his original demand for perfect obedience in the covenant of works. According to Puritan writers, the covenant of grace existed in the Old Testament but was hidden, awaiting its full revelation by Christ in the New Testament. In catechisms they state that though the Gospel—the covenant of grace—was issued after the Fall, it was obscured by the Old Testament's emphasis on outward works.[8]

Two conclusions followed this argument: the New Testament did not abrogate the authority of the Old Testament, and the Gospel promise of

---

Frewen, *Certaine Choice Grounds . . . Wherein the people of the Parish of Northiham . . . have been Catechized* (1611), pp. 232, 239; George Webbe, *A Briefe Exposition of the Principles of the Christian Religion* (1617), Sig. C6ᵛ.

6. Thomas Cartwright and Dudley Fenner, along with Perkins, were the first Puritan clerics to contrast a covenant of works to the covenant of grace. Calvin never referred to a covenant of works, although he occasionally mentioned a covenant of grace, e.g., *Institutes* 4,13,6. Specialists in religious history have noted that the parable of two covenants never appears in Calvin's writings and that references by continental Calvinists to the covenant of grace are not nearly as prominent in their writings as in Puritan writings. See Anthony Hoekema, "The Covenant of Grace in Calvin's Teachings," *Calvin Theological Journal* 2 (1972), pp. 133–34; Kendall, *Calvin and English Calvinism*, p. 27; George Marsden, "Perry Miller's Rehabilitation of the Puritans: A Critique," *CH* 39 (1970), pp. 103–4.

7. William Perkins, *Workes* (Cambridge, 1608–9), I. 32, 71.

8. See H.B., *Grounds Of Christian Religion*, pp. 15–16; Arthur Dent, *A Pastime for Parents* (1603), Sig. D6ʳ; John Randall, *Three And Twentie Sermons* (1630), p. 115.

salvation did not abolish God's original demand for outward obedience but provided another way of satisfying that demand. Thus, despite changes in the terms of the covenant, continuity characterizes the history of God's dealings with humanity, as they are recorded in both the Old and the New Testament. In this way Puritan clerics, such as Daniel Rogers, upheld the continuing efficacy of the Law under the Gospel, because "the covenant of obedience (works) is subordinated to the covenant of grace." In his *Practical Catechism* Rogers further stated that "the old covenant is not contrary to the new in point of direction to obedience." [9]

Evidently, more than an affinity for theological subtlety was responsible for the elaborate distinctions drawn by Puritan divines between different covenants. They expanded the scope of the simple covenant concepts of continental Calvinism in order to meet the radical challenge to their authority and doctrine that existed in heretical denials of the Law. Arguments over the two covenants occupy a prominent place in debates between Puritan clerics and radical heretics in pre-Revolutionary England. Emphasis on differences between the two covenants helped heretics to dismiss the Old Testament Law and to justify Antinomian varieties of religious experience, which had no need for an ordained ministry. To defend their radical forms of lay initiative, Antinomians separated what Puritans joined together, the heavenly contracts in the Old and New Testaments.

The author of an early seventeenth-century manuscript that defended Antinomian heresy erroneously referred to William Perkins as an authority to prove that "the whole law of Moses is wholly abolished." This author cited Perkins's remarks on differences between the covenants of works and grace to defend that which Perkins had abjured. [10] For the other side, Puritan clerics such as George Walker argued that "knowledge of the true differences of the Old and New Testament, and the covenant of works and the covenant of grace, the Law and the Gospel, will not only give us great light . . . but also may keep us from many dangerous errors." He and many other Puritan clerics, like Samuel Torshell, referred

9. Daniel Rogers, *A Treatise Of The Two Sacraments* (1635), p. 44, *A Practical Catechism* (1633), pp. 87–88. See also Thomas Cartwright, *A Treatise of christian religion* (1616), p. 168; Dent, *Pastime for Parents*, Sigs. D5ʳ-6ʳ; Henry Finch, *The Sacred Doctrine of Divinity* (1613), I. 12, II. 1; Samuel Hieron, *The Abridgement Of The Gospel* (1613), in *All The Sermons of Samuel Hieron* (1614), p. 124; Edward Phillips, *Certaine Godly And Learned Sermons* (1607), p. 99.

10. BoL, *MSS. Rawls.* D1350, ff. 109–14. Cf. the use of Perkins's works to refute Antinomian arguments against the Law in William Hinde, *The Office And Use Of The Morall Law* (1623), Sig. B1ᵛ, pp. 91, 94; Thomas Taylor, *The Rule Of The Law Under The Gospel*, (1631), p. 208.

to continuities between the two covenants in order to refute "Libertines and Antinomists," "the enthusiasts and vision boasters," and "such as receive not the testimony of the Old Testament."[11] These comments are instructive, for they point to radical forms of lay initiative—the Antinomian variety of religious experience—as the key issue which animated these debates over the heavenly contract.

FROM WHAT HAS BEEN SAID SO FAR, IT SHOULD BE EVIDENT THAT THE concept of covenant that was used to refute radical heresy bears little resemblance to a contractual transaction in the world of commerce. The heavenly contract appears to be, rather, a heavenly testament, a decree, enacted unilaterally rather than bilaterally. In antiheretical polemics, this unilateral aspect dominated Puritan discussion of the covenant: it is a decree, made in the remote past, that enjoins humanity to follow certain precepts (the Law under the Gospel) and practices (infant baptism). For example, in explaining the necessity of infant baptism, Puritan clerics portrayed the sacrament as an inherited right of children:

> Children of believing parents have a right to the sacrament . . . for the believing parent lays hold on the covenant not only for himself, but also for his seed. As in the title of lands at this day, a man does purchase lands to himself and his heirs after him.[12]

Although elements of mutuality exist in the relationship between God and the adult believer, no such reciprocity characterizes the covenant as it affects infant baptism. Neither the sins of parents nor the absence of faith in their offspring abridges a testamentarian right to the sacrament,[13] a right which derives not from one's parents but ultimately from Abraham.

This unilateral covenant more closely resembles the type of contract encountered in medieval political philosophy than that found in early modern thought, where bilateral features are more important. Many medieval writers attributed the institution of political sovereignty to a freely willed submission of a *populus liber*. But the pact of sovereignty created by this

11. George Walker, *The Manifold Wisdome Of God* (1641), pp. 2–3; Samuel Torshell, *The Questions Of Free Justification* (1632), pp. 256–97. See also Joseph Bentham, *The Christians Conflict* (1635), pp. 137–38; Cleaver, *Patrimony Of Christian Children*, p. 186; Robert Harris, *A Treatise Of The New Covenant* (1632), II. 151–52; Taylor, *Rule Of Law*, p. 186.

12. Samuel Smith, *The Ethiopian Eunichs Conversion* (1632), p. 440. See also William Attersoll, *The New Covenant* (1614), p. 211; John Ball, *A Treatise Of Faith* (1632), pp. 409–10; Perkins, *Workes*, II. 235.

13. Ames, *Marrow Of Sacred Divinity*, p. 207.

submission was seldom seen as a bilateral contract: the grant of sovereignty was irrevocable.[14] This type of contract theory appeared in the
writings of some sixteenth-century writers, such as Bodin, who described
the pact of sovereignty as "a form of a gift, not being qualified in any way
. . . being at once unconditional and irrevocable." Richard Hooker's
Laws of Ecclesiastical Polity also described the pact of sovereignty in terms
that minimized its bilateral aspects. Its provisions are "for the most part
either clean worn out of knowledge, or else known unto a very few." Instead of stipulating mutual duties and obligations between sovereign and
subject, the pact of government teleologically expresses a social order pre-
ordained by God.[15] The irrevocable nature of the original grant of sovereignty, and the teleological goals assumed to govern it, created a pact of
government and society that had more in common with a testament than
with a bilateral contract.

This derivation of sovereignty from a pact made in the remote past is
similar to the Puritan use of covenant concepts to refute radical heresy. To
the extent that the operation of the covenant depends solely on God's will,
it has, in Bodin's words, the form of a "gift." Puritan clerics described
this gift in terms of God's free and undeserved mercy. Of course, in political theory the gift is made by subjects to a sovereign, whereas in covenant theology the gift comes from God to man. But both doctrines involve
a unilaterally enacted contract, made in the depths of time, that established mutually binding relations between two parties.

This unilateral contract was most useful for Puritan efforts to refute
various tenets of radical heresy. Heretical arguments about infant baptism, the Law, and also free will[16] were challenged by Puritan clerics,
who portrayed the heavenly contract as an inheritance that heretics were
arrogantly rejecting. The agreement between God and humanity established by this inheritance was admirably suited to clerical needs, for it
demanded obedience to many precepts and practices but never required
more lay initiative than Puritan clerics thought was proper.

---

14. Otto von Gierke, *Johannes Althusius und die Entwicklung der natürrechtlichen Staats-
theorien* (Breslau, 1913), pp. 78–81; Walter Ullman, *Principles of Government and Politics in the Middle Ages* (London, 1974), pp. 232–37, 241, 297.

15. Jean Bodin, *Six Books of the Commonwealth* (New York, 1967), p. 27; Richard
Hooker, *Laws of Ecclesiastical Polity* (Oxford, 1845), II. 501 (8,2,11). See also J.W.
Gough, *The Social Contract* (Oxford, 1957), p. 74. At the same time, however, increasing
concern with the conditional nature of the pact of sovereignty was voiced by Buchanan and
Boucher and, somewhat later, by Althusius and Grotius.

16. BoL, *MSS. Bodleian* 53, f. 116ᵛ; John Bradford, *Defence of Election* (c. 1555), in
PS, V. 322, 327.

Separatists and the Generous Covenant

Efforts by Separatists to gather congregations of visible saints threatened the leadership of Puritan clerics just as much as radical heresy did. It is therefore not surprising to find these clerics, in their debates with Separatists, using covenant notions which they had first developed for use in antiheretical polemics. Nor is it surprising that they emphasized the unilateral aspects of the covenant, which minimized the need for individual initiative. As in the case of radical heresy, undesirable forms of lay initiative were at the center of conflicts between Puritan clerics and Separatists. By referring to the heavenly contract as an inheritance, the clerics defended a comprehensive church in opposition to radical heresy and Separatism, both of which promoted more exclusive forms of religious organization, which left no room for the sinful multitude. The clerics' response referred to the covenant as a generous legacy in order to show that only the obstinate practice of gross sin could disqualify laypersons from the privilege of attending Puritan worship in the church.

Whereas disputes with heretics focused on differences between the old and new covenants, those with Separatists more directly concerned the new covenant and the role of individual consent in it. Here, too, baptism was an issue, although in this case what was at stake was not the proper age for baptism but the eligibility of infants born to profane parents. Thus, a "godly woman" put the following Separatist query to a cleric, asking by "what right we, as a national church, dedicate to God our children, though the parents be not visible saints?" The cleric responded by observing that baptism was an infant's legacy, provided by the heavenly contract: "How shall you after the revolt of the parent deprive the child of a share in God's covenant?" [17]

Depicting the heavenly contract as a legacy or testament justified not only a comprehensive church but also coercive enforcement of universal membership. An agreement with God made by the first generation of the faithful was binding on subsequent generations. Though present members of the church may not have consented to it, the use of secular force to compel attendance

> is lawful and fit, which at the first entry of covenant had been injurious. Even as when a man has taken up his freedom, he is liable to taxes . . . which before could not be imposed . . . so it is for those that for themselves and for their seed have once voluntarily em-

17. BoL, *MSS. Rawls.* C597 pp. 51–52. See also Richard Allen, *A Plaine Confutation Of A Treatise Of Brownisme* (1590), p. 10.

braced covenant with God, if they or theirs after fall from it, they may be by censures of the church or civil power compelled to resume their covenant.[18]

Just as Richard Hooker defended Anglican polity, and Edmund Burke the *ancien régime* against Thomas Paine's support for the French Revolution, so Puritan clerics upheld the validity of a compulsory state church by removing, to the remote past, the effectual consent to an original contract.

Separatist leaders understood that Puritan arguments for remaining within the church relied on unilateral conceptions of the heavenly contract, which treated church membership as an inherited right (and obligation) of all Christians. A sectarian communion of visible saints required more active evidences of true belief from its members. The lay initiative implicit in this sectarian model of church organization was more compatible with bilateral than unilateral conceptions of the covenant. A bilateral covenant makes consent of believers to its terms a prerequisite for its existence. In fact, emphasis on mutual obligations between God and believers dominated Separatist thinking about the heavenly contract, from the Plumbers' Hall group in London, at the beginning of Elizabeth's reign, to the establishment of exile groups in Holland, who later colonized New England. Bilateral conceptions of the covenant were well suited to Separatist concern with church discipline: lack of rigorous discipline represented humanity's failure to uphold its part of the covenant. Over time, Separatists increasingly distinguished between covenants among believers, which established particular congregations, and the heavenly contract between individuals and God. But in both instances the issues of discipline and visible sainthood lay at the heart of their covenant formulations.[19]

Disagreement over the unilateral and bilateral aspects of the heavenly contract shaped doctrinal debates between Puritan and Separatist writers. Leaders of Separatism in late Elizabethan England repeatedly attacked a popular Puritan writer, George Gifford, who upheld a unilateral view of the covenant in defending the legitimacy of the Church of England. According to Henry Barrow, Gifford's defense of the Anglican church rested on the assertion that all Christians "are from ancient descent within the covenant." The anti-Separatist implications of this position were evident to Barrow, who observed, "If the interest in God's covenant . . . depend

18. BoL, *MSS. Jones* 30, ff. 21ᵛ-22ʳ. See also Robert Abbot, *A Triall Of Our Church-Forsakers* (1639), pp. 53–54.

19. Here I rely on Edward S. Morgan, *Visible Saints: The History of a Puritan Idea* (Ithaca, 1963), pp. 37–38; B. R. White, *The English Separatist Tradition* (Oxford, 1971), pp. 9, 58, 113.

not upon the faith of the next parents, but upon the ancient Christians, etc., then ought all to be received, and none to be kept out of the church. Then is the whole world within the covenant."[20] Barrow's rejoinder explicitly contrasted Puritan views to his bilateral conception of a covenant, which required specific actions by believers. For Barrow, the Puritan view was implausible: "[It is] as though the Lord plights his love to us, and requires not again our faith and obedience unto him in the same covenant. Let Mr. Gifford show one place of Scripture through the whole Bible where the Lord made his covenant unto us without this condition."[21]

The Puritan side of this debate developed along lines that subsequently became a prominent feature of Puritan covenant theology. In opposition to Separatist arguments about practices required by the heavenly contract, Puritan clerics developed the idea of a gracious covenant, in conformity with the general Protestant tenet of justification by faith. Puritan writers charged that Separatists espoused justification by works when they insisted that performance of specific religious practices was a condition for the continuance of the heavenly contract. In fact, the organizational principle of Separatism—exclusive membership, based on visible sainthood—and its doctrinal expression in bilateral conceptions of the covenant did blur distinctions between faith and works. Puritan writers seized this opportunity to tar their Separatist opponents with popish pitch.

At the height of the controversies over Separatism in late Elizabethan England, Puritan polemicists discerned Catholic tenets, on the efficacy of works, in writings on the covenant by Barrow, Browne, and Greenwood. According to one writer, Browne believed "that one breach of duty . . . breaks the covenant," an error ascribed to Browne's ignorance of the fundamental tenet of Protestantism: "Not by works, but by faith is the covenant on our part" upheld.[22] Subsequently, other churchmen, such as Thomas Adams and Joseph Hall, referred to the gracious dimensions of the heavenly contract in order to defuse sectarian arguments: "What though the miscellaneous rabble of the profane, as the Brownists term them, be admitted among us. Shall the lewdness of these disannul God's

20. Henry Barrow, *A Refutation of Mr. Giffard's Reasons* (1590/91), in *ENT*, V. 337, and *A Plaine Refutation* (1591), in *ENT*, V. 115. See also John Greenwood, *A Brief Refutation* (1591), in *ENT*, VI. 14–15. For another example of the Puritan doctrine, see Attersol, *The New Covenant*, pp. 219–20.

21. Barrow, *A Fewe Observations* (1591), in *ENT*, VI. 108.

22. Stephen Bredwell, *The Raising Of The Foundations Of Brownisme* (1588), p. 72. See also George Gifford, *A Short Treatise Against the Donatists of England* (1590), Sigs. A2–3, p. 66, *A Short Reply unto . . . Henry Barow and John Greenwood* (1591), pp. 43–47; Richard Sibbes, *A Learned Exposition*, p. 425; John Udall, *A Commentarie Upon The Lamentations of Jeremy* (1593), p. 22.

covenant with his [faithful followers]? Yea, say they, this is their mercy. God's is more."[23]

Emphasis on the dimension of grace in the heavenly contract enabled Puritan writers to refute the Separatist argument that lack of a rigorous church discipline annulled the heavenly contract. Puritan writers associated good works with true faith, but they charged Separatists with abridging God's merciful intent in substituting, by Christ's intercession, faith for works as the means of salvation. According to Puritan clerics, the sectarian doctrine on church membership—visible sainthood—presumed to judge secrets best left to God.

The anomaly of these debates between Puritan and Separatist is the fact that, in the final analysis, their covenant theologies were not diametrically opposed. Separatists repeatedly denied the suggestion that their doctrine upheld justification by works or that it dismissed the efficacy of God's grace. According to Barrow, only "obstinate and presumptuous transgression breaks the covenant," a point with which his Puritan antagonists certainly agreed.[24] The real dispute between them lay in the grounds of obstinacy, an issue which in the first instance did not stem from doctrinal disagreement but from pragmatic and pastoral conflicts between the sectarian impulse and efforts by Puritan clerics to work with the resources of a comprehensive church.[25] Separatists thought that retention of the existing church polity constituted obstinate disobedience to God; Puritan clerics did not. While the former demanded visible sainthood of church members, the latter were willing to leave secret judgments to God. Disputes over the unilateral and bilateral dimensions of the heavenly contract evolved as a doctrinal expression of this conflict over organizational priorities.

Lay Puritanism and the Covenant

Prior to the last decade of the sixteenth century, the idea of the covenant in English Calvinism was limited to polemical writings directed against radical heresy and Separatism. Beyond these polemics scant mention was

---

23. Thomas Adams, *Workes* (1629), p. 790; Joseph Hall, *A Common Apologie Of The Church Of England* (1610), p. 18.

24. Barrow, *A Fewe Observations*, p. 121, *A Plaine Refutation*, pp. 160–64, *Barrow's Final Answer To Gifford* (1591/92), in *ENT*, VI. 121, 165–69. See also Francis Johnson, quoted in Richard Clyfton, *An Advertisement Concerning A Book* (1612), pp. 60–61. For Puritan arguments, see Anon., *The Church of England is a true Church of Christ* (1592), p. 24.

25. Henry Barrow, *A Brief Discoverie of the False Church* (1590), in *ENT*, III.

made of the covenant. However, over the next fifty years Puritan divinity made far more extensive use of covenant concepts. They appeared not only in the context of polemics directed against heresy and sectarianism but in a new context, a pastoral context in which Puritan clerics described both the interior dimensions of faith and the external evidences of it that could provide certitude of salvation.

Beginning in the 1590s, Puritan clerics placed the idea of a heavenly contract at the doctrinal core of their casuistries, which described in minute detail the experience of spiritual regeneration. In so doing they created a distinctively Puritan form of covenant theology, which they presented in sermons and popular treatises. This was not a scholastic theology, if "scholastic" implies that it was intellectually accessible to only a few. Though it was developed by clerics as an intellectually consistent doctrine, it was primarily a practical theology, intended explicitly for a lay audience. It united the doctrinal tenets of Calvinism and their pastoral implications in a relatively simple system of divinity. It not only related Calvinist tenets to the introspective search for evidences of election but showed as well the role of Bible-reading, sermons, sacraments, and household religion in this personal search for spiritual assurance.

Organizational pressures animated this theological innovation. In chapter 4, we saw that the events of the 1590s formed a turning point in the rise of Puritanism.[26] Disabused of the hope that the public authorities might sanction a presbyterian reform of the church, an overall shift occurred in the direction of Puritan reform. Inspired by preachers like John Dod, Richard Greenham, Richard Rogers, and, above all, William Perkins, a new set of clerical leaders appeared who took little interest in ecclesiological issues. Instead they emphasized the pastoral aspects of the ministry, based on Protestantism's long-standing commitment to edification. The style of pulpit oratory and sermon literature they developed— one that chronicled the inner experience of regeneration and the spiritual warfare between the spirit and the flesh—became the hallmark of Puritanism. As the doctrinal basis of this pastoral activity, covenant theology enabled laypersons to detect evidences of election and reprobation in themselves and others. Instead of relying on a formal discipline, Puritan clerics sought to channel lay initiative in directions that led to the same end. They provided an orthodox doctrinal guide for a lay vanguard within the church that would maintain its integrity by individual practice of the evaluative tasks formerly associated with a disciplinary apparatus.

309–10; Greenwood, *Brief Refutation*, pp. 17, 29; Robert Browne, *An Answere To Mr. Fowler's Letter* (nd), in *ENT*, II 459–60.

26. See above, chap. 4, pp. 113–15.

In this pastoral context, the concepts of the covenant differed markedly from those found in polemical writings, which stressed the unilateral aspects of the covenant, treating it as an inheritance or testament. In pastoral writings, Puritans emphasized the bilateral dimensions of the covenant: the duties and obligations required of believers in exchange for God's covenanted promise of salvation. These conceptual changes in the covenant concept were consequences of the organizational pressures described above. Unilateral conceptions of the covenant in polemical writings were well suited to the task of attacking undesirable forms of lay initiative. Bilateral conceptions in pastoral writings were useful for encouraging other types of lay initiative which nonetheless retained a prominent place for clerics in religious life.

Moreover, covenant concepts in Puritan casuistry were compatible not only with clerical interests but also with the broad concerns of lay dissent. Covenant theology was fully consonant with the strongly dualistic outlook of lay dissent and its consequent emphasis on edification and its opposition to rituals associated with a sacral priesthood.

PURITAN VIEWS ON SACRAMENTS AND SERMONS REVEAL THE UTILITY OF covenant theology for encouraging forms of lay initiative that were compatible with clerical authority. In chapters 2 and 4 we saw how the dualistic outlook of popular dissent led it to emphasize edification at the expense of the sacramental aspects of worship. This emphasis inspired the lay Puritan belief that the sacrament of communion was administered improperly when it was not accompanied by a sermon, and it also inspired opposition to many ceremonies prescribed by the church for use in administering the sacraments, such as signing infants with the cross in baptism.

Instructive examples of the efforts Puritan clerics made to accommodate these lay Puritan concerns can be found in their discussions of the sacraments as "seals" of the covenant. Some Puritan clerics illegally substituted an oral declaration of baptism as a seal of the covenant in place of the ceremonial signing of infants with the cross. Among them was a Sussex minister who in the 1605 subscription campaign was charged with several counts of nonconformity because "he does not say the litany . . . neither does he in baptism sign with the sign of the cross, but with the sign of the covenant; neither does he wear the surplice." The motive behind this innovation clearly involved appeasing lay opinion. In a London parish led by John Davenport, baptism also ended with clerics using the phrase "I sign thee with the seal of the covenant" in place of the prescribed formula. This substitution is not surprising, given the disposition of Davenport's parishioners. When urged by another cleric to use the prescribed ceremony, Davenport warned him, "If you breach such things you will spoil my parish, for none will suffer you to use the cross to the children."[27]

Describing baptism as a seal of the covenant was not an innovation of Puritan ministers. This was a legacy of the struggle against radical heresy that originated on the Continent at the outset of the Reformation. What was unique was the extent to which Puritan clerics described this sacrament, and communion also, as a covenant seal. Indeed, this became a hallmark of Puritanism. Two large charts, preserved in the Public Record Office, portray the two sacraments in simple language, with diagrams, as covenant seals. As bishop of London, Laud ordered the removal of these charts from several churches.[28] Some Puritan clerics assumed that their parishioners were thoroughly familiar with the covenant doctrine of the sacraments. When Richard Sibbes in a sermon defined baptism as "the seal of the covenant of grace," he added, "You are well enough acquainted, I imagine, with the thing. Therefore I will not enter into the commonplace. It is needless."[29]

Discussion of communion as a covenant seal was unique to the Puritan ministry. Its occurrence is a predictable feature of Puritan catechisms, and it is seldom encountered in writings by clerics who were avowedly hostile to Puritanism.[30] This treatment of communion reflected a relatively high level of intellectual rationality compared to that achieved in more conservative Anglican writings. The dualistic outlook implied by this rationality precluded any conception of Christ's corporeal presence in the Lord's Supper. Instead, Puritan covenant theology described the Lord's Supper as a visible sign and seal of the heavenly contract. This view was wholly compatible with the ethical religiosity and emphasis on edification promoted by a dualistic outlook.

As a sign and seal of the covenant, the function of communion was limited to its portrayal of the nexus of obligation between God and the communicant. Puritan covenant theology minimized the sacramental connotations of communion by treating it as an instructional aid for understanding the heavenly contract and as a symbol of the believer's consent to

27. *Sussex Archaeological Collections* 49 (1906), p. 54; *CSPD* 1629–31, p. 142; David A. Kirby, "The Radicals of St. Stephen's, Coleman Street, London, 1624–1642," *Guildhall Miscellany* 3 (1970), pp. 98–119. See also *CSPD* 1638–39, p. 362.

28. PRO, *SPD* SP 16/154/ff. 183–84; *CSPD* 1629–31, p. 142.

29. Sibbes, *Lydias Conversion* (n.d.), in *Works*, VI. 530. See also Edward Elton, *An Exposition of the Epistle . . . to the Colossians* (1615), p. 398.

30. E. Brooks Holifield, *The Covenant Sealed: The Development of Puritan Sacramental Theology in Old and New England, 1570–1720* (New Haven, 1974), p. 51. This view of the Lord's Supper also appears in catechisms by Puritan authors such as Nicholas Byfield, Arthur Dent, John Dod and Robert Cleaver, Robert Jenison, Elnathan Parr, and Thomas Taylor.

that contract. This doctrine upheld lay Puritan demands for an edifying style of worship, for it not only minimized sacramentalism but also made knowledge of the ethical bond between God and believers in the covenant a prerequisite for admission to communion. Because the sacrament represented and signified assent to the covenant, it was useless to communicants who were ignorant of the covenant. According to Puritan clerics, "If men come often to the sacraments, and do not before and after meditate on the covenant of grace, they should not receive much good thereby." Participation in communion demanded that communicants "be able in some measure to understand the covenant of grace."[31]

This doctrine differs sharply from the sacramental doctrines held by the Anglican opponents of the Puritan ministry. Their efforts to retain a prominent place for sacramentalism in worship were incompatible with the more rigorously dualistic outlook of Puritanism. The Puritans, who viewed sacraments as signs and seals of the covenant, stressed their role as edifying and symbolic aids to worship. Conservative Anglicans argued that communion embodied the mystery of Christ's divinity and sacrifice. In a polemical work against Puritan nonconformity, one author explained why ceremonial flourishes prescribed by the church were appropriate: they are "agreeable to the reverent majesty of sacred mysteries. For what can be more agreeable to holy mysteries than the sign of that which was the consummation and accomplishment of all holy mysteries?"[32] Supporters of these ceremonies regarded communion in ways that were antithetical to the Puritan emphasis on the edifying function of the sacrament: they described communion as a material representation of the incomprehensible. The Puritan view of communion as an aid in giving informed consent to the heavenly contract left no room for excessive ritualism, such as kneeling during communion, which conservative Anglicans regarded as the reverence due to a holy mystery.

The primary means of edification in worship was, of course, preaching. It is not surprising, then, that Puritan clerics referred to preaching as the way in which the heavenly contract was offered to believers. They stated that "the preaching of his word is the covenant of grace," because

31. Samuel Smith, *Davids Blessed Man* (1617), p. 137; Cartwright, *Treatise of christian religion*, p. 216. See also John Dod and Robert Cleaver, *Ten Sermons* (1632), pp. 13, 16; Henry Scudder, *The Christians Daily Walke* (1637), pp. 166–67; Thomas Taylor, *Davids Learning* (1617), p. 121.

32. Leon Hutton, *An Answere To A Certaine Treatise* (1605), p. 26. See also the debates on this issue presented in William Ames, *A Reply to Dr. Mortons Generall Defense* (1622), p. 36; Lancelot Andrewes, *Ninety-Six Sermons* (Oxford, 1841), I. 41–43; Hooker, *Laws Of Ecclesiastical Polity*, II. 85–86, 89 (5,67,7–8 and 5,67,12).

"we renew our covenant in every sermon, for God declared what he will be unto us and what he requires of us back again."[33]

This doctrine provided a convenient way for clerics to explain the relationship between preaching and communion in ways that were agreeable to lay Puritans. Preaching announced the terms of the heavenly contract, and communion signified individual consent to those terms. In almost the same words, leading Puritan clerics, such as Paul Baynes and Richard Rogers, explained that "the sacraments are helps necessarily adjoined unto the preaching of the word, and do visibly confirm and ratify that which the word does teach, and the covenant made betwixt God and the believer is most surely sealed up."[34] Analogies with worldly contracts and seals also sustained the view that sacraments must be administered with sermons: without the contract, a seal is meaningless. In this view, the sacrament existed somewhat below preaching in order of importance. "The sacrament in some respects has its place below the word, in that the word is the covenant, and the sacrament does but increase the validity and force of the covenant."[35]

Household religion was another lay Puritan practice that Puritan clerics dealt with in their covenant theology. From 1590 to 1640, Puritan sermon literature devoted much attention to the special duties of householders as one aspect of the heavenly contract. As with communion and preaching, Puritan discussion of household religion advanced bilateral conceptions of a covenant that required specific actions by believers. This is understandable in view of the lay initiative involved in conducting study and worship in the home.

However, in this case the heavenly contract demanded more than individual consent to its provisions: heads of households had also to compel wives, children, and servants to fulfill their religious duties. In a treatise on the covenant first published in 1596, the author observed that Christian householders always were expected to catechize their children and lead family prayers, and "by these and other means was God's covenant repeated, renewed and continued from generation to generation." This "continual repeating of the covenant" occurred in the household when

33. John Downame, *The Christian Warfare* (1634), p. 117; John Angier, *An Helpe To Better Hearts* (1647; sermons delivered before 1640), p. 308. The same point was made by a London pewterer who composed a small manuscript, BoL, *MSS. Rawls.* C765, p. 33.

34. Richard Rogers, *Seven Treatises* (1610), p. 233; Paul Baynes, *Brief Directions Unto A Godly Life* (1637), pp. 116–17. See also Edward Elton, *The Triumph Of A True Christian* (1623), p. 7; BoL, *MSS. Rawls.* C825, p. 177; William Gouge, *A Short Catechisme* (1635), Sig. B2ʳ; Randall, *Three and Twentie Sermons*, I. 72–73.

35. Angier, *An Helpe to Better Hearts*, p. 302. See also Phillips, *Certaine Godly Sermons*, p. 149.

children "confess the article of Christian faith, and when they promise to obey God's commandments." And in a book on catechizing, probably written by the same author, it is stated that "the covenant between God and his church . . . cannot continue except youth be instructed."[36]

This emphasis on the mutual duties of God and believers in the covenant pervades discussion of household religion in writings by other Puritan clerics. Some argued that a condition of God's promise to include children of the faithful in his covenant was the parents' effort to keep themselves and their offspring in covenant with God. George Estey pointed to the following duty of prospective parents: "Before they ever have children to endeavor to be in the covenant of God, that their children may be."[37] Estey's argument appeared as a point of casuistry in sermons by Nicholas Bownde, Richard Greenham, and Arthur Hildersham, who were leading exponents of the Puritan practice of household religion and who were closely related by family and professional ties.[38] Hildersham remarked in his weekly lectures, "We have good assurance that ourselves are within God's covenant" if "we have done our endeavor to bring up our children in God's fear." Other prominent Puritan preachers who taught laymen to discern their inclusion in the heavenly contract by their success in rearing their children included John Dod, Robert Cleaver, and Richard Sibbes.[39]

Puritan concern with edification, preaching, and household worship was also expressed by Sabbatarianism. As a distinct doctrine that upheld the necessity of these activities on Sundays, Sabbatarianism was another pastoral feature of Puritanism that clerics incorporated in their covenant theology after 1590.[40] Covenant concepts in Sabbatarianism were also strongly bilateral in nature. A condition imposed on believers by the covenant was devotion of entire Sundays to religious observances in church and at home. According to one preacher, "The way to lay hold of the cove-

36. J.F., *The Covenant Betweene God And Man* (1616), pp. 63–64, 68–69, *The Necessities And Antiquitie Of Catechizing* (1617), Sig. B2ʳ.

37. George Estey, *An Exposition upon the Tenne Commandments* (1601), in *Certaine Godly And Learned Expositions* (1603), f. 55ᵛ. See also Thomas Gataker, *Davids Instructor* (1620), pp. 30–31.

38. Bownde married Greenham's daughter and was also a member of a combination lectureship at Bury St. Edmunds that included George Estey. Hildersham was a friend of Greenham and wrote a memorial of Greenham's life.

39. Arthur Hildersham, *CVIII Lectures Upon The Fourth Of John* (1632), p. 180. See also John Dod and Robert Cleaver, *Seven Godlie And Fruitfull Sermons* (1614), p. 50; Sibbes, *The Returning Backslider* (1639) in *Works*, II. 356.

40. See Patrick Collinson, "The Beginnings of English Sabbatarianism," *SCH* 1 (1964), p. 211; Christopher Hill, *Society and Puritanism in Pre-Revolutionary England* (New York, 1967), pp. 170, 501.

nant is to keep the Sabbath; there is some hope of a man's salvation when he makes conscience of keeping the Sabbath."[41]

Occasionally, when Puritan clerics discussed the appropriateness of making private vows to God on the Sabbath, they described this as "covenant-making." Like the more general covenant of grace, vows involved an element of mutuality between God and the believer. Referring to private vows made for specific purposes, a preacher, in 1614, noted that Sundays were "most fit for those covenants." Other references to covenant-making as vows exist in Puritan diaries.[42] However, Puritan clerics distinguished between the general covenant relation and specific vows, arguing that the former preceded and subsumed any vows.[43] The Puritan doctrine of Sabbatarianism primarily concerned the heavenly contract, whose provisions applied equally to all. It was "God's covenant," the covenant of grace, that required Sunday religious observances.[44]

Puritan clerics related the nature of Sabbath observances to the heavenly contract in terms similar to those used to explain the sacraments. Like the sacraments, God established Sabbath observances as a sign of his contract with the faithful. Outward observances in communion, and more generally throughout the Sabbath day, had as their common rationale the function of edification, explaining the mutual bonds that united God and the faithful in the heavenly contract. Richard Greenham compared this edifying function of the Sabbath and the Lord's Supper when he remarked that the Sabbath "is called a sign . . . as we may see in the sacraments . . . whereby we should know what He is unto us, and wherein we should learn what we should [be] to him." Other Puritan clerics observed that the Sabbath was established as "a sign of God's covenant" which reminded believers of the mutual obligations uniting them to God.[45]

Puritan clerics used this doctrine when they debated Sabbatarianism with the Anglican hierarchy. In opposition to Puritan insistence that Sundays be devoted to preaching and household religion, church leaders in

41. George Abbot, *Vindiciae Sabbath* (1641), p. 112.

42. BoL, *MSS. Rawls.* C475, p. 198. See also M.M. Knappen, ed., *Two Elizabethan Puritan Diaries* (Chicago, 1933), pp. 67–82; E. Hockliffe, ed., "The Diary of Rev. Ralph Josselin, 1616–1683," *CS* 3d ser. 15 (1908), p. 18.

43. See William Fenner, *Workes* (1658), I. 427; Richard Greenham, *Workes* (1612), p. 477; John Preston, *The Saints Daily Exercise* (1629), p. 102; Sibbes, *A Learned Commentary* (1656; published posthumously), in *Works*, IV. 406.

44. See Joseph Bentham, *The Societie Of The Saints* (1630), p. 149; Robert Cleaver, *A Declaration Of The Christian Sabbath* (1625), pp. 57–58; William Fenner, *Of The Sabbath* (n.d.), in *Workes*, II. 71.

45. Abbot, *Vindiciae Sabbath*, p. 109; Greenham, *Workes*, pp. 132–33, and see p. 841. See also Bentham, *Societie Of The Saints*, p. 151; Cleaver, *Declaration Of The Sabbath*, pp. 66–68.

the early seventeenth century claimed as one of their prerogatives the right to establish the form and even the day of Sabbath observances. Puritans defended their Sabbath practices in arguments that traced their origins to the supersession of the old by the new covenant.[46] One such cleric composed a treatise that was banned along with other "dangerous books" in the 1630s. Its author, George Walker, was a London preacher who was implicated in the practice of baptizing infants with the sign of the covenant. According to Walker, the Lord's day "can no more be abrogated and abolished than God's covenant"; foremost among Sabbath duties is "preserving the knowledge and memory of the covenant," for on this day occurred "the greatest blessing which God gave to the world . . . God's entering into the covenant of grace."[47]

THE SAME LINKS BETWEEN IDEOLOGY AND ORGANIZATION ARE EVIDENT in Sabbatarianism as in Puritan writings on preaching, the sacraments, and household religion. Taken collectively, these writings provide three types of evidence—biographical, chronological, and hermeneutic—that enable us to relate the development of covenant theology to organizational pressures on Puritan clerics.

Biographical evidence shows that some of the prominent clerical proponents of a renewed emphasis on pastoral work had been only peripherally interested in or even explicitly indifferent to the classis movement. These include Bownde, Cleaver, Dod, Greenham, Hildersham, and Perkins, who were also the first Puritan clerics to use covenant theology in popular sermons and treatises to explain the necessity and nature of preaching, sacraments, and household religion in Sunday worship. This use of covenant theology went beyond its earlier, polemical use as a weapon against radical heresy and Separatism, a use with which these clerics were certainly familiar.[48]

Chronological evidence points to the fact that before 1590 covenant concepts appeared almost entirely in the context of arguments against radical heresy and Separatism. This use of covenant concepts retained many features of the embryonic covenant theology developed on the Continent at the outset of the Reformation by Bullinger, Calvin, and Zwingli and later by Beza and the Heidelberg theologians. It was after 1590 that a distinctively Puritan variety of covenant theology emerged, focusing on

46. See Abbot, *Vindiciae Sabbath*, pp. 49–50; John Ley, *Sunday A Sabbath* (1641), p. 87; John Traske, *A Treatise Of Libertie From Judaisme* (1620), pp. 27–28; Thomas Young, *The Lords-Day* (1672), pp. 165–67 (this work first appeared in Latin, in 1639).

47. BoL, *MSS. Tanner*, 70, f. 209ʳ; *CSPD* 1629–31, p. 142; George Walker, *The Doctrine Of The Weekly Holy Sabbath* (1641), pp. 65, 67, 134.

48. See above, chap. 5, pp. 132–34, 139–40.

pastoral issues. Of course, the fact that a revised covenant theology appeared at the same time as Puritanism underwent an organizational reorientation cannot by itself be viewed as proof of a causal relationship. But when biographical and conceptual issues are taken into account, chronological evidence further confirms the existence of a causal relationship between organizational and ideological developments.

Hermeneutic evidence strongly supports these conclusions. Until 1590, covenant concepts were overwhelmingly unilateral in nature because of the pragmatic use to which these concepts were put in combating radical forms of lay initiative. Unilateral conceptions of the heavenly contract were most expedient for this purpose. Bilateral conceptions of the heavenly contract dominated Puritan discussion of preaching, sacraments, household religion, and Sabbatarianism after 1590, when Puritan clerics were developing a doctrinal framework for types of lay initiative that did not openly flout clerical authority.

This newer covenant theology provided a precise doctrinal identity for important concerns of lay Puritanism that derived from an older tradition of popular dissent. It provided a Calvinist rationale for subordinating sacramental to edifying aspects of worship and for encouraging male householders to enforce piety among their wives, children, and servants. At the same time, covenant theology also channeled these focal concerns in directions that were compatible with continuing clerical guidance from within the church. Thus, covenant theology after 1590 balanced the spiritual interests of the clerics and the laity. Though Puritan preachers did not presume to manipulate sacral forces, they did claim for themselves a primary role in spiritual edification. Clerics were responsible for proclaiming the conditions of the heavenly contract, while satisfaction of those conditions had to be accomplished by individual believers.

Two further considerations complete this analysis of the development of Puritan covenant theology. I have emphasized the significance of changes in the covenant concept. In response to organizational pressures, Puritan clerics used bilateral covenant concepts to incorporate pastoral aspects of religion in a covenant theology that previously had been limited to polemics against heresy and Separatism.

This does not imply, however, that Puritan clerics were the first to use a bilateral conception of the covenant, for isolated passages in the Bible and in the writings of continental reformers also point to the mutual duties of God and believers in the heavenly contract.[49] This has led several histo-

---

49. See Bullinger, *Decades*, II. 169–72; Calvin, *Institutes*, II. 477, 505–6 (4,13,6 and 4,14,19), *Tracts And Treatises On The Doctrine And Worship Of The Church* (London, 1958), II. 214; Zacharias Ursinus, *The Summe Of Christian Religion* (1645), p. 124. See also Kenneth Hagen, "From Testament to Covenant in the Early Sixteenth Century,"

rians to conclude that Puritan covenant theology was almost entirely derivative of continental Calvinism and of scriptural inspiration.[50] But the
existence of these precedents does not explain why the bilateral conception
appeared in Puritan thought after 1590, almost a half-century after the
initial introduction of continental covenant theology in England. Moreover, the biblical and continental precedents existed in isolated, rudimentary references, whereas Puritan covenant theology after 1590 united pastoral aspects of religious worship in a compact system of divinity. Thus,
the salience of intellectual *precedents* for Puritan covenant theology can be
understood only with reference to organizational *pressures* acting on Puritan clerics.

A second consideration concerns the pastoral use of covenant theology
by the Puritan laity. Their practical interest in being assured of salvation
was at least as strong as, if not stronger than, their doctrinal commitments. Yet, so far, my discussion of covenant theology has been limited to
doctrinal and liturgical issues regarding the necessity of preaching, sacraments, and household religion. How did this theology serve as a practical
guide to the laity's use of these religious ordinances in the matter of greatest spiritual interest to them? If covenant theology was as important as I
have suggested, we would expect it to have influenced Puritan casuistry
and to have guided lay initiative in the introspective search for evidences
of election.

In fact, the elaborate casuistry produced by Puritan writers was doc-
trinally grounded in covenant theology. The idea of a heavenly contract
was the conceptual keystone of Puritan divinity, because it united doctrinal tenets and their casuistical implications in Calvinism. Puritans referred to the covenant of grace in order to describe the inner experience of
spiritual regeneration in terms of the Calvinist tenets of election, faith,
and grace. This explains the importance attached to the heavenly contract,
in the form of the covenant of grace, by Puritan clerics; it was indeed the
"marrow of Puritan divinity," as Perry Miller suggested nearly fifty years
ago.[51]

Sixteenth-Century Journal 3 (1972). Michael McGiffert, "William Tyndale's Conception
of the Covenant," *JEH* 32 (1981), notes that unilateral and bilateral covenants appear in
Tyndale's writings.

50. E.g., Everett H. Emerson, "Calvin and Covenant Theology," *CH* 25 (1956),
pp. 136–44; John Dykstra Eusden, *Puritans, Lawyers, and Politics in Early Seventeenth-
Century England* (New Haven, 1958), p. 28; David Little, *Religion, Order, and Law: A
Study in Pre-Revolutionary England* (Oxford, 1970), p. 258; John New, *Anglican and Puritan: The Basis of Their Opposition* (London, 1964), pp. 92–95; Marsden, "Perry Miller's Rehabilitation of the Puritans," pp. 99–100.

51. More recently some have downplayed the importance of covenant theology in Puritan thought. New, *Anglican and Puritan*, pp. 93–94, argues that it is not as important as

The Covenant of Grace

In the half-century prior to the English Revolution, covenant theology became almost synonymous with Puritanism. As bishop of London and later as archbishop of Canterbury, William Laud sought to limit Puritan teaching on the subject. At about the same time, a leading Puritan preacher, John Preston, said of the covenant:

> It is the main point that the ministers of the gospel can deliver at any time. Neither can they deliver a point of greater moment, nor can you hear any, than the description of the covenant of grace . . . There is no ground you have to believe you shall be saved, there is no ground to believe that any promise of God shall be made good to you . . . I say, there is no other ground at all but upon this covenant. All that we teach you from day to day are but conclusions drawn from this covenant.[52]

The importance of the covenant for Puritan ministers later appeared in the first of the "fast sermons," which were delivered before the Long Parliament during the Revolution. Cornelius Burges presented the first such sermon on the morning of 17 November 1640, and in it he referred to God's covenant with humanity no less than 240 times. He anticipated some objection to this and so defended his concern with the covenant against "some jeerers," who suggested that it betrayed a "Puritan humor." That afternoon Stephen Marshall preached a second sermon in which he argued that "The presence of God in his covenant of grace with any people is the greatest glory and happiness that they can enjoy."[53]

Perry Miller has suggested because, instead of finding frequent references to the covenant in Puritan writings, "I had to look for it." Obviously, the importance of one concept in a belief system is not a function of the frequency with which it is expressed. Michael Walzer, *Revolution of the Saints: A Study in the Origins of Radical Politics* (Cambridge, Mass., 1965), p. 167n, cites the views of John Eusden, *Puritans, Lawyers, and Politics*, p. 29, that some Puritan divines, such as Paul Baynes and Richard Rogers, were "pointedly against covenant." Eusden may have mistaken Puritan rejection of the Catholic notion of a meritorious covenant for a rejection of a Calvinist covenant theology; see Paul Baynes, *The Mirrour Of Miracle Of Gods Love* (1619), pp. 59–62, and John Ball, *A Treatise Of Faith* (1632), pp. 88–89.

52. See above, p. 143, for actions by Laud as bishop of London, and also "Reports of Cases in the Courts of Star Chamber and High Commission," *CS* new ser. 39 (1886), pp. 236–37. For Archbishop Laud, see PRO, *SPD* SP 16/260/f. 190ᵛ. John Preston, *The New Covenant* (1629), pp. 350–51.

53. Cornelius Burges, *The First Sermon, Preached To The Honourable House of Commons* (1640), in *FS*, I. 74; Stephen Marshall, *A Sermon Preached before the Honourable House of Commons* (1640), in *FS*, I. 107. For a discussion of the political uses of covenant theology at this time, see John F. Wilson, *Pulpit in Parliament: Puritanism during the English Civil Wars, 1640–1648* (Princeton, 1969), pp. 166–96.

The covenant of grace encompassed major doctrinal and pastoral aspects of Puritan religion. It was a theological catchword that represented all obligations and promises uniting God and humanity, all duties and rewards attendant upon election. With regard to rewards and promises, John Preston and Richard Sibbes taught that God "makes a covenant, and as branches of the covenant gives many promises." [54] With regard to duties and obligations, another preacher referred listeners to Puritan doctrine on the covenant "as it has been approved for many years by sundry learned professors of the Gospel": it revealed "the sum of that which the Lord requires of us . . . if we will be saved." [55] From these clerics the laity learned that different rewards of faith were determined by provisions of a heavenly contract. In identical words John Ball and Richard Sibbes stated that "faith does not effect and perform these things by any excellency, force or efficacy of its own . . . but in regard of the office whereunto it is assigned in the covenant of grace." [56]

According to Puritan clerics, knowledge of the covenant was not to be gained from revelation but from the Bible. Indeed, the Bible was regarded principally as a written record of God's covenant with humanity. For Perkins, "the stipulation of the covenant of grace is the substance of the Gospel." Many other Puritan writers equated the Bible and the covenant, including the author of a catechism that instructed its readers as follows:

Q. What is the word of God?
A. The books of the holy canonical scriptures containing the covenants, both of our obedience to God, and of his saving grace in Christ to us. [57]

Some lay religious writers, including a legal authority and a London pewterer, also thought that "The word of Christ is the doctrine of the covenant of grace." [58]

54. Richard Sibbes, *A Miracle Of Miracles* (1638), in *Works*, VII. 188. See also John Preston, *Foure Godly And Learned Sermons* (1636), p. 300.

55. John Brinsley, *The Third Part Of The True Watch* (1622), Sig. A5ʳ. In Brinsley's estimation, Greenham and Perkins were foremost among the "learned professors of the Gospel," who also included Baynes, Bownde, Crooke, Daniel Dyke, Dod, John Downame, and Hall (*Third Part Of The True Watch*, pp. 389–90).

56. Ball, *Treatise Of Faith*, p. 135. For Sibbes, see his epistle to Ezekiel Culverwell, *Treatise Of Faith* (1623), in Sibbes, *Works*, I. xci. See al ɔ Thomas Goodwin, *The Glory Of The Gospel* (1625), in *Works*, IV. 245.

57. Perkins, *Workes*, II. 327; Henry Wilkinson, *A Catechism* (1624), Sigs. C2ᵛ-3ʳ. See also Bentham, *Societie Of The Saints*, p. 179; Cartwright, *Treatise of christian religion*, pp. 80–81; Elton, *An Exposition*, pp. 64, 443–44; Preston, *The Cup of Blessing*, p. 30; Randall, *Three And Twentie Sermons*, I. 192–93, 199.

58. Finch, *Doctrine Of Divinitie*, I. 15. The pewterer is John Frethorne, BoL, *MSS. Rawls.*, C765, p. 33.

THOUGH IT WAS A SOLIDLY CALVINIST DOCTRINE, PURITAN COVENANT theology modified Calvinism in subtle ways. Several historians have suggested that this modification made Calvinism more palatable for laypersons, effacing some of its harsher features.[59] Covenant theology struck a balance between hope and despair, between certitude of either salvation or damnation. Overemphasis on either could lead to complacency, which was antithetical to the life of continuous introspection that clerics expected of their parishioners. Covenant theology avoided complacency because the idea of a heavenly contract implied that salvation rested on an agreement between God and the believer. This focused attention on the nature and role of human consent in salvation, in place of a fixed and unknowable decree made by God at the beginning of time.

However, what has not yet been adequately explained is how and why covenant concepts were used to achieve these goals. In what follows, I show how Puritan clerics translated the major tenets of Calvinism into a contractarian doctrine; then I explain how this doctrinal innovation made Calvinism more easily received by the laity.

Emphasis on the heavenly contract was adequate, both conceptually and socially, for creating a belief system that was intended for popular consumption. Contractual references were sufficiently complex to be useful for explaining Calvinist doctrines of election, faith, and grace. Yet these references were also intelligible to lay Puritans. References to principles of worldly contracts and other financial instruments were cognitive resources which Puritan clerics used in creating a compact system of Calvinist divinity. As the doctrinal core of Puritan casuistry, covenant theology guided the search for evidences of election by treating them in terms of economic practices and legal maxims that were associated with the use of contracts in everyday life. It was this development in Puritanism that solved a key pastoral problem that Max Weber saw as an obstacle to lay acceptance of Calvinism: reconciling the rigidly deterministic doctrine of election with continuous efforts by believers to achieve salvation.[60]

This modification of Calvinism solved a fundamental problem that has confronted many social movements: balancing a deterministic world view with the need for activism by individual members. The utility of a deterministic theory of history or salvation lies in supplying the members of a movement with the conviction that their actions are in accord with objective historical laws or with God's will. But, at the same time, initiatives by individuals must be justified. It is not enough that the members of a

59. E.g., Hill, *Society and Puritanism*, p. 489; M.M. Knappen, *Tudor Puritanism* (Chicago, 1966), p. 395; Perry Miller, *The New England Mind: The Seventeenth Century* (Cambridge, Mass., 1939), pp. 394–96; New, *Anglican and Puritan*, p. 128.

60. H.H. Gerth and C.W. Mills, eds., *From Max Weber* (New York, 1958), pp. 111–12.

movement uphold the existence of historical laws or of God's will: they must also act to implement them. These twin imperatives introduce an irreducible element of ambiguity into the ideological formulations of many movements whose successes rest in part on their ability to fortify individual activism with a deterministic world view.

For example, in orthodox Marxism it is the party organization that aligns individual efforts with objective historical laws. In Puritanism, the ambiguity of activism and determinism appeared in the contrast between contract and grace in the heavenly contract. Like the theory of the party in orthodox Marxism, Puritan covenant theology did not resolve the ambiguity of activism and determinism in an intellectually consistent manner. The strength of both doctrines lay in combining the irreconcilable in an ideologically plausible manner.

THE AMBIGUITY OF ACTIVISM AND DETERMINISM IS EVIDENT IN THE core concept of Puritan covenant theology, the covenant of grace. Covenants implied a mutual exchange of rights and obligations, whereas grace, in Calvinist doctrine, originated entirely and freely in God. In catechisms and sermons, Puritan clerics taught that the covenant of grace replaced the covenant of works after the Fall of Adam. Adam's sin violated the covenant of works, which required perfect observance of all its conditions: Adam precipitated his Fall by "breaking the covenant in taking of the forbidden fruit." [61] This interpretation of original sin equated unregenerate persons with covenant-breakers. Puritan clerics regarded the keeping of one's covenants as a precept of natural law, and sometimes they called the first covenant the "covenant of nature." [62]

Adam's Fall thus signified the inability of humanity to fulfill its part of a divine agreement whose contractual provisions followed the natural law precept of *quid pro quo*. In view of this inability, God made a new covenant, one that was guided by grace, not natural law. This was the covenant of grace, "God's second contract with mankind after the Fall," which "succeeds the former covenant and was made upon the breach thereof." [63]

The dimension of grace in the new covenant created a heavenly contract which severely qualified the precept of *quid pro quo*. Instead of requiring

61. Immanuel Bourne, *The Rainbow* (1617), p. 10. See also Ames, *The Marrow Of Sacred Divinity*, p. 57; Samuel Crooke, *The Guide Unto True Blessednesse* (1613), p. 21; John Frethorne, *MSS. Rawls*. C765, p. 19; John Preston, *Life Eternal* (1634), II. 87; Sibbes, *A Learned Commentary*, p. 144.

62. See Nicholas Byfield, *The Patterne Of Wholesome Words* (1618), p. 200; Thomas Goodwin, *Aggravation of Sin* (1638), in *Works*, IV. 182; Perkins, *Workes*, II. 280; Walker, *Manifold Wisdome Of God*, pp. 40, 50.

63. Crooke, *Guide Unto True Blessednesse*, p. 39; Cartwright, *A treatise of christian religion*, p. 167.

obedience to his Law in exchange for salvation, God undertook to fulfill both his and humanity's part of the contract: "God, who seeing the first Adam could not stand in the covenant of works . . . has renewed with the faithful, in the second Adam, a covenant of grace, in which he has undertaken to work all our work for us."[64]

The covenant of grace lay within the reach of human ability aided by grace, for this covenant accepted sincere intent and faith, in place of the outward obedience demanded by the old covenant. "In the covenant of grace," declared Sibbes, "our performances, if they be sincere, they are accepted."[65] This substitution of faith, aided by grace, for outward obedience was related to Christ's intercession and sacrifice. "Christ is the maker good of the covenant of grace between God and man." He satisfied the demand for perfect obedience by the old covenant, and his sacrifice "seals all the covenant of grace . . . because it ratifies unto us the cancellation of that handwriting of the old covenant which we had transgressed, and wiping off all old scores and debts, it confirms our entrance into the new covenant."[66]

Puritans interpreted the general tenet of justification by faith to mean that humanity's obligation under the covenant of grace was faith: "the means to be in this covenant is to perform the condition of faith."[67] But in conformity with Calvin's emphasis on the utter depravity of humanity after the Fall, Puritans declared that performance of the condition of faith was beyond the reach of human ability unaided by God's grace. Faith itself was a gift of God, gratuitously given to some according to his decree of election. Consequently, faith in the covenant of grace was both humanity's duty and God's gift.

The covenant of grace was a gracious contract for three reasons. First, divine mercy modified its contractual form: "The covenant of grace is so called because God is so gracious to enable us to perform on our part."[68]

64. Phineas Fletcher, *Joy In Tribulation* (1632), p. 243. See also John Preston, *The New Covenant* pp. 363–64, 501–2; Frewthorne, *MSS. Rawls.* C765, p. 24; Sibbes, *Faithful Covenanter*, pp. 3–5.

65. Sibbes, *A Learned Commentary*, p. 61, and also *The Art Of Contentment* (1629), in *Works*, V. 187. For other writers, see Nicholas Byfield, *The Marrow Of The Oracles Of God* (1640), pp. 360–61; Elton, *Triumph Of A True Christian*, p. 6; Perkins, *Workes*, III. 335.

66. Randall, *Three and Twentie Sermons*, I. 192; Thomas Taylor, *Christs Victorie Over The Dragon* (1633), p. 605. See also Elton, *Triumph Of A Christian*, p. 17; Preston, *New Covenant*, p. 330.

67. John Downame, *A Treatise Of Securitie* (1622), p. 98. See also Perkins, *Workes*, III. 122; Randall, *Three and Twentie Sermons*, I. 203; John Rogers, *Doctrine Of Faith*, p. 256; Thomas Wilson, *Saints by Calling* (Barbican, 1620), p. 95.

68. Sibbes, *Bowels Opened* (1639), in *Works*, II. 183, and also *Josiahs Reformation* (1629), in *Works*, VI. 31, 350. For other writers, see Harris, *Treatise Of The New Cove-*

Second, it *obligated* God to provide grace to the elect, enabling them to believe and thus perform their part of the heavenly contract. This obligation, or pledge, was entered into freely, as a gift. "By covenant [God] is bound to man, but his covenant is established upon his own promise . . . there never was, nor could be anything in man to move God to enter into covenant with [man]."[69] Third, an element of mercy existed in God's willingness to use contracts—a human invention—in his dealings with humanity. To encompass his will within the limits of human understanding, God "stoops so low as to make use of terms that are used in human matters and contracts," declared Sibbes. This was further evidence of his merciful intent for the saints: "that his word may be the better foundation for faith, it is conceived under the manner of a covenant."[70]

Contrasting principles of contract and grace in Puritan thought established an ambiguous relationship between activism and determinism. When Puritan clerics discussed the contractual dimensions of the heavenly contract, they referred to a mutual exchange of obligations between God and humanity, which required specific actions on the part of believers:

> Let us see what this covenant is, what are the articles of agreement between God and us, and what things each party interchangeably covenants and contracts each toward the other.[71]

Activism took the form of the will to believe, a condition clearly stipulated in the bilateral conceptions of the covenant. But the will to believe was determined in advance by God's electing will. Puritans emphasized the unilateral aspects of the covenant in order to represent this deterministic element of predestination. Here the covenant appeared as an unqualified gift or legacy, in which grace was freely bestowed upon the elect. This ambiguity of activism and determinism appeared in sermons by Perkins and Sibbes, who explicitly contrasted the dimensions of contract and grace in the heavenly contract. In explaining God's promises to the faithful, Sibbes remarked, "though they be conditionally propounded

---

nant, I. 48, II. 118; Ball, *Treatise Of Faith*, p. 273; Preston, *Life Eternal*, pp. 86–87, *New Covenant*, p. 389.

69. William Gouge, *A Learned And Very Useful Commentary On The whole Epistle To The Hebrews* (1655, published posthumously), p. 242. See also Hieron, *An Abridgement Of The Gospel* (1613), in *Sermons*, p. 125; Thomas Hooker, *The Soules Vocation* (1638), p. 83; Smith, *Christs Last Supper* (1620), p. 121.

70. Sibbes, *A Learned Commentary*, pp. 454, 521, and see *Yea And Amen* (1638), in *Works*, IV. 132, and *Faithful Covenanter*, pp. 23–24.

71. Attersoll, *New Covenant*, p. 96. Additional examples are scattered throughout the writings of Perkins, Preston, Sibbes, and other Puritan divines repeatedly cited in this chapter.

(for God deals with men by way of commerce—he propounds it by way of covenant and condition) yet in the covenant of grace, which is truly a gracious covenant . . . he performs the condition by the Spirit working our hearts to believe."[72]

There was no resolution of this ambiguity of contract and grace in Puritan thought. Indeed, Puritan clerics could no more resolve this than they could the problem of free will and determinism. As a contract, the covenant of grace required human consent to its provisions. But without God's grace, which converted the naturally unregenerate disposition, such consent was impossible.

This did not imply that God was responsible for the reprobate's lack of consent to the heavenly contract. Though grace made consent possible, humanity's free will was the source of disbelief. Puritan preachers pointed out that "there be a free will to do that, for the not doing of which they shall be condemned."[73] This solved the theodicy problem posed by the doctrine of election. God did not create the vast majority of humanity in order to condemn them; instead, he created free will, leaving reprobates, not him, responsible for their own damnation. Fortunately, the formal logic of this position was irrelevant to its practical utility. Clerics informed their audience that there was a heavenly contract made by God, in Christ, to humanity; that this contract required their consent to its condition of faith; and that, if this condition was not met, they had only themselves to blame. God's promise of salvation belonged to the elect and "not to the wicked, because the covenant is not made with them, by reason they agree not to the condition of becoming God's people."[74]

The utility of the conceptual ambiguity in Puritan covenant theology lay in its ability to justify individual initiative in seeking evidences of election. While this theology retained the doctrine of election, it also depicted salvation as a conditional offer; it proclaimed the conditions of the heavenly contract but did not probe the secrets of God's electing will. Though the election decree was secret, the results of election could be known according to the provisions of the heavenly contract: "[Election] is a secret . . . hidden from us till we believe . . . But the covenant is a publishing, a proclaiming from heaven, [of] this his meaning, that so the church

72. Sibbes, *A Learned Commentary*, p. 394, and see *Yea And Amen*, p. 122; Perkins, *Workes*, I. 167–68, II. 282–83.

73. John Preston, *The Saints Qualifications* (1633), p. 236. See also Ball, *Treatise Of Faith*, p. 9; Fenner, *Workes*, II. 41; Perkins, *Workes*, II. 706; Sibbes, *The Souls Conflict With Itself* (1635), in *Works*, I. 175.

74. Daniel Dyke, *Two Treatises* (1618), p. 88. See also Nicholas Byfield, *A Commentarie* (1623), p. 789; Perkins, *Workes*, I. 7; Preston, *New Covenant*, p. 456; Smith, *The Great Assize Or Day of Jubilee* (1631), p. 243.

might not lie in darkness . . . he would speak to her very heart in his
covenant." [75] Proclamation of the heavenly contract, by preaching, offered
salvation to all upon the condition of faith. Satisfaction of this condition
guaranteed salvation to all, though only the elect were able to believe and
repent.

COVENANT THEOLOGY PERFORMED A VITAL FUNCTION IN LINKING PUB-
lic doctrine with the private experience of spiritual regeneration. The
conditions of the heavenly contract, proclaimed to all in sermons and
treatises, were reflected subjectively in the elect. These conditions informed the Puritan's private search for evidence of election. Comparisons
of these conditions with introspective evidence enabled Puritans to learn
retrospectively whether they were among the elect. This was the doctrinal
basis of Puritan casuistry, which informed the laity that spiritual self-
examination involved the search for evidences of a contract. Thus, the
appearance of a distinctively Puritan form of covenant theology was in-
separable from Puritan casuistry. Both developments characterized Puritanism after 1590, and their seminal source for subsequent generations
of Puritan clerics was the work of William Perkins. [76]

Covenant theology structured a simple doctrine of casuistry. In explaining how to interpret inner experience as evidence of one's spiritual standing, Puritan clerics referred to a bilateral covenant. The basic provision
of the covenant that made faith the condition of salvation was offered publicly in preaching. Evidence of an effectual agreement was revealed privately. Affirmation of faith through self-examination was "the inward
means whereby God revealed his covenant of grace." To a company of
English merchants on the Continent, one preacher declared that, *if* they
were indeed among the elect, they should find within themselves "all the
promises of God in Christ, being written therein, by the spirit, according
to the covenant." [77]

In explaining this casuistical point, Puritan clerics cited four biblical
passages (Jer. 31:33 and 32:40 and Ezk. 11:19 and 36:26–27) where

75. Daniel Rogers, *A Practical Catechism*, II. 7. This view can be traced to one of the
early proponents of covenant theology in Scotland, Robert Rollock; see his *A treatise of
God's effectual calling* (1603), pp. 1–2 (this work first appeared in Latin, in 1596). Later,
a lay Puritan writer, Edward Leigh, argued that though only the elect are truly in
the covenant, it is openly proclaimed to all; see his *A Treatise of The Divine Promises*
(1633), p. 39.

76. See Norman Pettit, *The Heart Prepared: Grace and Conversion in Puritan Spiritual
Life* (New Haven, 1966), p. 14.

77. Crooke, *Guide Unto Blessednesse*, p. 58; John Forbes, *A Letter First Written and
Sent by Jo. Forbes . . . unto certen of the companie of Marchants Adventurers at Stoade*
(Middleburgh, 1616), p. 28.

God promised to inscribe his Law in the conscience of his faithful and to renew their hearts. In Puritan parlance, renewed hearts meant regenerate dispositions, prepared by God's grace to believe. Introspective evidence of faith was thus evidence of God's promise at work, enabling believers to fulfill their part of the heavenly contract. This was the key to Puritan casuistry: "The condition of the promise being already formed in you by the grace of God, you may safely assure your soul of so much favor from God."[78] Certitude of salvation rested on introspective evidence that confirmed the publicly announced conditions of the heavenly contract. Puritan preachers therefore asked their parishioners, "Is the Law of God thus written in your hearts? Have you had experience of this? Then certainly you are within the covenant."[79]

But what degree of faith was necessary in order to be sure of an effectual agreement with God? Puritan casuistry specified that the smallest evidence of faith provided proof of an effectual agreement. The idea that "the very least measure of saving grace" offered such proof was developed by William Perkins and then appeared in writings by other prominent Puritan preachers, such as John Preston and Richard Sibbes. They compared true faith to sparks of flame and seeds out of which grew raging fires and towering trees. According to them, "in the covenant of grace, God requires the truth of grace, not any certain measure."[80]

This casuistical point reflected the more general tenet that God in the covenant of grace accepted faith in place of the perfect obedience demanded by the covenant of works. Thus, the least amount of faith that indicated inclusion within the covenant was the will to believe. "If you can bring your hearts to will to consent . . . this argues a hearty and full consent and a true faith . . . Nay, if you can bring the heart but to desire to receive Christ and enter into the covenant . . . this argues a true and firm consent."[81] This was a major premise of Puritan casuistry in pre-Revolutionary England. By 1631 one author could cite a long list of Puritan worthies—including Baynes, Byfield, Culverwell, Crooke, Downame, Dyke, Forbes, Greenham, Gouge, Perkins, Rogers, Taylor, and Wil-

78. Byfield, *Marrow Of The Oracles*, p. 28. See also Sibbes, *The Tender Heart* (1639), in *Works*, VI. 31.

79. Preston, *New Covenant*, p. 427. See also Harris, *Treatise Of The New Covenant*, I. 46, II. 76, 96; Randall, *Three And Twentie Sermons*, I. 120; Taylor, *Davids Learning*, pp. 131–32.

80. Perkins, *Workes*, I. 628; Sibbes, *The Bruised Reed And Smoaking Flax* (1630), in *Works*, I. 58. See also Preston, *The Breast-Plate Of Faith And Love* (1634), I. 110, *New Covenant*, p. 508, *Saints Qualifications*, p. 177.

81. Scudder, *Christians Daily Walke*, pp. 618–19. See also Leigh, *Treatise Of Divine Promises*, p. 140.

son—in support of his assertion that "What graces you unfained desire . . . you have."[82]

Of course, Puritan clerics were not content to urge their followers to find minimal evidence of their inclusion in the heavenly contract, so remarks on minimal evidence were followed with strictures on the necessity of increasing one's faith. This was another requirement of the heavenly contract: individuals contracted to God were to labor ceaselessly to grow in faith. The conversion experience of regeneration did not occur at one point in time, as Calvin thought. It was a life-long experience of spiritual growth. This provided a context for Puritan remarks on minimal evidence of true faith: "In the condition of the covenant of grace, we must live and grow by grace by little and little and not all at once."[83]

Covenant theology not only urged individuals to grow in grace but also instructed them how to do so through meditation and prayer. Because God obligated himself to help believers fulfill their part of the heavenly contract, individuals who were parties to it could presume that God would provide grace. Indeed, they had a right to grace in ever increasing amounts. "It is no presumption but true obedience to assure ourselves from God of whatsoever he has . . . entered into bond and covenant freely to give."[84]

In this way, Puritan theology sharply revised Calvin's portrayal of a remote and unfathomable God. Fealty to God now lay in confidently assuming that he would observe his part of the heavenly contract. Puritan preachers went so far as to urge laypersons to acquire additional grace through a litigious challenge to the almighty.[85] If God promised to provide grace to work the believer's part of the heavenly contract, then those with an interest in that contract could urge God to keep his promise:

> Like a household servant that is in covenant with his master, comes in from his work and calls for his dinner . . . so may we, as many as are in covenant with God, go to him in the like manner: Lord I want faith, give me it . . . As if he had said you are in covenant with me, and therefore perform your bargain; as you have allotted me work,

---

82. Robert Bolton, *Instructions For a Right Comforting Afflicted Consciences* (1631), in *Workes* (1640), III. 145–50, 392–94. See William Sclatter, *The Sick Souls Salve* (Oxford, 1612), p. 33.

83. Sibbes, *A Learned Commentary*, p. 61. See also Pettit, *The Heart Prepared*, pp. 55–56.

84. Ball, *Treatise Of Faith*, p. 238.

85. A point previously made by Christopher Hill, *Puritanism and Revolution* (New York, 1964), pp. 240–41; Miller, *The New England Mind*, pp. 389–90; John von Rohr, "Covenant and Assurance in Early English Puritanism," *Church History* 34 (1965), pp. 198–99.

so you must find me tools wherewithal to work . . . It is a flat bargain between us, therefore stand to it.[86]

Preston and Sibbes told the godly to approach God in prayer and meditation and "urge him on his promise." They should institute spiritual lawsuits because God's promises were like the "bonds and obligations of a rich man," and when a believer stirs up his faith, he can "put those promises in suit." God was "content to be sued on his own bond"; "you may sue him of his own bond written and sealed, and he cannot deny it."[87]

AN ENORMOUS DISTANCE SEPARATES PURITAN THEOLOGY FROM CONtinental Calvinism, which did not encourage assertiveness and familiarity—implied by contracts and lawsuits—in humanity's dealings with God. In its broad outlines, Puritan covenant theology was clearly Calvinist in inspiration, but Calvinism's deterministic elements tended to recede behind the encouragement given by Puritanism to individual initiative in spiritual life. Calvin's strictures on the depravity of human nature and his doctrines of free grace and predestination remained doctrinal tenets of Puritanism. Translation of these tenets into a contractarian idiom provided far greater room for individual initiative than Calvin provided. What he described as an election decree made by God in the remote past was transformed by Puritan covenant theology into a conditional offer that confronted believers in the present. Thus, the deterministic tenets of free grace and predestination were balanced by elements of activism in Puritan thought.

Believers who discerned evidence of their interest in the heavenly contract could be sure of the future consummation of that contract. They could even remind God of his obligations to them under provisions of the heavenly contract. In this way, the inscrutable and remote God of Calvin appeared in Puritanism as a more familiar and intelligible power—indeed, as a heavenly contractor, whose promises and obligations were openly proclaimed in the covenant of grace.

Biographical, chronological, and hermeneutic evidence suggests that these modifications of Calvinism emerged most directly from the organizational context in which Puritan clerics sought to promote reform. Developments among lay dissenters were most salient in determining this

86. Harris, *Treatise Of The New Covenant*, I. 42–43. See also Leigh, *Treatise Of Divine Promises*, p. 84.

87. Preston, *The New Creature*, pp. 22–23; Sibbes, *The Churches Riches* (1638), in *Works*, IV. 505, *A Learned Commentary*, p. 350 (and see also p. 362), and *Yea And Amen*, p. 125; Leigh, *Treatise of Divine Promises*, p. 50; Preston, *Breast-Plate Of Faith And Love*, I. 75, and *New Covenant*, pp. 477–78.

context. Though Puritan covenant theology was formulated by clerics, it was influenced decisively by the activities and mentalities of radical heretics, Separatists, and lay Puritans. Puritan clerics conceived of God as a heavenly contractor because this enabled them to cope with the worldly obstacles and opportunities created by intellectual initiatives among the godly.

6
The Heavenly Contract – II

As the lands and goods of one man are made over unto another by deed of gift, sale, exchange or some like conveyance of law, both for title and use, even so the righteousness of Christ, by virtue of the free gift of God, according to the tenure of the covenant of grace, is truly and really conveyed unto us and made ours.

Thomas Newhouse, *A Learned And Faithfull Sermon* (1612)

Look as a man may say of his inheritance, his house and lands, *these be mine*, so he may as truly say of God, *God is mine*, I am righted and interested in him. This privilege is conferred upon us in the covenant of grace.

Daniel Dyke, *Two Treatises* (1618)

So far this analysis of Puritan theology has referred to intellectual precedents and organizational pressures. Puritan clerics used precedents, from the Bible and from the writings of continental reformers, to modify Calvinism in response to organizational pressures. The source of these pressures has been shown to be an intractable dilemma created by the dual role played by Puritan clerics. They were the nominal leaders of a popular religious movement that displayed high levels of lay initiative, and they were also ordained ministers in a comprehensive church that upheld the principle of lay subordination to the clergy. Puritan covenant theology was a modified Calvinism that provided more room for individual initiative but channeled it in directions that did not threaten the pastoral authority of clerics in a comprehensive church.

However, Puritan covenant theology also derived from another source: secular precedents established by use of contracts in daily life. To develop the idea of a heavenly contract as a pastoral guide to the introspective search for evidence of election, Puritan clerics turned to principles and practices associated with the use of worldly contracts. The operation of the heavenly contract followed these principles and practices: they were conditions not only of economic success but of spiritual success as well. Puritan clerics identified a normative structure in the worldly use of contracts which they urged their followers to apply to their spiritual life. Obtaining evidence of election required the same pattern of methodical discipline and record-keeping that people used in their contractual dealings; it also displayed the same notions of equity and justice as those implicit in the use of economic contracts.

These secular precedents provided Puritan clerics with a valuable resource. Their modification of Calvinism could have achieved its goals only if it was intellectually accessible to the Puritan laity. Puritan clerics created this modified Calvinism by translating doctrinal tenets into a contractarian idiom that was intelligible to laypersons. Its viability as a popular divinity rested on lay familiarity with the general principles and practices of worldly contracts.

Discussion of the heavenly contract by Puritan clerics invoked, explicitly and implicitly, the principles and practices of marital as well as economic contracts. Puritan views of marital contracts were similar to those of economic contracts. Indeed, the former was treated as a specific case of the latter. In both cases, Puritan clerics referred to lay knowledge of the principles and practices of contracts in order to explain doctrinal points and draw out their pastoral implications.

These principles and practices concern a very specific type of contract: the type used in acquisitive activities governed by a market rationality. Notions of exchange, ownership, and accumulation in this rationality all had their spiritual counterparts in Puritan divinity. Considered collectively, these notions are identical to what C.B. Macpherson describes as a doctrine of "possessive individualism,"[1] the basis of liberal ideology in market societies. Central to the Puritan doctrine of grace and central also to pastoral advice on how to acquire it was a model of society as contractual interaction. This model pervaded Puritan theology and informed its treatment of the deepest mysteries of religion.

Of course, the social implications of a market rationality and of possessive individualism, which underpin a model of society as contractual interaction, would not have met with Puritan approval. Amoral individualism in economic or political life was anathema to Puritanism. It is, then, ironic that Puritan clerics placed at the center of their divinity the logic and language of the acquisitive society. But it is also evidence of the resilience of this economic ideology, even in its infancy.

THE PRINCIPLES AND PRACTICES OF ECONOMIC CONTRACTS HAD A SPEcial relevance for the social basis of lay Puritanism. In chapter 2 I linked this social basis to early capitalist development, which created a highly differentiated rural economy organized around specialized regional and national markets. Along with this, there appeared a highly ramified stratum of independent producers and small employers, drawn from the ranks of the gentry, the yeomanry, and the artisans. What united the different vocational groups within this stratum—along with their urban

1. C.B. Macpherson, *The Political Theory of Possessive Individualism* (Oxford, 1962).

counterparts—was their autonomy and their independence, based on their role in price-making markets. Also uniting them was the practical rationalism demanded by their entrepreneurial role and their consequent affinity for relatively critical and independent mental habits. This was why the highly rationalized beliefs of popular dissent and, later, Puritanism, received their greatest support from these groups.[2]

This also explains why the idea of a heavenly contract was well suited to the task of creating a popular form of Calvinist divinity. The principles and practices of contractual interaction had special relevance for the secular life of the Puritan laity, because these principles and practices provided the foundation of the social groups that were most receptive to highly rationalized beliefs.

From 1500 to 1640, contractual transactions in pursuit of profit became a familiar feature of everyday economic life. They encompassed a broad variety of economic activities in the countryside as well as in urban centers. In parts of the rural economy transformed by early capitalist development, use of written contracts was not limited to the sale of products; it also appeared in credit arrangements for sale of crops in advance of harvest. In addition, yeoman farmers frequently invested in bills of debt: upon retirement, they converted their holdings into money for making loans, for which they received written bonds. Along with other contracts, these documents were drawn up by parish officials or literate yeomen, as is shown by the journal of one farmer, which "contains copies of petitions, bonds, and contracts of various kinds that [he] drew up for his neighbors." A contemporary writer defended the rudimentary education available in villages by noting, "This is all we go to school for: to read common prayers at church; and set down common prices at markets; write a letter and make a bond." Literary skills needed for drawing up these financial instruments were readily available in the villages.[3] It may safely be presumed that opportunities for drawing up contracts were even more widespread in London and provincial towns, where many public notaries and scriveners resided.[4]

The general principles of contract were well known to contemporaries, who possessed modern notions about the content and form of a contractual agreement. They also used these notions as standards for measuring

2. See above, chap. 2, pp. 47–49.

3. See above, chap. 2, p. 36.

4. In 1574 there were said to be 120 public notaries in London who drafted business contracts, conveyances, and wills; see R.H. Tawney, editor's introduction to Thomas Wilson, *A Discourse upon Usury* (London, 1925), pp. 96–97. For notaries and scriveners in provincial towns, see Alan Everitt, "The Marketing of Agricultural Produce," in Joan Thirsk, ed., *The Agrarian History of England and Wales* (Cambridge, 1967), IV. 555.

equity, justice, and truth. The content of a contract—free and mutual consent—was associated with premarital contracts as well as with economic agreements. In ecclesiastical courts, which had cognizance of premarital contracts, "Judges upheld no contracts clearly shown by the evidence to have been vitiated by coercion." In economic life, the essence of exchange was said to be free and mutual consent: buying and selling "is a voluntary contract, made by the mutual consent of two parties . . . trade has in it such a kind of natural liberty as it will not endure to be forced by any."[5]

Contemporaries defined the form of a contract in terms of the formal equality between contractors. Use of contracts in economic life meant that social distinctions became increasingly irrelevant for the pursuit of profit. This, of course, contradicted the still prevalent preoccupation with feudal statuses, a contradiction that was evident to some contemporaries. When offering ruinous loans to the earl of Shrewsbury, Sir Horatio Palavicino lectured him "on the difference between business and friendship":

> Where question is of doing your honour service I am to do it in such manner as becomes a man of my estate to an honourable personage whom I greatly reverence; and when question is of matter of contract (because that to my judgement they are things greatly different) then I take myself bound to sincerity & plainness without blameworthy deceit, but yet with due regard to traffic for my self profitably . . . so your honour may not compt it ill if in the point of profit a man honestly every ways regard his own commodity.[6]

But what determined honesty? In a contemporary dialogue on usury, a merchant argued, "I would have all things weighed by reason in matters of contracts and bargains." In this context, appeals to reason were an attack on tradition in the name of utility. From 1500 to 1640, notions of reason and reasonableness increasingly referred to a market rationality: what was reasonable in economic affairs was that which was mutually agreed to by contractors. This led to Hobbesian notions of justice. Equity in economic life "is nothing else but a mutual voluntary estimation of things." "Truth is none other but a man to be true and faithful in all his promises, covenants, and words."[7]

5. Ralph Houlbrooke, *Church Courts and the People during the English Reformation, 1520–1570* (Oxford, 1979), p. 64; Edward Misselden, *The Circle Of Commerce* (1623), p. 112.

6. Lawrence Stone, *An Elizabethan: Sir Horatio Palavicino* (Oxford, 1956), p. 40.

7. Wilson, *A Discourse Upon Usury*, pp. 238–39; Edmund Dudley, *The Tree Of Commonwealth* (1510), edited by D.M. Brodie (Cambridge, 1948), p. 38; Werner Sombart, *Der moderne Kapitalismus* (Munich and Leipzig, 1922), II. 46, citing Gerard Malynes, *Lex Mercatoria* (1622). For a general discussion of changing conceptions of reason in this

Use of contracts in an emerging marketing economy thus cultivated the kind of contractarian world view conventionally associated with the work of Hobbes. Although this world view coexisted uneasily with older views, it was not especially controversial for many contemporaries. For its adherents, it reflected common features of everyday life that were taken for granted as part of a natural and immutable order of things. By 1601 a writer on behalf of the Merchant Adventurers could argue that "there is nothing in the world so ordinary and natural unto all men as to contract, truck, merchandise, and traffic one with another, so that it is almost impossible for three persons to converse together two hours, but they will fall into talk of one bargain or another, chopping, changing or some other kind of contract."[8] This is the economic world as Adam Smith described it nearly two centuries later, and if it occupied a smaller place in pre-Revolutionary England than in the England of Smith's day, it nonetheless was governed by the same seemingly self-evident principles and sturdy self-confidence.

Lessons from Worldly Contracts

Worldly analogies and metaphors for spiritual matters exist in the Bible, and they were also a hallmark of Puritan rhetoric. All things in domestic life had spiritual counterparts in the Bible's portrayal of God's kingdom: "here are the houses, the tents, chambers, stairs, doors, beds, curtains, gardens, sheds, hedges, arbors, fountains, all spiritual, all representations." It was a sign of God's mercy, said Sibbes, "to speak to us in our own language": "seeing God has condescended to represent heavenly things to us under earthly terms, we should follow God's dealings therein."[9]

Puritan interest in analogies and metaphors for spiritual realities had a Calvinist rationale. Without such devices, God remained beyond human comprehension. According to Francis Bacon, "God himself condescends to the weakness of our capacity . . . inoculating, as it were, his revelations into the notions and comprehensions of our reason." This belief indicates why Puritan clerics modified Calvinism with contractarian ideas: in the form of a heavenly contractor, God became less remote and unknowable. No longer was God unaccountable, for God condescended to use a human

---

era, see Christopher Hill, *Change and Continuity in 17th-Century England* (London, 1974), pp. 103–23.

8. John Wheeler, *A Treatise Of Commerce* (1601), p. 6.

9. BoL, *MSS. Rawls.* C526, p. 15; Richard Sibbes, *Bowels Opened* (1639) and *The Souls Conflict With Itself* (1635), both in *Works* (Edinburgh, 1862–63), I. 185, II. 60. See also Thomas Taylor, *The Parable Of The Sower* (1623), p. 17.

device, a contract, in his dealings with humanity. Thus, one preacher described the action of God's spirit on the soul as "the cooperation and joint working together of both, like fellow and fellow well met (if I may so speak)."[10] Rules governing the interaction of "fellow and fellow well met" were used by God to encapsulate his unfathomable will within the limits of human understanding. Puritans thought that God created a heavenly contract because he knew that contracts were the way individuals dealt with each other on earth.

Obviously, this line of thought made little sense if Puritan preachers could not assume that use of contracts was widespread. Without that assumption there would be little rationale for a doctrine which states that "we are to know God, not as he is in himself, but as he has revealed himself unto us in the covenant of grace."[11] Puritan covenant theology presupposes lay familiarity with the principles and practices of contracts. This is why "God will argue with us from our traffic and commerce with men." This is why he "stoops so low as to make use of terms that are used in human matters and contracts": "that his word may be the better foundation for faith, it is conceived under the manner of a covenant."[12]

In view of these presuppositions, it is not surprising to find Puritan clerics explaining the operation of the heavenly contract in terms of principles governing its worldly counterparts. References to such principles, however, did not invoke precise legal issues; they concerned general maxims about contracts that clerics thought were common objects of knowledge among their parishioners. For example, clerics glossed over technical distinctions between contract and covenant, using the terms interchangeably. But to explain the dimension of grace in the heavenly contract—God's promise to enable the elect to believe and thus to fulfill their part of the covenant—clerics cited general differences between wills and contracts (or covenants). "Testaments and covenants are not all one among men, but in matters of grace and salvation betwixt God and man they are all one."[13] By equating contracts with bilateral agreements and wills with unilateral decrees, clerics explained the role of God's electing will in the heavenly contract:

10. Francis Bacon, *The Dignity and Advancement of Learning* (1605), in Joseph Devey, ed., *The Physical and Metaphysical Works of Lord Bacon* (London, 1873), p. 371; John Randall, *The Great Mystery Of Godliness* (1624), in *Workes* (1629), p. 90.

11. William Perkins, *Workes* (Cambridge, 1608–9), II. 300.

12. John Wing, *The Best Merchandise* (Flushing, 1622), pp. 2–3; Sibbes, *A Learned Commentary* (1656, published posthumously), in *Works*, IV. 454, 521. See also Sibbes, *Yea And Amen* (1638) and *The Faithful Covenanter* (1638), in *Works*, IV. 132, VI. 23–24.

13. John Randall, *Three And Twentie Sermons* (1630), I. 113–14. A popular treatise on legal terminology states, "Contract is a bargain or covenant between two parties . . . as if I sell my house for money, or if I covenant to make you a lease of my manor . . . in

All the gracious promises of the Gospel are not only promises upon condition, and so a covenant, but likewise the covenant of grace is a testament and a will (a will is made without conditions; a covenant with conditions), that as he has made a covenant what he would have us to do, so his testament is that we shall have the grace to do so.[14]

While the contrast between contracts and wills is overstated (provisions of wills can stipulate conditions), the general point remains clear enough.

IN DISCUSSING FAITH, GRACE, AND SPIRITUAL INTROSPECTION PURITAN clerics relied routinely on lessons that could be drawn from worldly contracts and applied to spiritual matters. These lessons referred to the broadest principles and most general practices that characterize the form and content of contractual agreements. Four lessons were most important: (1) the heavenly contract, like its earthly counterparts, requires for its enactment the mutual consent of both parties; (2) consent must be informed consent, given by persons capable of understanding the heavenly contract and its provisions; (3) this contract remains in effect only if its conditions are met; (4) formal equality among contractors on earth also applies to God and believers in the covenant of grace.

Of all these lessons, the most important one deals with the voluntary consent of both parties to a contract. In the heavenly contract the condition to which consent must be given is, as we saw in chapter 5, the condition of faith. Discussion of this point by Puritan clerics referred invariably to worldly precedents that were thought to be self-evident to laypersons. A troublesome Puritan preacher in London, George Walker, observed, "The word covenant in our English tongue signifies, as we all know, a mutual promise, bargain, and obligation between two parties." It "signifies all covenants in general, both God's covenant with men, and also the covenants which men make among themselves."[15] So argued many other Puritan divines, such as Perkins, who reduced the mystical bond between

---

consideration of xxli that you shall give me. These are good contracts because there is one thing for another" (John Rastell, *An exposition of certaine difficult . . . termes of the lawes* [1579], Sig. 48ᵛ-49ʳ).

14. Sibbes, *Christs Exaltation Purchast By Humiliation* (1639), in *Works*, V. 342, and see also Sibbes, *The Brides Longing* (1639), in *Works*, VI. 542, and *The Christian Work* (1639), in *Works*, V. 18; Perkins, *Workes*, II. 282. See also Elnathan Parr, *The Grounds Of Divinity* (1614), in *Works* (1632), pp. 12–13: "The doctrine of grace . . . is called in regard of the form of convention and agreement between God and man, a covenant; and in regard of the manner of confirming it, a testament." For a lay religious writer's plagiarism of this passage, see Edward Leigh, *A Treatise Of The Divine Promises* (1633), p. 69. For another layman's views, see Henry Finch, *The Sacred Doctrine Of Divinitie* (1613), I. 12, II. 4.

15. George Walker, *The Manifold Wisdome Of God* (1641), pp. 39, 48.

God and humanity to the essence of a contractual relationship: "to the making of a contract, the consent of both parties (at the very least) is required. Christ gives his consent in the word . . . and we give our consent to him."[16]

The essence of worldly contracts, mutual consent, thus defined the nature of God's dealing with the faithful. As the Puritan cleric Sibbes observed, "There is a reciprocal and natural passage between God and the soul, for in covenants there must be consent on both sides." This lesson appeared not only in sermons and doctrinal treatises but also in catechisms:

Q. After what manner was the covenant made?
A. After the manner that covenants are made between man and man, as in covenants between man and man matters are first agreed upon by both parties, then articles of agreement written, sealed and delivered.[17]

As with worldly contracts, the use of force was proscribed in the heavenly contract because, according to Preston, it "is required to be done out of love. It is a rule in the Civillian Law, *contractus qui fit per minus, nullus est*, . . . so it is between Christ and us."[18] However, most clerics did not refer so precisely to legal maxims but instead appealed to more popular notions that conveyed the same point: faith played the same role in the heavenly contract as mutual consent did in worldly contracts.

Consent had to be given not only freely but knowledgeably. It was an informed consent that, on the believer's part, enacted the heavenly contract, for "where there is no knowledge, there is no consent."[19] This too reflected worldly practices. Walker explained the necessity of religious knowledge by citing requirements of worldly contracts where "in a true and lawful contract, both parties must be of pure hearts, free from all deceits and sophistry, and must deal faithfully and mean plainly and sincerely in every point and article."[20] This overstates the case, but the point is clear: where knowledge of its implications is lacking, consent to a contract may be void. According to Puritan clerics, what made a contract oblig-

---

16. Perkins, *Workes*, II. 339, and see also II. 86, III. 672.

17. Sibbes, *Discouragements Recovery* (1629), in *Works*, VII. 62; Lewes Hughes, *The Covenant of Grace and Seales thereof* (1640), Sig. B11. See also Robert Harris, *A Treatise Of The New Covenant* (1632), II. 160; Samuel Hieron, *An Abridgement Of The Gospel* (1613), in *All The Sermons Of Samuel Hieron* (1614), pp. 124–25; Leigh, *Treatise Of The Divine Promises*, p. 63; Edward Phillips, *Certaine Godly And Learned Sermons* (1607), pp. 97, 131.

18. John Preston, *A Cup Of Blessing*, (1633), p. 27.

19. Perkins, *Workes*, I. 168, and see III. 646; Jeremiah Dyke, *A Worthy Communicant* (1636), pp. 104–5.

20. Walker, *Manifold Wisdome Of God*, p. 40.

atory under natural law was consent given to it by those who, regardless of their age, enjoyed the "use of reason."[21]

Consent to the heavenly contract required that believers understand all of its provisions and implications. Prospective saints ignorant of this could no more contract with God than could the ignorant profit from contracts with other persons. "Natural fools are unfit to enter covenant with men. Spiritual fools are as unfit for God's covenant." This principle animated Puritan insistence that knowledge of the covenant was necessary for admission to communion, the seal of the covenant.[22]

A third lesson drawn from worldly contracts concerned the consequences of consent, the necessity to discharge the obligations assumed by it. This lesson showed that the heavenly contract remained in effect only if these obligations were met. As God was faultless, only the believer's lack of faith—the principal obligation—was to blame for nonperformance of the covenant. Referring explicitly to lay knowledge of worldly contracts, a popular Puritan preacher in Banbury, William Whately, declared, "The Lord has made many great promises in his word . . . And it has pleased God to limit these promises to those who do such and such things, requiring (as you would say) certain conditions to be performed on his part that would enjoy these promises."[23] Other Puritan preachers also made this point in order to instruct laypersons about the conditional nature of salvation. According to Thomas Wilson, "as in human contracts there is no enjoying the bargain if the condition be broken; so it is here if we bring not this condition of faith with us, God is not bound to stand to the covenant." In these remarks, worldly contracts provided a precedent for explaining the role of faith as a condition of salvation, "for when men intend to covenant and contract one with another, they set down articles as well on the one side as on the other."[24]

---

21. See above, p. 154, for covenant-keeping as a precept of natural law. According to William Ames, "Those that are under age, and are come to the perfect use of reason . . . if on mature counsel they do bargain, that contract considered in itself, according to the court of conscience, seems to be of force" (*Conscience With The Power And Cases Thereof* [1639], IV. 227). This view appears in contemporary theories of natural law; see Hugo Grotius, *De Jure Belli et Pacis* (1625), edited by William Whewell (Cambridge, 1853), II. 38 (2,11,5).

22. Alexander Grosse, *Sweet And Soule-Persuading Inducements* (1632), p. 380. See above, pp. 143–44, for knowledge of the heavenly contract as a requirement for admission to communion.

23. William Whately, *Gods Husbandry* (1619), p. 46. See also George Estey, *Exposition upon the Lords Supper* (1603), in *Certaine Godly And Learned Expositions* (1603), f. 2ʳ.

24. Thomas Wilson, *Saints By Calling* (1620), pp. 95–96; William Attersoll, *The New Covenant* (1614), p. 98.

Clerics also referred to the conditional nature of worldly contracts in their casuistry, in explaining how to detect introspective evidence of election. In electing some to salvation, God guaranteed performance of their part of the heavenly contract. Evidence of such performance—the will to believe—thus could be interpreted as a sign of election. This reasoning guided clerical remarks on how to discover whether one was within the covenant: "First, see what God has done for you. Second, what you have done for him again. For something there is to be done on both sides, you know, in every covenant."[25] The aside "you know" is instructive, for it shows how references to the *quid pro quo* nature of contracts could help clerics explain their casuistry to the Puritan laity.

A sermon by Thomas Gataker contains several extended passages on worldly contracts that explain the conditional nature of salvation. Contracts between landlords and tenants, in which the former justly refuse to accept any sum less than the stipulated rent, illustrate the operation of the heavenly contract. Anything less than true faith will be refused by God, because, as in "a lease made upon condition of diverse acts, . . . one fail, or once failing, is enough to make all the rest of no effect, and to cause a forfeiture of the whole." Accordingly, Gataker warned his auditors that in their dealings with God, "If we look that he should keep covenant with us, let us be sure that we keep covenant with him," because,

> where agreements between parties are founded and grounded on conditions or covenants (for I stand not now on the precise distinctions of law terms) to be mutually and interchangeably performed on either side, he that in such case breaks off first does thereby free the other party. Nor is it therefore unfaithfulness in God (whose promises of life and salvation are so conditional) to deny to make his promises good unto those that have no care to keep in touch with him.

Gataker's disclaimer about the precise juridical status of his remarks is significant: he clearly had in mind the general principles of contract, with which he thinks his audience was familiar. This presumption becomes even more evident in his subsequent remarks on God's refusal to accept any service less than that stipulated by the heavenly contract:

> It is an unreasonable thing for us to expect that he should keep covenant with us, when we have no care to keep the like with him. An unreasonable thing is it . . . for a servant to expect wages covenanted from his master, when he keeps no covenants at all with his master, when he refuses to work.[26]

25. Harris, *The New Covenant*, I. 46.
26. Thomas Gataker, *Christian Constancy* (1624), pp. 5, 9. See also Thomas Adams,

So a general understanding of contracts, attributed by Gataker to his lay audience, extended to what was reasonable and unreasonable in contractual obligations.

A fourth lesson drawn from worldly contracts reinforced the general Protestant tenet that the spiritual condition of an individual was independent of his or her social status. Social distinctions were irrelevant to the heavenly contract, whose provisions applied equally to all believers:

> There is a difference in men by nation . . . there is some difference in men in respect of condition, some are bond & some are free. So there is a difference in respect of sexes . . . [But] there is no difference at all in nation, condition or sex in respect of the covenant of grace.[27]

Spiritual equality existed among the godly, according to Perkins, because their claim to heaven came not "by descent in the blood or birthright . . . this right they have is brought to pass in the covenant." A preacher to a company of English merchants on the Continent made the same point by analogy: "No man is born a natural merchant; neither can any be naturally religious."[28]

These comments clearly reflect the universalistic values of the bourgeois ideology of economic achievement. The relevance of these values for Puritan thought becomes apparent if we remember that they emerged from a world view that regarded civil society as the product of contractual interaction.[29] Universalism in this case reflected the growing irrelevance of social distinctions for an economic order created by early capitalist development. Contracts were both the means by which this social develop-

---

A Commentary Or, Exposition Upon The Divine Second Epistle Written by St. Peter (1633), p. 1502. For similar remarks on the Lord's Day, see John Dod and Robert Cleaver, A Plaine And Familiar Exposition Of The Ten Commandments (1622), pp. 150–51; William Fenner, Of The Sabbath (n.d.), in Workes (sermons delivered before 1640), II. 84. According to Dod and Cleaver, cited above:

> if we hire a day laborer and give him wages, and he covenant to do our work for the whole day, and after an hour or two should leave off all and go to follow his pleasure . . . we would count him little better than a thief or a deceiver.
>
> But God has covenanted with us to reward us; and we with him to obey him. And therefore what is it but theft to take away part of his day . . . for our own lusts and pleasures?

27. Randall, Three And Twentie Sermons, I. 171–72.

28. Perkins, Workes, III. 226; Wing, The Best Merchandise, p. 9. See also Dyke, Worthy Communicant, Sig. A4'; Robert Preston, The Doctrine of the Sacrament of the Lords Supper (1621), pp. 115–16.

29. I have discussed this point in "From Political Philosophy to Social Theory," Journal of the History of the Behavioral Sciences 17 (1981).

ment occurred and the basis for its ideological representation in secular and religious thought.

The formal equality among contractors was the model for universalistic values in Puritan covenant theology. This formal equality extended not only to relations among the godly but also to the relationship between God and the believer. Here is another way in which the awesome and remote God of Calvin became the far more familiar and predictable God of Puritan thought. Preston and Sibbes asked their auditors to consider the implications of God's willingness to "abase" himself by entering into a contract with humanity: "He is in heaven, and we are on earth; he the glorious God, we dust and ashes; he the creator, and we but creatures; and yet he is willing to enter into covenant, which implies a kind of equality between us." [30] Another preacher of the new covenant also pointed to this contractual equality between humanity and its creator. Just as indifference to the social qualities of contractors characterized worldly contracts, so the heavenly contract led to familiarity between God and humanity; for God

> is willing to enter into bonds . . . and to enter into a kind of familiarity with the sons of men. For, so you know, there must be a familiarity in some degree where contracts are made between any. [31]

Once again we see how the clerical author of these remarks explicitly presupposed that his lay audience was acquainted with a general principle of contractual interaction in economic life.

Images of the Heavenly Contract

In addition to the general principles of contract, Puritan covenant theologians also referred frequently to specific types of contracts and contractual practices. Doctrinal tenets and pastoral precepts were explained in terms of earnests—small payments that signified ratification of a contract to be fulfilled later—and of seals. In addition, the heavenly contract was compared to bills or bonds of debt and to premarital contracts. These comparisons provided Puritan clerics with an extensive body of imagery, which enhanced the rhetorical effectiveness of Puritan preaching by making covenant theology intellectually accessible to the laity. The casuistry of detecting election, the meaning of Christ's intercession, the issue of theodicy, which in Calvinism created a great divide between heaven and earth—these were among the doctrinal and pastoral matters illuminated by this body of imagery.

---

30. John Preston, *The New Covenant* (1629), p. 331. See also Sibbes, *The Faithful Covenanter*, p. 6.
31. Harris, *The New Covenant*, I. 32.

Like the general principles of contract, images of the heavenly contract were important for Puritan divinity because they referred to what clerics thought were familiar features of lay knowledge. This is especially evident in the case of earnests. Earnests were used to ratify worldly contracts that were consummated at some future date. God's grace was a spiritual earnest given to the elect to assure them of the salvation that was promised in the heavenly contract.

The wide use of this analogy in Puritan sermons evidently depended on the preachers' assumption that parishioners were well acquainted with earnests in worldly contracts. Commenting on biblical passages that compare the spirit to an earnest (Eph. 1:14, 2 Cor. 1:22), Sibbes observed that the term "is borrowed from human contracts" and, more significantly, inferred the following reason for its presence in the Bible: "God is pleased to condescend to our weakness; he stoops to the lowest capacity, and frames his speech to the understanding of the simplest soul, for which purpose this term earnest is here borrowed."[32] Many other Puritan writers made the same point with the following parenthetical observation: "The nature of an earnest (we know) is to bind any contract or bargain."[33]

Comparing grace to worldly earnests helped Puritan clerics explain the pastoral implications of the heavenly contract. With regard to detecting election, they taught that one provision of the heavenly contract was God's promise to supply grace to the elect. Upon detecting introspective evidence of this grace, individuals could presume that an effectual agreement existed between them and God. This comparison of God's donation of grace and the worldly practice of "laying earnest" played an important role in Puritan divinity. It provided the laity with a casuistical guide that linked the subjective dimension of religion to the publicly proclaimed provisions of the heavenly contract. "Now where an earnest is, there is: 1. A contract or bargain; namely, the covenant between God and us . . . 2. The earnest confirms the seller, that he shall receive the whole price . . . so the gift of regeneration confirms us that we shall receive whatsoever is promised in the covenant."[34]

This casuistry channeled lay initiative in the direction of seeking evidences of election, and it provided strong encouragement for such activity. Just as worldly earnests assured individuals of a contractual right to

32. Sibbes, *Yea And Amen*, pp. 140–41.

33. Adam Harsnet, *A Touch-stone Of Grace* (1633), pp. 254–55. See also John Downame, *The Christian Warfare* (1634), p. 115; John Randall, *St. Pauls Triumph* (1629), in *Workes*, p. 102; John Wing, *Jacobs Staffe* (Flushing, 1621), p. 73.

34. Thomas Taylor, *The Parable Of The Sower And Of The Seed* (1623), p. 283. See also Paul Baynes *A Commentarie Upon The First Chapter of the Epistle of Saint Paul* (1618), p. 293; Nicholas Byfield, *The Marrow Of The Oracles Of God* (1640), p. 389; Edward Elton, *The Triumph Of A True Christian* (1623), p. 522; Perkins, *Workes*, III. 363–64.

some object, so introspective evidence of spiritual earnests confirmed the existence of an effectual contract of salvation: "As the earnest-penny confirms the whole bargain among men, so the earnest of the spirit gives us full assurance of full holiness." Puritan clerics took for granted the intelligibility of this analogy, for "will any man reason thus: such a man has had the earnest of a bargain, and therefore he will not have the bargain?" The apparent intelligibility of this reasoning allowed clerics to use it to warn laypersons of the necessity of introspection. "Where the earnest is not, the bargain will not follow."[35]

Whether used as encouragement or warning, discussions of grace as an earnest of the heavenly contract taught the laity to pursue their spiritual interests with the same care they used in securing gainful bargains in economic life. Clerics urged those "as are already in covenant with God . . . to deal as good husbands . . . when they light upon a good bargain." What good husbands did to secure good bargains was apparently known to all: "Here you know what a man will do: lay earnest of the bargain, draw writings . . . the same must we do."[36]

Two additional points of casuistry were dealt with by comparing grace to worldly earnests. The first concerns the degree of grace that conveys assurance of salvation; the second stresses the vast distance that separates spiritual experiences in this life from the full sanctification of the saints in heaven. References to grace as an earnest dealt with both points simultaneously.

Though spiritual rewards in this life are meager in comparison to those in the next, their value consists in providing assurance of obtaining all such rewards. Spiritual earnests derived their value with regard to salvation in the same way that worldly earnests derived theirs as guarantees of the future consummation of an economic agreement. According to Sibbes, "we value an earnest not for the worth that is in itself, but because it assures us of a great bargain."[37] What makes an earnest valuable is not its intrinsic worth but its signification of an effectual agreement. Thus, the spiritual earnest represents the least degree of true faith that, as we saw in chapter 5, was sufficient evidence of an effectual agreement between God and the believer.

This doctrine also enabled clerics to maintain a strict Calvinist separation between heaven and earth. The only continuity between them con-

---

35. Thomas Taylor, *The Progresse Of Saints To Full Holinesse* (1630), p. 365; Thomas Hooker, *The Soules Vocation Or Effectual Calling* (1638), p. 127; Sibbes, *Faith Triumphant* (1639), in *Works*, VII. 437. See also William Whately, *The New Birth* (1618), p. 59; Wing, *The Best Merchandise*, p. 13.

36. Harris, *The New Covenant*, II. 90.

37. Sibbes, *A Learned Commentary*, p. 470.

sisted in the contractual assurance that spiritual experience on earth provided for future salvation. Here is another way that the worldly practices associated with economic contracts provided an exemplar for lay conduct of a religious life: "Haply a shilling or ten shillings [are] given in earnest for the payment of a hundred pounds or more. So are the special gifts and graces of God given here to God's children but a small thing in comparison of that fulness of grace they shall receive in the kingdom of heaven."[38]

THE SAME CASUISTICAL ISSUES DEALT WITH BY EARNESTS WERE ALSO dealt with by comparing grace to the seals that were used to ratify contracts. In this context, "seals" did not refer to the sacraments but to the inward action of the spirit on the soul. The function of such seals was the same as the donation of a spiritual earnest: they signified ratification of the heavenly contract. Just as a seal set in wax ratifies worldly contracts, so "the spirit does leave an impresion on the soul." This imagery also helped clerics present pastoral guidance to laypersons by asking this question: "Have you not the seals of God's covenant for yourself, yea, in yourself?"[39]

Discovery of the imprint of the spirit on the soul revealed, as his seal, God's consent to enter into covenant with a believer. This analogy, like that of spiritual earnests, informed laypersons about the introspective search for evidences of salvation. It also showed that certitude of salvation revealed by introspection followed the same principles of assurance that were used by merchants who set their seals to economic agreements, for "God here stoops so low as to make use of terms that are used in human matters and contracts."[40]

IN ADDITION TO EARNESTS AND SEALS, PURITAN CLERICS ALSO REferred to bonds, contracts, and leases as written evidences of agreement. These references illuminated the same casuistical issues as those discussed in conjunction with earnests and seals, and they also clarified important doctrinal issues. For example, Puritan clerics cited written evidences in economic life in explaining the imputation of Christ's righteousness to the saints. They portrayed this as a contractual conveyance of right and title to

38. Elton, *Triumph Of A Christian*, p. 528. See also Baynes, *A Commentarie*, p. 295; Phillips, *Certaine Godly Sermons*, p. 286; Timothy Rogers, *Saving-Beliefe* (1644; sermons delivered before 1640), pp. 89–90; Sibbes, *Yea And Amen*, p. 141.

39. Hooker, *Soules Vocation*, p. 48; Phineas Fletcher, *Joy In Tribulation* (1632), p. 112. See also Downame, *Christian Warfare*, p. 115; Richard Sibbes, *The Fruitful Labour* (1639), in *Works*, VI. 376.

40. Sibbes, *A Learned Commentary*, p. 454, and see *Yea And Amen*, p. 132; Baynes, *A Commentarie*, p. 289.

property: "As the lands and goods of one man are made over unto another by deed of gift, sale, exchange or some like conveyance of law, both for title and use, even so the righteousness of Christ, by virtue of the free gift of God, according to the tenure of the covenant of grace, is truly and really conveyed unto us, and made ours."[41]

References to written evidences also applied to casuistical issues. The self-interest that prompted concern with written evidences in economic life provided an exemplar for religious life. No evidence, no contract: a person who lays claim to the heavenly contract must have introspective evidence, otherwise he or she "lays a claim without title, and claims a title without evidence, reckoning upon a bargain without the consent of the party to whom he would contract."[42]

The pastoral utility of this imagery becomes apparent if we recall the litigiousness for which early modern England was notorious. Recourse to lawsuits was a familiar feature of economic life, and it typically involved prolonged wrangling over possession and interpretation of written bonds, contracts, and leases.[43] Clerics referred, enviously, to this preoccupation with written evidences as a model that the godly should emulate when they sought for introspective evidence of their ultimate religious interest. "For tenures of lands, for conveyances, for leases, for bonds . . . what ado there is among men! . . . Alas that we which are so politic for our bodies, should be so simple and silly for our souls!"[44]

References to the worldling's concern with written evidences of economic agreements helped Puritan clerics explain to laypersons the necessity of introspection as a source of spiritual assurance. Testing one's faith in the court of conscience offered the same assurance in spiritual life that scrupulous concern with bonds, contracts, and leases provided in economic life. Thus, many Puritan clerics observed that it was important to "look to our faith to consider whether it be a right faith or no. If a man has evidences upon which his lands and estate depend, if one should come and tell him they are false evidence, it would affect him, he would at the least be ready to look and to examine them."[45]

ONE FINAL TYPE OF IMAGERY REMAINS TO BE DISCUSSED. BASED ON two specific kinds of contracts, bonds of debt and premarital contracts, it

---

41. Thomas Newhouse, *A Learned And Faithfull Sermon* (1612), Sig. C1ᵛ. See also Thomas Gataker, *A Discussion Of The Popish Doctrine Of Transubstantiation* (1624), p. 21.

42. Sibbes, *Souls Conflict*, p. 265. See also Baynes, *A Counterbane against Earthly Carefulnes* (1618), pp. 6–7.

43. For example, see *LL*, II. 421–23.

44. Hieron, *The Spiritual Sonne-Ship* (1611), in *Sermons*, pp. 359–60.

45. John Preston, *The Breast-Plate Of Faith And Love* (1634), I. 170. See also Atter-

was widespread in Puritan writings, no doubt because bonds of debt and premarital contracts were widely used at this time. Moreover, their use provoked lively debates, which of course only increased their utility for Puritan rhetoric.

Comparison of sin to a debt, and sinners to debtors, is, of course, one of the oldest rhetorical devices in Christianity. For centuries, this comparison had been used to explain the nature of original sin: it arose as a consequence of the Fall of Adam, which made humanity a spiritual debtor to God. Puritan writers easily adapted this parable of the divine creditor and human debtor to their covenant theology. In order to explain sin, they referred to its "similitude and resemblance to civil debts. For, first, every debt arises of some contract between the creditor and the debtor. So God is the great creditor, man is the debtor, whose debt arises out of the contract and first covenant of works."[46]

However, Puritan writers altered this analogy of sin as a debt when they discussed the dimension of grace in the second contract between God and humanity, the covenant of grace. They reversed the roles of God and humanity in the creditor-debtor parable in order to explain God's covenanted obligation to provide grace to the elect to enable them to satisfy their part of the heavenly contract. Christ's intercession and sacrifice not only "ratifies unto us the cancellation of that handwriting of the old covenant which we had transgressed . . . wiping off all old scores and debts"; it also engages God as a debtor to the elect, a debtor obligated to pay off their spiritual debts. "Now as the man that is bound for payment of a sum of money may have the condition of his bond performed by another . . . so may we have the condition of righteousness performed for us by Christ." "Whereas we only by our sins were debtors to him," after enactment of the covenant of grace, "he is not only a merciful creditor to us, content to release the debts of our sins, but also by his promise become our debtor."[47]

This use of the creditor-debtor parable provides another piece of evidence of the distance separating Puritan covenant theology from Calvin's writings. Preston and other Puritan preachers called attention to the startling implications of God's willingness to become, in the heavenly con-

---

soll, *New Covenant*, p. 40; John Ball, *Treatise Of Faith* (1634), p. 244; Paul Baynes, *Christian Letters* (1637), pp. 211–12; Elton, *Triumph Of A Christian*, p. 648; Leigh, *Treatise Of Divine Promises*, p. 17; Randall, *St. Pauls Triumph*, p. 109; Taylor, *Progresse Of The Saints*, p. 365.

46. Thomas Taylor, *Davids Learning* (1617), p. 23.

47. Elton, *Triumph Of A Christian*, p. 18; Thomas Taylor, *Christs Victorie Over The Dragon* (1633), p. 605; Timothy Rogers, *The Righteous Mans Evidence for Heaven* (1632), pp. 197–98.

tract, a debtor to humanity, and they asked laypersons to consider "how great a mercy it is that the glorious God . . . should be willing to indent with us, as it were, that he should be willing to make himself a debtor to us . . . that he should tie himself and bind himself to become a debtor to me."[48] Here is another way in which the unfathomable God of Calvin became in Puritan thought not only more intelligible but also more predictable. This aspect of the creditor-debtor parable shows how the contractual limitation of God in Puritan covenant theology reinforced elements of assurance and comfort. That "God has made himself our debtor," said Sibbes, "ought to be a comfort to us." The debtor's obligation assumed by God as a result of Christ's intercession and sacrifice placed limits on God's dealings with humanity. "Seeing therefore our saviour Christ has fully discharged our debt . . . God cannot in equity extract of us a second payment, no more than the creditor may justly require that his debt should be twice paid."[49] What remained to be paid by the elect corresponded not to the severity of the debt of original sin but to the more gracious terms of the covenant of grace.

Premarital contracts were also widely used by Puritan clerics in their explanations of the heavenly contract. This imagery depicted the faithful as prospective brides of Christ, the spiritual suitor "who does woo, contract himself unto, consummate the match with, and perform all duties of a husband to all true believers."[50] This imagery reflected the emphasis placed by Puritan clerics on the *de futuro* contract of marriage, which was a commitment to marry and which I will refer to as a premarital contract. Summarizing the teachings of many Puritan preachers, William Gouge listed the following "three steps or degrees commended unto us by which marriagable parties are . . . to proceed unto marriage": "(1) a mutual liking; (2) an actual contract; (3) a public solemnization of marriage."[51] The rationale for using premarital contracts was to signify the mature consent to a marriage on the part of the prospective spouses.

48. Preston, *The New Covenant*, pp. 330–31. See also Thomas Hooker, *The Faithful Covenanter* (1644), p. 22; Leigh, *Treatise Of Divine Promises*, p. 49; William Sclatter, *Sermons Experimentall* (1638), p. 46; Wing, *The Best Merchandise*, p. 35.

49. Richard Sibbes, *The Christians Work*, p. 18; Downame, *Christian Warfare*, p. 208. And see Edward Elton, *An Exposition Of The Epistle of St. Paule to the Colossians* (1615), p. 624. Cf. John Dykstra Eusden, *Puritans, Lawyers, and Politics in Early Seventeenth-Century England* (New Haven, 1958), p. 31, where Eusden says that covenant theology "was hardly a signal alteration of the Calvinist doctrine of God." It "is more correctly seen as an intensification of the fundamental idea of God's rule."

50. Joseph Bentham, *The Societie Of The Saints* (1630), p. 203.

51. William Gouge, *Domesticall Duties* (1626), p. 114. See also, Ezechiel Culverwell, *Time Well Spent* (1635), pp. 60–62; Perkins, *Workes*, III. 672; Randall, *Three And Twentie Sermons*, II. 258; Henry Smith, *A Preparative To Marriage* (1591), in *Sermons* (1631), p. 9.

Mature consent was a controversial issue for Puritans and others in early modern England. It involved the propriety of forced marriages and the relative importance to be accorded to parents' approval and their children's desires. It was further complicated by lawsuits to compel performance of premarital contracts, which were widespread at all levels of society at this time.[52] Though Puritan clerics supported the need for parental approval, they argued against the validity of forced marriages and upheld the necessity of premarital contracts, for which "free and full consent of the parties . . . is indeed the very soul and life of the contract."[53] The premarital contract signified mutual consent to marry and, according to Greenham and Preston, created an obligation greater than verbal promises made privately,[54] even though such a contract *per verba de praesenti* was, legally, just as binding. The actual marriage ceremony followed the signing of a premarital contract, after certain conditions had been met or a specified period had elapsed.

Puritan preachers used this imagery to explain to laypersons the contractual dimensions of the covenant and the role of faith as consent. According to Sibbes, "Though God's grace do all, yet we must give our consent; and therefore the covenant is expressed under the title of marriage." The rationale for this analogy was as follows: "Believing is a spiritual marriage. In marriage there must be consent. This consent is faith."[55] But parallels between civil and spiritual marriage explained more than the demand for the believer's consent, through faith, to the heavenly contract. The covenant bond between God and humanity was, after all, a reciprocal bond, requiring the mutual consent of both parties, so that "[Just] as, in a simple contract of marriage, there is a mutual & reciprocal giving and taking made between man & wife of each other, so in this holy, happy and spiritual contract . . . there is a mutual giving and taking of each other."[56]

References to premarital contracts also appeared in discussions of the

---

52. Houlbrooke, *Church Courts and the People*, pp. 56–57; *LL*, IV. 362, VI. 140–41, 148.

53. Perkins, *Workes*, III. 681; Richard Cawdrey, *A Godly Forme Of Household Government* (1603), pp. 120–22. Controversies over this issue are discussed by Mildred Cambell, *The English Yeoman under Elizabeth and the Early Stuarts* (London, 1967), pp. 283–88; M.M. Knappen, *Tudor Puritanism* (Chicago, 1966), pp. 455–56; Louis B. Wright, *Middle-Class Culture in Elizabethan England* (London, 1964), pp. 206, 209.

54. Richard Greenham, *Workes* (1612), p. 123; John Preston, *The Golden Scepter* (1638), II. 2–4.

55. Sibbes, *Faithful Covenanter*, pp. 8–9, *The Fountain Opened* (1638), in *Works*, V. 515, and see also Sibbes, *The Brides Longing* (1639), in *Works*, VI. 541, *The Church's Visitation* (1634), in *Works*, I. 390, and *The Spouse* (1638), in *Works*, II. 201; Ball, *Treatise Of Faith*, pp. 163, 418.

56. Thomas Tuke, *A Theologicall Discourse* (1617), pp. 30–31. See also Samuel Crooke, *The Guide Unto True Blessednesse* (1613), pp. 42–43; Edward Elton, *The Com-*

sharp separation between this life and the one hereafter. Like spiritual earnests, marital imagery in covenant theology helped clerics explain why spiritual experience in this life fell far short of the communion of the saints in heaven. It stressed the meagerness of the one in comparison to the other by defining spiritual experience, simply and concisely, as evidence of future salvation. Central to this point was the distinction between a premarital contract and the actual marriage, a distinction which pointed to differences between grace in this life and glorification in heaven.

In this life, consent through faith ratifies the covenant as a premarital contract; the marriage itself occurs in the life hereafter. This was why Puritan clerics referred to the faithful as brides, not spouses, of Christ. "They must first be contracted, then after married. The contract is when a man is regenerate and born anew."[57] Regeneration signals the beginning of the conversion experience whose culmination, glorification, occurs in heaven. In this view, death permits fulfillment of the premarital contract, an idea that provided convenient points of consolation in funeral sermons by clerics who rhetorically asked, "To be with Christ is to have the marriage consummated. Is not marriage better than the contract?"[58]

A religious life spanned the interval between a premarital contract and marriage. Grace bestowed by God and human faith were like love tokens exchanged between contracted lovers in advance of the wedding, for the "stay between the contract & the marriage [is] the time of longing." Thus, like spiritual earnests, the marital imagery of the covenant helped clerics to explain the nature of the process of detecting election. Signs of spiritual longing were evidences of an effectual agreement between God and the believer. "Faith unites Christ and the believer, and contracts them together. Now when once the contract is passed, there follows the longing for the marriage day. And this longing after the marriage day is the sign of a contract made by faith."[59]

This casuistical doctrine was consistent with other Puritan prescriptions for interpreting spiritual experience in terms of contractual assurances.

---

plaint *Of A Sanctified Sinner* (1618), pp. 57–59; Rogers, *Saving-Beliefe*, p. 40; John Wilson, *Some Helpes To Faith* (1625), p. 207.

57. Samuel Smith, *The Great Assize* (1631), p. 229. See also Thomas Adams, *Workes* (1629), p. 1197; Thomas Draxe, *The Earnest Of Our Inheritance* (1613), p. 14; Samuel Hieron, *The Bridegroom* (1613), in *Sermons*, pp. 6–7; George Webbe, *The Bride Royall* (1613), pp. 64–65.

58. Sibbes, *Christ Is Best* (1634), in *Works*, I. 339, and see also his *A Learned Commentary*, p. 442; John Barlow, *Hierons Last Fare-well* (1618), p. 72; Thomas Gataker, *Two Funeral Sermons* (1620), p. 13.

59. Smith, *Preparative To Marriage* p. 9; Dyke, *The Worthy Communicant*, p. 304. See also Hooker, *Soules Vocation*, pp. 258–59; Rogers, *Saving-Beliefe*, p. 115; Sibbes, *Bowels Opened*, p. 58.

Interpreted as love tokens, introspective evidences of faith and grace linked spiritual experience on earth with salvation; this did not, however, undermine the notion of a sharp separation between heaven and earth. To understand the meaning of grace, Puritan preachers urged laypersons to "receive them as love tokens and pledges of further grace, sealing up unto us the covenant and that spiritual marriage between Christ and us. A small token . . . of a lover to his spouse is therefore most welcome because it assures of the marriage."[60] This link between heaven and earth—revealed by grace and faith, which are like love tokens exchanged by engaged lovers—provided the same contractual assurance that was conveyed by spiritual earnests and seals.

References in Puritan theology to principles and images derived from worldly contracts were nowhere more evident than in clerical efforts to transform doctrinal tenets into pastoral precepts for the laity. The importance of these contractual precedents is further suggested by the consistency with which many Puritan preachers related specific principles, practices, and types of worldly contracts to the operation of the heavenly contract. What emerges from this is further support for my argument that covenant theology, as a popular divinity intended for lay consumption, was developed by clerics who modified Calvinism by translating its major tenets into a contractarian idiom.

Possessive Individualism in the Heavenly Contract

Thus far I have interpreted the contractarian features of Puritan thought by locating them within their social and intellectual contexts, which I have described, respectively, in terms of organizational *pressures* and intellectual *precedents*. Precedents refer both to religious ideas about God's covenant and to secular forms of contractual interaction as they existed in early modern England. Though the importance of the secular precedent for Puritan thought is suggested by the consistency with which clerics used lessons and images derived from economic contracts, this importance is by no means conclusively demonstrated. It could be argued that the contractarian features of Puritan thought reflect a universal principle of reciprocity that characterizes cultural forms in all societies.[61]

---

60. Taylor, *Davids Learning*, p. 290. Exchange of "tokens" among friends as well as between lovers was a widely practiced social custom in early modern England; see *LL*, II. 362–65.

61. This has been suggested by Ernest Gellner and Steven Lukes in private correspondence. No doubt they have in mind a work by Marcel Mauss, *The Gift* (Glencoe, 1954), and also Claude Lévi-Strauss, *Structural Anthropology* (New York, 1963).

Lessons and images derived from economic contracts would, then, be far less significant than I have suggested, their presence in Puritan theology being merely a reflection of a transcultural principle of reciprocity. In this view, the social and intellectual contexts of Puritan thought would be seen to have influenced only its epiphenomenal features, the concrete examples and illustrations by which Puritan clerics gave expression to a far more fundamental principle of reciprocity. This being the case, the historically specific contexts of Puritan thought would be of secondary importance for understanding its contractarian features, these contexts shaping merely the surface expression of a universal cultural form. For example, Puritan theology might have related the mutual obligations between God and humanity to a covenant modeled on a peace treaty instead of on an economic contract.[62] But in neither case would the largely derivative metaphor of the peace treaty or the economic contract be important for understanding the sources of Puritan theology.

Obviously, a study like this one cannot resolve the issue of the universality of reciprocity as a cultural form. However, this issue is peripheral to this study because the contractarian features of Puritan theology cannot be understood simply in terms of a general principle of reciprocity. Though reciprocity is central to Puritan theology, so are many principles of accumulation and ownership that are not transcultural in nature but are part of the historical context of Puritanism. More than reciprocity structures the contractarian features of Puritan thought: at its core lies the logic of acquisitive behavior that is governed by a market rationality.

Central to this logic is the premise that individuals privately own the properties which, motivated by self-interest, they exchange through contractual interaction. This premise informed Puritan writings on the heavenly contract, which portrayed it as a relationship between God and the believer that consisted essentially of an exchange of self-proprieties. It was this exchange of self-proprieties that allowed the two parties to the heavenly contract to exercise their respective claims on each other. For the elect, their propriety in the person of God (in Christ) enabled them to obtain all of the spiritual and temporal blessings promised in the covenant. Such blessings were attributes of God, and they accrued to believers as a consequence of their proprietary right to God.

Readers familiar with C.B. Macpherson's study of seventeenth-century philosophy will immediately see how Puritan notions of spiritual ownership strongly resemble the core doctrine of possessive individualism that

62. For examples of the covenant described as a peace treaty, see William Gouge, *A Learned And Very Useful Commentary On The Whole Epistle To The Hebrews* (1655; composed before 1640), p. 240; Grosse, *Soule-Perswading Inducements*, p. 59; Harris, *The New Covenant*, I. 32; Preston, *The New Covenant*, p. 330.

Macpherson discerns in Hobbes and Locke.[63] Possessive individualism in political philosophy is the notion that private property is an extension of its owner's personal attributes. From this notion emerged a defense of the institution of private property, a defense that formed the basis of classical liberal ideology in market societies.

However, this notion apparently antedates the origins assigned to it by Macpherson, for it underlies Puritan remarks about the exchange of self-proprieties in the heavenly contract. Reciprocal claims between God and the believer were, according to Puritan clerics, a function of spiritual ownership. Reciprocity in the heavenly contract—the exchange of spiritual rights and obligations—presupposed ownership of these things as attributes of the parties to the contract.

One possible reason for the attention given by Puritan clerics to spiritual ownership in the heavenly contract is that it filled a doctrinal lacuna created by the Reformation. Spiritual ownership in Puritan covenant theology resolved a problem posed by the Reformation's attack on the church as an institution that mediated between God and the believer. In Protestantism, the individual believer became, in place of the church, the repository of all claims to grace. The doctrine of spiritual ownership in Puritanism explained how, if not through the intercession of the church, individuals acquired grace. Though not as concise as Catholic doctrine on the purchase of merits, spiritual ownership in covenant theology was within the intellectual grasp of ordinary laypersons. Moreover, this doctrine was fully compatible with the relatively high level of intellectual rationality in Puritan theology. Proprietary right to divine things, established by spiritual ownership in the heavenly contract, did not lessen the sharp separation between heaven and earth that was characteristic of a strongly dualistic world view.

The idea of spiritual ownership appeared frequently in Puritan sermons and treatises on the heavenly contract. According to Sibbes, parties to the heavenly contract can confidently assert that "Christ is mine, and myself am Christ's. He has my soul . . . he has a property in me." This is why, said Sibbes, "you see a mutual interest and owning between Christ and the church." Most Puritan writers used the term "propriety" rather than "property" to describe the spiritual ownership enacted by the heavenly contract. At this time, property meant propriety, which referred not to an object but to exclusive rights to the use of an object. Parliamentary opposition to Stuart absolutism produced the idea of self-propriety, meaning the capacity of individuals to develop and exploit skills and talents over which they had propriety. This was what Lilburne had in mind when

63. Macpherson, *Political Theory of Possessive Individualism.*

he protested that his jailers had seized his self-propriety, and it is what Locke meant when he declared that "every man has a property in his own person."[64]

In the second fast sermon delivered before the Long Parliament, Stephen Marshall echoed the teachings of two generations of Puritan preachers when he observed that "God's presence in the covenant of grace" implied for the saints that "they have a propriety in God and God has a propriety in them."[65] This idea of spiritual propriety in Puritan covenant theology derived from Perkins, who argued that consent to the heavenly contract produced an exchange of self-proprieties between God and the believer. Subsequent generations of Puritan clerics discussed this point in terms similar to those used by Perkins. Daniel Dyke remarked that

> Every true Christian . . . has a peculiarity and special propriety in God. Look as a man may say of his inheritance, his house and lands, *these be mine,* so he may as truly say of God, *God is mine,* I am righted and interested in him. This privilege is conferred upon us in the covenant of grace . . . We assenting to the conditions of this covenant, to be God's, God forthwith becomes ours, so that we may now lay claim to him as our own.[66]

Thus, the heavenly contract was based on more than the mere principle of reciprocity. It consisted of an exchange of self-proprieties between God and the believer, and it was this exchange on which all other benefits and rights depended.

This doctrine of spiritual proprietorship lies at the core of Puritan explanations of how believers acquired various graces promised by the heavenly contract. Grace was an attribute of God, and by acquiring a proprietorial right to God (in Christ), believers obtained the right to grace as an attribute of his person: "Whosoever he be that has Christ, he has also the benefits of Christ . . . whatsoever Christ did . . . it is by the covenant of grace truly and really his who is one with Christ and who has Christ for himself."[67]

---

64. Sibbes, *Bowels Opened,* pp. 175, 177. On the seventeenth-century meanings of "property" and "propriety," see G.E. Aylmer, "The Meaning and Definition of 'Property' in Seventeenth-Century England," *P&P* 86 (1980); Michael Levy, "Freedom, Property and the Levellers: The Case of John Lilburne," *Western Political Quarterly* (1983), pp. 118–22; Judith Richards et al., "'Property' and 'People': Political Usages in Locke and Some Contemporaries," *Journal of the History of Ideas* 42 (1981), p. 36.

65. Stephen Marshall, *A Sermon Preached before the Honourable House of Commons* (1640), in *FS,* I. 113.

66. Daniel Dyke, *Two Treatises* (1618), p. 87. See also Elton, *Triumph Of A Christian,* p. 761; Gore, *The God Of Heaven* (1638), in *Certayn Sermons,* p. 21; Perkins, *Workes,* III. 594; Randall, *St. Pauls Triumph,* p. 13; Wing, *Jacobs Staffe,* p. 11.

67. Elton, *Triumph Of A Christian,* p. 763.

What makes this idea of spiritual ownership all the more striking is that it was not, after all, logically necessary for explaining how believers, in covenant with God, obtain grace. A reciprocal agreement, without any mention of propriety in the persons of God and believers, would have been sufficient. But Puritan clerics stipulated that the spiritual blessings promised by the covenant were an attribute of God and that the saints acquired these in virtue of their proprietorial right to the person of God (in Christ). They argued that "all temporal blessings, and spiritual, are annexed to the person of Christ, whom [the saints] possess by faith."[68] In this way, they linked the role of faith to spiritual self-interest. Religious self-interest led believers to spiritual transactions that gained them a contractual right to divine goods, just as the pursuit of economic self-interest led worldlings to enter into contracts that gave them right and title to economic goods.

Puritan clerics often referred to the institution of civil marriage in order to explain more fully the relationship between the right to the person of God (in Christ) and the right to the attributes of that person. Possession of a spouse through civil marriage conveyed with it the right and title to his or her wealth and debts, which, for better or worse, were attributes of that person. The same was true in the spiritual marriage effected by the heavenly contract. Just as the prospective rise in a bride's fortunes, due to a lucrative match, depended primarily on her claim to the person of her husband, so the proprietorial right to Christ was the basis of the Christian's spiritual fortunes. In each case, the right to property of the spouse followed ineluctably from marriage to the spouse, because property was regarded as an attribute of the person. According to John Preston:

> When a virgin marries with a man that is rich, she looks upon all his possessions, and sees so many thousand sheep, so many fair houses, and so much land. He has so much gold and silver, and she says thus with herself: now he is my husband, all this is mine . . . So look now upon the Lord, consider when you have choosen him to be your portion. Though you should be content to have him alone, yet all this comes together with him; it cannot be separated from him.[69]

It now becomes evident why Puritan divines invoked the idea of spiritual ownership when they explained how the saints obtained grace. They did so because, like Hobbes and Locke, they conceived of property, whether worldly or spiritual, as an attribute of its owner. This becomes even more

68. Elnathan Parr, *A plain exposition upon the whole 8th-12th chapters of . . . the Romanes* (1620), in *Workes*, p. 61. See also Ball, *Treatise Of Faith*, p. 358; Downame, *Christian Warfare*, p. 1022; Wing, *Jacobs Staffe*, p. 43.

69. Preston, *The New Covenant*, pp. 79–80. See also Baynes, *A Commentarie*, p. 232; Downame, *Christian Warfare*, p. 278; Sibbes, *Bowels Opened*, p. 24, and *The Life Of Faith* (1629), in *Works*, V. 363.

apparent when Puritan clerics dutifully warned their auditors not to regard the heavenly contract in an excessively pecuniary manner. Obviously, that contract offered many benefits to the saints, but these benefits, according to the preachers, followed first and foremost from unfeigned acceptance of Christ. According to Preston and other prominent Puritan preachers, "First we must have Christ, and then look to the promises . . . for it is an adulterous affection for a wife not to think of the husband, but to think only what commodity she shall have by him, what honors, what riches, what conveniences . . . It is true indeed you shall have all of this into the bargain, but first you must have the person of your husband."[70] Just as the wife's acceptance of the husband made her right to his property unobjectionable, so the saint's affiance for Christ brought spiritual wealth in its wake as a more or less honorable consequence.

AN INTERESTING ASPECT OF THIS DOCTRINE OF SPIRITUAL OWNERSHIP is its implications for temporal goods. When discussing the conditions under which property rights had God's blessing, Puritan clerics referred to the heavenly contract and the doctrine of spiritual ownership. Because the entire universe is God's creation, temporal as well as spiritual goods are attributes of God's person. The propriety acquired by the saints in God provided them not only with grace but also with the divine right to own worldly goods—to worldly proprietorship.

This view is quite different from the older doctrine of stewardship in Christian thought. This held that individuals, as God's stewards, were entrusted with goods and talents which they should use for the general welfare of society. Criteria for this religious approbation of temporal propriety were defined objectively, though imprecisely: specific social utilities had to be maximized by worldly proprietors, e.g., on behalf of the poor, to maintain hospitality, or to support the visible church. This traditional doctrine of stewardship appeared frequently in sermons and other writings by the clerical leaders of early Protestantism, who used it to denounce the enclosing and engrossing of land, depopulation, and usury, which they thought were among the chief causes of social unrest.[71] And this use of stewardship continued to appear in Puritan sermons in the late sixteenth and early seventeenth centuries.

70. Preston, *Breast-Plate Of Faith*, I. 44–45. See also Attersoll, *The New Covenant*, p. 267; Hooker, *Soules Vocation*, p. 158; Phillips, *Certaine Godly Sermons*, p. 402; Sibbes, *Fountain Opened*, p. 516.

71. For example, see Thomas Becon, *A Pleasant New Nosegay* (1542) and *A New Catechism* (1564) in *PS*, II. 225, III. 115; Robert Crowley, *An informacion and Peticion agaynst the oppresours of the pore Commons* (1548), Sigs. A4ʳ, A6ʳ, A8ʳ-B1ᵛ; William Tyndale, *The Obedience of a Christian Man* (1528), in *PS*, XLII. 201–2.

However, this traditional doctrine was the product of an older religious world, dominated by a church that laid claim to a monopoly of Christ's merits. A natural affinity existed between the doctrine of stewardship and the medieval church because this doctrine required that the criteria for the just use of worldly things should be established institutionally, by the church. The ethical imperative to place one's goods and talents in the service of society had a secure foundation when the church determined that the giving of alms, the maintenance of hospitality, and so on, would be rewarded by merits dispensed by the church. Central to the doctrine of stewardship was the church's authority to determine the criteria of the social good, an authority enforced by the church's role as a mediating agency between God and humanity.

The Reformation's attack on the church as a mediating agency dissolved, albeit unintentionally, the institutional basis of stewardship. To be sure, this traditional doctrine continued to be upheld and defended by Puritan preachers. But alongside this traditional view another doctrine appeared, containing different criteria for deciding what constituted a religiously just use of worldly things. Focusing on the godliness of the proprietor, this newer doctrine glossed over the social considerations that were implicit in the older doctrine of stewardship. Instead, it made divine right to worldly things a function of an individual's right and title to the person of God. By providing saints with a proprietary right to God in Christ, the heavenly contract also conveyed the right to use and own temporal things, which, like grace, were attributes of God's being: "By his being ours in covenant, all other things become ours."[72]

A religious right to own worldly things was often mentioned in terms of a right to God's "creatures." The term "creatures" referred generally to nature; and the right and title to the natural world had been forfeited by Adam, whose sin caused the creatures to rebel against him. This rebellion signified loss of divine right to worldly things. Restoration of a prelapsarian right to worldly dominion followed the believer's entrance into the heavenly contract. According to Preston, Sibbes, Taylor, and many other Puritan preachers, "it is an express branch of the new covenant that the Lord will work our peace with the creatures." The saint in covenant with God regained right to the creatures and "receives earthly blessings as gifts of the covenant" because "in the covenant of grace God promised . . . to confer temporal blessings . . . as God gives temporal things to his people

---

72. Sibbes, *Souls Conflict*, p. 272. See also, Elton, *Triumph Of A Christian*, p. 765. Two historians see in the rise of Puritanism a decline in the "strain of social commentary that had marked the teachings of Latimer and a number of other early reformers" (Felicity Heal and Rosemary O'Day, editors' introduction to *Church and Society in England: Henry VIII to James I* [Hamden, Ct., 1977], p. 9).

in covenant, so does faith receive them as tokens of special goodwill and favor in Jesus Christ, in and whom of free grace, son-like right and title to the creatures is restored."[73]

This doctrine was fully consonant with the more general tenets of the Reformation, for it made divine right to worldly things a consequence, not a cause, of certitude of salvation. Now individual conscience, not institutionally defined criteria—private not public actions—determined when divine sanction accompanied temporal proprietorship. Puritan clerics did argue that good works that upheld the general welfare were outward signs of a good conscience. But these outward signs, which corresponded to the social goods defended by the traditional doctrine of stewardship, occupied a secondary place behind the primary importance attached to the individual's covenant with God.

Entrance into the heavenly contract was the essential prerequisite for a religiously just propriety in temporal things.

> This is the plea of the Lord against us, that we dwell in a land where we are but usurpers and have no right. No man is of so reprobate a sense but he will grant that whatsoever we have, we have it at the Lord's hand. But are these free gifts without all condition? No . . . if we keep the Lord's statutes, we keep the condition and consequently have a good right . . . Therefore when we bless ourselves for our riches, and say, the Lord be blessed for my wealth . . . we must also say . . . all this I have of the Lord, and hold whatsoever I have of him. Do I keep that part of the covenant which is of my part, as he has performed his part of the covenant with me? If I do, then I am no usurper, for he has given me a condition and I have kept it.[74]

An enormous distance separates this doctrine and the older doctrine of stewardship. No longer do predetermined standards of social utility—e.g., alms, hospitality, purchase of merits—establish what is a just use of worldly things. Instead, individuals must seek, above all else, private evidence of their inclusion in the heavenly contract, because certitude of faith and self-assurance of good intent must precede all outward actions.

This shift from institutional to introspective criteria of a religiously just use of the world had important consequences for acquisitive behavior. Whereas the older criteria subordinated acquisitive behavior to the social good, the newer criteria passively facilitated private accumulation. The Puritan doctrine of temporal proprietorship lacked an objective standard

---

73. Taylor, *Japhets First Publique Perswasion* (Cambridge, 1612), p. 38; Ball, *Treatise Of Faith*, pp. 260, 363. See also Leigh, *Treatise Of Divine Promises*, pp. 78, 109, 120; Preston, *The New Covenant*, pp. 481–83; Sibbes, *The Privileges of the Faithful* (1638), in *Works*, V. 262, 271; Taylor, *Davids Learning*, p. 254; Walker, *Manifold Wisdome Of God*, pp. 42–43, 50, 53–54.

74. Greenham, *Workes*, p. 786.

for covetous behavior, for it insisted that covetousness be evaluated from the vantage point of individual conscience. For Perkins, Preston, and other Puritan preachers, "covetousness may be defined to be a sinful desire of getting, or keeping money or wealth inordinately." But levels of desire that are inordinate vary from case to case, depending on the worldly calling and rank of the individual: "There is a necessity in respect of your condition and place, as men in higher rank and calling need more than men of inferior degree to maintain their place and dignity."[75] As one of its provisions, the heavenly contract provided divine sanction for possessing worldly things in proportion to one's worldly station. "The Lord by his covenant has promised to furnish his people with all needful blessings pertaining to this life."[76] What was "needful," however, remained for each individual to decide in accordance with the dictates his conscience. Thus, the Puritan doctrine of proprietorship was in effect a mirror that legitimated secular expectations about appropriate levels of wealth by reflecting them in the individual conscience as ethically acceptable intentions.[77]

Making pious intent the criterion for legitimate aspiration, the Puritan doctrine of proprietorship promoted acceptance of newer standards of acquisitive activity that followed a market rationality. Although this activity was a well-established feature of early modern England, it continued to generate much debate and criticism because of its corrosive effects on the old ideals, which subordinated the individual to the community. Puritan arguments inadvertently circumvented this debate and criticism. There was no absolute quantity of concern with temporal matters that established, for all persons, what constituted covetous behavior, because "it is not the having of riches, but the coveting of them that proves a man to be a covetous man. For not only great usurers and oppressing landlords are covetous worldlings . . . covetousness may be in a beggar."[78] Puritan remarks like this were a comfort to those whose consciences informed them

75. John Preston, *Sins Overthrow* (1633), II. 25, 32, and see also *Foure Godly And Learned Treatises* (1636), p. 35; Jeremiah Dyke, *A Counterpoison Against Covetousness* (1619), p. 14; Elton, *Triumph Of A Christian*, p. 119; Fenner, *Workes*, I. 60; Perkins, *Workes*, II. 148–49, III. 163.

76. Ball, *Treatise Of Faith*, p. 357. See also Preston, *The New Covenant*, pp. 38, 107–8, 126–28; Sibbes, *The Returning Backslider* (1632), in *Works*, II. 386.

77. This thesis has been explored by Christopher Hill in "Protestantism and the Rise of Capitalism," in *Change and Continuity*, pp. 92, 96–99, and also in his *Society and Puritanism in Pre-Revolutionary England* (New York, 1967), pp. 315, 488. For an earlier version of this thesis, see R.H. Tawney, *Religion and the Rise of Capitalism* (New York, 1926), pp. 226–27, 231–32, 272–73.

78. Fenner, *Workes*, II. 400–401. See also William Gouge, quoted in Hill, "Protestantism and the Rise of Capitalism," p. 96; Sibbes, *Souls Conflict*, p. 150; William Whately, *A Caveat For The Covetous* (1604), pp. 22–24. Cf. Knappen, *Tudor Puritanism*, pp. 406–14, who argues that Puritan views on covetousness were essentially medieval in their emphasis on good works.

that their acquisition of wealth was in conformity with their worldly station and with God's will.

Spiritual Accumulation

Assumptions about worldly accumulation were as important to Puritan covenant theology as were assumptions about property as an attribute of its owner. Both sets of assumptions provided Puritan clerics with resources for making their covenant theology intellectually accessible to the laity. They also had in common an economic logic dictated by a market rationality.

Clerics used assumptions about accumulation in order to explain pastoral issues not dealt with by the idea of spiritual proprietorship. Assumptions about property as an extension of its owner helped to explain doctrinal tenets regarding the role of faith, the imputation of grace, and the necessity of introspection. Assumptions about accumulation guided clerical remarks on how to implement these tenets. Puritan clerics referred to worldly accumulation when they wanted to describe behavioral qualities that were necessary in religious devotion. Here again we see how Puritan clerics incorporated in their covenant theology what they thought were common objects of knowledge among their lay followers. Puritan clerics relied on lay knowledge of the instrumental utility of diligent, methodical behavior for economic success in explaining why the devout had to be diligent and methodical in seeking to enter into the heavenly contract.

Puritan clerics described grace as a heavenly commodity that true believers came to acquire through spiritual bargaining. Often they invoked certain biblical parables (e.g., Matt. 13:45, Prov. 22:23) that compared the devout individual to the merchant. Spiritual self-interest required of the devout the same diligent care taken by merchants in their buying and selling.

> You must bargain for Christ, and so you shall be assured that he is your own . . . do then as the buyer: 1. See you want the commodity; 2. That it is to be had; 3. . . . . what a benefit to you to have it; 4. Thereupon take a liking to it . . . 5. Consider upon what terms and at what rate it is to be had . . . 6. Consent thereto to give God his asking . . . If thus you consent to it . . . the bargain is stricken up, Christ is yours.

It is important to note, however, that spiritual bargaining created an exchange in which the believer did not obtain grace because of any specific work. This would, of course, violate the tenet of justification by faith.

Grace was instead provided upon condition of good intent; diligence and desire itself were its price: "The price is this, to prefer it in account and estimation before all things, and to make it our chiefest labor to attain it."[79] Puritan clerics taught that the Apostles referred to true believers as buyers of grace, not because they had actual merits to exchange for it, but because "God here asks diligence, painfulness, industry and labor of the spirit in the use of the means." The true believer is a spiritual merchant because "as a buyer he makes an exchange, not of money nor money-worth, but uses all good endeavor and labor, by prayer and diligence . . . which price God does set upon grace, and on which condition an exchange is made."[80]

Moreover, it was not only an initial purchase of grace but a continuous accumulation of grace that characterized the religious life. Puritan preachers warned their lay followers that no person could maintain spiritual grace if they did not ceaselessly seek to increase it. According to the famous Puritan preacher of Banbury, William Whately, "A good man follows goodness as a tradesman does his trade"; and this, said Thomas Taylor, required "a diligent and constant using of the means of increase."[81] Though merely the least degree of true faith indicated inclusion in the heavenly contract, confirmation of this evidence required spiritual growth: "We may make our claim by the very least grain of true grace we have gotten, but our claim is confirmed by our increasing therein and gaining of more."[82]

To understand the necessity of spiritual growth, Puritan clerics instructed the laity to examine the exigencies of economic life: "He that has true grace indeed is not content with that measure of grace which he has for the present . . . For though he be no niggard of it, yet he is withal a good husband with it, and labors daily to increase it . . . For as a good deal laid up in a napkin will quickly come to nothing, so a little well improved will quickly be increased."[83] Not only did this analogy instruct the

79. Rogers, *Saving-Beliefe*, pp. 89–90; Hieron, *Truths Purchase* (1613), in *Sermons*, pp. 49–50. See also Downame, *Christian Warfare*, p. 1119.

80. Jeremiah Dyke, *Divers Select Sermons* (1640), p. 339; Thomas Taylor, *Three Treatises* (1633), p. 87. See also Hieron, *Truths Purchase*, p. 42; Thomas Hill, *The Trade Of Truth* (1642), in *FS*, III. 303; Thomas Stoughton, *Two Profitable Treatises* (1616), pp. 211–12.

81. Whately, *Gods Husbandry*, pp. 125–26; Taylor, *Progresse Of Saints*, p. 218. See also Elton, *An Exposition*, pp. 32–33; Rogers, *Saving-Beliefe*, p. 173; Sibbes, *The Rich Pearl* (1637), in *Works*, VII. 256.

82. Wing, *Jacobs Staffe*, p. 73. See also Downame, *Christian Warfare*, p. 264; Elton, *An Exposition*, p. 929; Thomas Gataker, *The Joy Of The Just* (1623), pp. 143–44.

83. William Harrison, *Two Treatises* (1639), p. 66. See also Baynes, *Christian Letters*,

laity about the necessity of spiritual accumulation, it also pointed to behavioral qualities that were requisite for successful accumulation. Clerics
thought that this latter point was virtually self-evident: spiritual merchants must attend to their religious transactions with the same consistent
and methodical care that worldlings used in their pursuit of gain. Puritan
preachers accordingly asked their lay followers to consider:

> How do men bestir themselves to add to their gains . . . How
> thrifty husbands: 1. Forecast to get and plod to add to their stock?
> 2. Carefully save that which is gotten, avoiding expenses, & much
> more excesses? 3. Having got a good portion, yet still desire and
> seek more? . . . Should we not be now as thrifty for our souls as for
> our bodies?[84]

These remarks did not refer merely to worldly avarice and greed but to a
specific type of avarice, to accumulation governed by a market rationality.
Though Puritan clerics occasionally cited enterprises of the very rich,
more frequently they referred to the marketing activities of small independent proprietors, to thrifty yeomen and diligent tradesmen. Systematic care with economic affairs was especially important for this stratum of
small proprietors, given their precarious position: below them was an increasingly impoverished rural labor force; above them was an elite based
on large estates and monopolies obtained by court connections. Their precarious situation was reflected in popular consciousness as part of the economic folklore of early modern England, which glorified the diligence
and industriousness of small proprietors.[85]

Puritan clerics associated this stratum of small entrepreneurs with a
normative structure that stressed the virtue and utility of diligent, methodical activity in economic life. They evidently thought that the importance of this normative structure for their lay followers made it a useful
exemplar for the extensive care required by religious devotion. The instrumental utility of diligent, methodical behavior in the worldly callings
of small proprietors became a model for the general calling of Christians.
The intelligibility of all this was taken for granted by Puritan clerics: the
godly Christian was an accumulating Christian, and accumulation required a most methodical discipline.

Among the behavioral qualities requisite for success in acquisitive activities, control of time was of paramount importance. The utility of such

---

pp. 189–90; Hieron, *Truths Purchase*, p. 60; Hooker, *Soules Vocation*, p. 620; Wing,
Best Merchandise, p. 90.

84. Taylor, *Progresse Of Saints*, p. 228. See also Ball, *Treatise Of Faith*, pp. 406–7;
Robert Cleaver, *A Plaine Exposition . . . of the Proverbs of Salomin* (1614), p. 113;
Whately, *Gods Husbandry*, pp. 112–13.

85. Wright, *Middle-Class Culture in Elizabethan England*, pp. 186–200.

qualities as diligence and methodicalness rests on the assumption that time itself is money, that it is a commodity of opportunity which, well spent, creates wealth and which, misused, leads to lost revenue. In the Middle Ages, this view of time was at odds with a more traditional view, upheld by the church, which insisted that time belonged to God and was not, as merchants regarded it, a dimension subject to proprietorial claims and profit.[86] It was this latter conception of time that Puritan clerics invoked in urging laypersons to take advantage of the spiritual opportunities offered in this life.

"Opportunity of time is a rich commodity," said Elnathan Parr; "As merchants observe carefully the seasons of buying in and vending their merchandise, so buy you and redeem time to do good."[87] Other preachers compared the time of mortal life to the hours of a market, asking, "[Why] be careless when our chief market days come?" In spiritual as in worldly markets, carelessness was misuse of the commodity of time:

> If he goes and sits and talks away the market time in the alehouse, bibbing and twatling with this and that idle companion, before he minds it the market is over and done . . . He cannot buy because through negligence and idleness he has lost his market time.[88]

Thomas Goodwin warned his readers that "however you may account it, yet the balance of the sanctuary thus estimates your time, calls it your money," for "this stock of time afforded you by God's goodness" is "riches indeed." For spiritual merchants, time was opportunity to accumulate grace. "It is the praying Christian that alone employs the riches of the promises, which we usually let lie by us like dead stock, unimproved, while he like a wise and diligent merchant looks abroad upon all the affairs of Jesus Christ that are afloat here in this world, and adventures in all of them."[89]

Disciplined use of time was the central theme of these admonitions by Puritan clerics. Religious discipline involved the same behavioral qualities, the same kind of asceticism, that the market rationality imposed on small proprietors. This pastoral precept presupposed that the instrumen-

86. See Jacques Le Goff, "Au Moyen Age: Temps de l'Eglise et temps du marchand," in *Pour un autre Moyen Age: Temps, travail et culture en Occident* (Paris, 1977), pp. 46–65.

87. Elnathan Parr, *Abba Father* (1632), in *Workes*, p. 24. See also John Dod and Robert Cleaver, *A Plaine Exposition Of The Ninth and Tenth Chapters of the Proverbs* (1612), p. 89.

88. Greenham, *Workes*, p. 384; Dyke, *Divers Select Sermons*, pp. 359–60. See also Preston, *The New Covenant*, pp. 178, 601–5.

89. Thomas Goodwin, *Aggravation Of Sin* (1638) and *The Return Of Prayers* (1636), in *Works*, III. 356, IV. 194.

tal utility of such discipline derived from its maximization of time in both spiritual and worldly markets. It was, moreover, the link between ascetic behavior and self-interest in a market rationality that provided the exemplar for religious life, and many Puritan clerics urged their lay followers to imitate this secular exemplar:

> All worldly men seek never for pleasure while profit does drop, as we may see in them that live on fairs and markets . . . So long as they hope to gain a penny, how wait they, how diligent are they, how little play they, how busy are they? And why? Forsooth, it is their harvest, it is their market, which (say they) they must attend upon . . . Behold, the policy of the world may teach us what we ought to do for our souls.[90]

But worldly and spiritual accumulation required more than certain behavioral qualities, more than diligence, industriousness, and a methodical use of time. Equally important was systematic monitoring of the success of one's methods. For the advancement of spiritual growth, the Puritan clergy commended to lay Puritans the care with which they recorded their losses and profits from economic transactions. Just as acquisitive activity in the economic market required diligent bookkeeping, so successful transactions in spiritual markets required introspective account-taking.

The spiritual market of paramount importance was, not surprisingly, defined by Puritan clerics as public worship, where sermons announced the conditions of the heavenly contract. It was a commonplace of Puritan divinity to argue that "The profitable and heavenly spending of the Sabbath is the market of the soul."[91] After public worship, spiritual merchants ought to audit the results of their efforts to grow in grace: "[Just] as market-folks returning from market will be talking of their markets, as they go by the way, and be casting up of their penny-worths, [and] when they come home reckon what they have taken, and what they have laid out, and how much they have gotten, so should we after we have heard the word publicly."[92]

90. Greenham, *Workes*, p. 169, and see also p. 384; Immauel Bourne, *The Godly Mans Guide* (1620), pp. 19–20; Daniel Dyke, *The Mystery Of Selfe-Deceiving* (1614), p. 230; Stoughton, *Two Treatises*, p. 207; Taylor, *Three Treatises*, p. 35; Wing, *The Best Merchandise*, p. 129.

91. An observation made by Hill, *Society and Puritanism*, p. 175. The quotation is from Richard Rogers, *Seven Treatises* (1610), p. 180. See also Nicholas Byfield, *The Patterne Of Wholesome Words* (1618), p. 399; Greenham, *Workes*, p. 841.

92. Thomas Gataker, *True Contentment* (1620), pp. 37–38. See also Dod and Cleaver, *A Plaine And Familiar Exposition*, p. 160; Hieron, *Truths Purchase*, p. 51; Randall, *Three And Twentie Sermons*, II. 146–47; Daniel Rogers, *Davids Cost* (1619), pp. 359–60; Sibbes, *The Demand Of A Good Conscience* (1640), in *Works*, VII. 513.

As in their remarks on the diligent use of time, Puritan clerics lamented the fact that, though the diligent record-keeping of economic transactions provided a model, few laypersons were as attentive to their spiritual accounts. In their economic affairs, individuals are "very careful to keep their books of receipt and expense, poring over anon on them, running oft over their reckonings and casting over their accounts to see how they thrive." "And were we as careful for the state of our souls," Puritan clerics observed, "we would be as careful . . . of keeping and oft casting up our accounts concerning the one, as they are theirs concerning the other."[93]

AT THIS POINT WE CAN STATE SUMMARILY SEVERAL ANSWERS TO THE question posed at the beginning of this chapter. The reasons why Puritan clerics translated the major tenets of Calvinism into a contractarian idiom are intellectual and social in nature. First, this idiom was intellectually adequate for the task: its conceptual complexity enabled it to encompass and express a wide variety of doctrinal and pastoral issues in a relatively compact system of divinity. The general principles and specific practices of contract illuminated such doctrinal tenets as the role of faith, the imputation of grace, and the meaning of Christ's intercession and sacrifice, and they also guided explanations of the chief pastoral problem of Calvinism: the introspective search for evidences of election. Puritan casuistry taught the laity that discovery of these evidences followed the same logic of assurance that was implicit in worldly contracts. It also taught that the same behavioral qualities that were needed for the successful use of worldly contracts were needed for entering into the heavenly contract. The contractarian format of Puritan theology was well suited for all these issues.

This format was socially as well as intellectually adequate for the task of imparting to parishioners a systematic understanding of the Calvinist economy of grace and salvation. This undertaking would, of course, have been impossible if the Puritan laity had been unfamiliar with the general principles and the specific practices of contract; but textual evidence indicates that Puritan clerics regarded these principles and practices as matters of common knowledge among the Puritan laity. Contractual principles and practices had special relevance to the social stratum from which Puritanism derived its strongest support, for the precarious economic independence of this stratum rested on skills in market transactions. Contrac-

93. Thomas Gataker, *The Spiritual Watch* (1622), pp. 92–93, *True Contentment*, pp. 32–33. See also William Chibald, *A Tryall Of Faith* (1622), p. 86; Samuel Smith, *The Chief Shepheard* (1625), p. 206; Taylor, *Davids Learning*, pp. 120, 291, and *Three Treatises*, pp. 42–43.

tual interaction, governed by a market rationality, formed an emergent pattern of social order for this stratum. This pattern of order—with its assumptions about accumulation, consent, ownership, and the disciplined use of time—is isomorphic to the contractarian format of Puritan covenant theology.

Discovering the importance of worldly contracts for Puritan thought does not, however, prove the implausible: that Puritan theology was a reflection of economic forces. We can explain the Puritan clerics' use of a contractarian idiom and logic from economic life only with reference to the organizational dynamics of Puritanism, to the specific constraints and opportunities confronting these clerics in their dual role as ministers in a comprehensive church and as leaders of a popular religious movement. The context in which Calvin's ideas were molded to English circumstances was provided by organizational developments internal to Puritanism as well as by economic developments. Indeed, the latter derived their salience for Puritan theology only from the former: economic ideas appeared in Puritan thought as a consequence of clerical efforts to channel popular dissent in directions compatible with the pastoral authority of clerics in a comprehensive church. The language and logic of commerce appeared in Puritan divinity because it helped clerics cope with worldly obstacles to their heavenly goals.

7
Conclusion

The influence of popular activities and beliefs on Puritan religion has formed the central theme of this book. I have shown how they affected many aspects of Puritanism, including its theological tenets, its pastoral precepts, and its rituals. Two major sets of conclusions have emerged. First, this study resolves—or provides additional evidence on—several issues, long debated among historical specialists, concerning the origins and content of Puritan theology and the place of an emergent individualism in seventeenth-century England. Second, it raises some broader theoretical questions, of interest to sociologists, concerning the sociological analysis of ideology and, more specifically, Max Weber's analysis of religion and rationalization.

In chapter 5, I referred to debates among historical specialists over the originality of covenant concepts in Puritan thought. My study suggests that, to explain the origins of Puritan covenant theology, it is not sufficient to establish whether this theology was foreshadowed by precedents in the Bible or in writings by continental divines. Nor is it sufficient to point to practical precedents, established by the growing reliance on contracts in early capitalism.[1] It is necessary as well to demonstrate the salience of these intellectual and practical precedents in terms of the organizational context in which Puritan covenant theology developed.

1. For discussion of precedents in the Bible and in the writings of continental divines, see above, chapter 5, notes 1, 6, and 50. For practical precedents created by contracts in early capitalism, see chapter 1, note 14.

The salience of these precedents for clerics who created a distinctively Puritan version of Calvinism lay in their utility for resolving problems of clerical control over a popular religious movement. Puritan covenant theology arose as a response to organizational problems that threatened this control. It emerged as clerics seized on various precedents in order to cope with challenges from above, issuing from their ecclesiastical superiors, and from below, issuing from a lay religious vanguard that existed partly within and partly outside the church. Doctrinal and pastoral dimensions of covenant theology helped Puritan clerics to resolve, albeit temporarily, the conflicting demands placed on them by their dual role as ordained ministers in a comprehensive church and as nominal leaders of a popular religious movement.

For English clerics, the salience of intellectual precedents in the embryonic covenant theologies of Beza, Bucer, Bullinger, Calvin, Zwingli, and the Heidelberg theologians appeared chiefly in conjunction with their efforts to contain radical trends in the English Reformation. For refutation of the doctrines put forward by heretical groups and, later, by the Separatists, they relied on these continental sources, which emphasized unilateral conceptions of the covenant.

The salience of practical precedents—found in the types of commercial agreements and practices used by small employers and independent producers—appeared chiefly in conjunction with the clerics' efforts to provide a pastoral foundation for a variety of lay initiatives in religious life. They sought to channel lay initiatives in directions that were amenable to clerical supervision within a comprehensive church. In their casuistical guides for the laity, Puritan clerics referred to practical precedents from economic life because such precedents were objects of common knowledge, and the precepts and practices of contractual interaction were thus useful exemplars for explaining religious precepts and practices.

This last point indicates why a far broader significance belongs to the role of contractual ideas in Puritan theology than has previously been asserted. The heavenly contract occupies a central place in Puritan divinity[2] because of—not in spite of—the pervasive individualism that is implicated in the idea of contract.[3] The significance of the heavenly contract

2. See above, chapter 5, note 51.

3. The contrary opinion has been voiced by those who deny major links between Puritanism and individualism. James Johnson, for example, says, "Too much . . . has been made of Puritan individualism. Giving the covenant theology proper weight would require a rethinking of those [R.H. Tawney's] theses which emphasize puritan individualism" (Johnson, "The Covenant Idea and the Puritan View of Marriage," *Journal of the History of Ideas* 32 [1971], pp. 107–8). See also John S. Coolidge, *The Pauline Renaissance in England* (Oxford, 1970), pp. 147–51.

clearly lies not in its originality but in the reasons for its appearance in Puritan divinity. For Puritan clerics, the utility of contractarian ideas depended on lay acceptance and understanding of the pervasive individualism implicit in those ideas.

Puritan clerics taught the godly to look for evidence of election in the same way that worldlings used contractual instruments in pursuit of gain. They defined introspective evidence of faith as evidence of an effectual agreement, regarding salvation, between God and the believer. This was not incompatible with the doctrine of predestination, because the existence of the heavenly contract depended on the prior electing decision of God. Thus predestination was not abolished but complemented by pastorally treating certitude of salvation as a problem of verifying the existence of a heavenly contract.

In addition, Puritan casuistry relied on lay knowledge of economic contracts in order to teach parishioners how to look for evidence of election. Behavioral qualities associated with economic success, such as methodical labor and diligent record-keeping, were cited in Puritan covenant theology as exemplars to be followed in the search for evidence of election. This theology, by comparing the instrumental properties of such behavior in religious and economic life, showed that the pursuit of one's ultimate religious interest had the same dimensions of accumulation, exchange, and ownership as the pursuit of one's economic self-interest. Here Puritan theology relied on a very specific model of economic life, one governed by a market rationality. In this model, acquisitive activities are governed by purely contractual patterns of interaction, and they are justified by the doctrine of possessive individualism. These secular themes appeared in Puritan theology because Puritan clerics assumed that contractual precepts, the instrumental properties of ascetic behavior in markets, and the ethics of possessive individualism were familiar features in the everyday lives of their parishioners.

This conclusion provides support for regarding Puritanism as an important factor in the rise of English individualism. This is, of course, an old assertion, and one that is currently unfashionable among historians. It has been advanced most notably by R.H. Tawney and Christopher Hill, who argue that Puritanism unleashed a corrosive individualism that undermined the corporate solidarity and structure of communal life and thus paved the way for capitalist society. According to Tawney, "The individualism congenial to the world of business became the distinguishing characteristic of a Puritanism which had arrived."[4] Critics such as Trevor-

---

4. R.H. Tawney, *Religion and the Rise of Capitalism* (London, 1938), p. 233; see also pp. 229–51. For the views of Christopher Hill, see "Protestantism and the Rise of Capi-

Roper dismiss this argument about Puritanism and individualism as a piece of Whig historiography. Some historians follow the lead of Knappen and cite the "hyperconservatism" of Puritan thinking on economic matters. Other historians, such as Walzer, call attention to repressive elements in Puritanism, which subordinated spontaneity to church discipline and individual needs to those of corporate groups.[5]

Recent studies of economic and political thought in seventeenth-century England also seem to cast doubt on the Tawney-Hill thesis. They suggest that individualism in a recognizably modern form does not appear until the end of the seventeenth or the beginning of the eighteenth century. J.G.A. Pocock argues, in opposition to Macpherson, that in the seventeenth century "a classical bourgeois ideology and a market theory of personality" have not yet appeared. And in her study of economic ideology, Joyce Appleby concludes that not until the 1690s were explicit assumptions made about "the invariable desire of market participants to seek their profit when reaching a bargain."[6]

The sociological analysis of Puritan covenant theology that I have presented provides strong support for the broad outlines of the Tawney-Hill

talism," in *Change and Continuity in 17th-Century England* (London, 1974) and *Society and Puritanism in Pre-Revolutionary England* (New York, 1967), passim.

5. A.G. Dickens, *The English Reformation* (London, 1964), p. 317; John Dykstra Eusden, *Puritans, Lawyers, and Politics in Early Seventeenth-Century England* (New Haven, 1958), p. 55; Charles H. George, "Puritanism as History and Historiography," *P&P* 41 (1968); Charles H. George and K. George, *The Protestant Mind of the English Reformation* (Princeton, 1961), pp. 144–73; J.H. Hexter, *On Historians* (Cambridge, 1979), pp. 231–33, 237–40; M.M. Knappen, *Tudor Puritanism* (Chicago, 1966), pp. 401–43; H.R. Trevor-Roper, *Religion, the Reformation, and Social Change* (London, 1972), p. 193; Michael Walzer, *The Revolution of the Saints: A Study in the Origins of Radical Politics* (Cambridge, Mass., 1965).

David Little's study, *Religion, Order, and Law: A Study in Pre-Revolutionary England* (Oxford, 1970), seeks to rescue Weber's analysis, as interpreted by Parsons and Bellah, from these criticisms. It represents the most recent sustained effort in this direction. My comments on Weber, below, apply also to Little.

6. J.G.A. Pocock, "Early Modern Capitalism: The Augustan Perception," in Eugene Kamenka and R.S. Neale, eds., *Feudalism, Capitalism and Beyond* (New York, 1975), p. 83; Joyce Oldham Appleby, *Economic Thought and Ideology in Seventeenth-Century England* (Princeton, 1978), pp. 247–48.

A radically different view is provided by Alan Macfarlane, *The Origins of English Individualism: The Family, Property, and Social Transition* (Cambridge, 1979), who argues that economic individualism in England dates back to at least the middle of the thirteenth century. Macfarlane's analysis would obviously vitiate the analytic thrust of my study. However, I do not find his argument compelling, either in its use of contemporary descriptions that support the idea of English "exceptionalism" or in its use of late medieval historical data. On this latter point see Zvi Razi, "Family, Land, and the Village Community in Later Medieval England," *P&P* 93 (1981).

argument. Rhetorical use of contractual themes by Puritan clerics makes sense only in view of their assumption that godly parishioners were familiar with the principles and practices dictated by the rational pursuit of self-interest in markets. Indeed, textual evidence indicates how this assumption explicitly animated Puritan rhetoric. Puritan clerics discerned a normative structure underlying the market activities of their followers, and they systematically translated doctrinal tenets and practical precepts into the terms of this normative structure, which today we call possessive individualism.

To be sure, my argument provides evidence on the emergence of economic individualism that is, in one sense, less direct than that provided by economic tracts composed in the seventeenth century by theorists and by the spokesmen for different guilds and corporations. I have had to derive interpretatively the forces that led clerics to modify Calvinism with a contractarian idiom borrowed from the marketplace. In another sense, however, the evidence on economic individualism that I have presented here is more direct than that contained in the writings of economic ideologues, who were conducting debates largely within an elite culture. The question of economic individualism in early modern England, as it touches on the larger issues of social change and conflict, concerns chiefly the existence of a pervasive orientation among economic actors rather than a consistent doctrine among ideologues. The evidence provided in my study is directly concerned with this orientation, and it is, for this reason, especially useful in sustaining the arguments put forward by Tawney and Hill.

Tawney and Hill both draw inferences about lay attitudes from writings by clerics. For example, Hill remarks that lay audiences may have selectively listened to sermons in which the lawfulness of acquisitive behavior was hedged with qualifications and restrictions.[7] My sociological account of covenant theology supports and extends the general argument of Tawney and Hill because my interpretation of clerical writings emerges from a precise analysis of the organizational context which led clerics to incorporate a market rationality at the core of their theology. My analysis is more circuitous than Tawney's or Hill's, but this seems unavoidable if its interpretative component is to be firmly wedded to a precise account of the organizational constraints and opportunities that influenced Puritan theology.

At several points in this study I have alluded to its implications for Max Weber's thesis on Protestantism and the rise of capitalism.

---

7. Hill, *Change and Continuity*, p. 96, and *Puritanism and Revolution* (New York, 1964), p. 230.

These implications are not unambiguous. On one level, they force us to conclude that the Weber thesis—as commonly understood and debated—cannot be sustained. On another level, they support Weber's contention that an intimate link exists between Puritanism and early capitalism. On yet another level, they undermine an important premise that led Weber to look for this link between religion and economic life.

As commonly understood and debated, the Weber thesis points to the ethical core of Calvinism, especially seventeenth-century Calvinism, as an independent source of the modern capitalist mentality.[8] This thesis preoccupied Weber in his early work, *The Protestant Ethic and the Spirit of Capitalism*, and it reappeared as a major theme in his sociology of religion and in *Economy and Society*. In the early work, he said that his goal was to demonstrate "correlations between forms of religious belief and practical ethics" in order to show how "religious forces have taken part in the qualitative formation and quantitative expansion of that [capitalist] spirit all over the world." In *The Religion of China*, he reasserted this theme: "Only the Puritan rational ethic . . . brought economic rationalism to its consistent conclusion." Referring to "the consistent development of Calvinism" in the seventeenth century, he noted, in *Economy and Society*, that it "attained the union of religious postulate and bourgeois style of life."[9]

Though Weber presented Calvinism as an independent source of the spirit of capitalism, he did not argue that it was either causally sufficient or more important than economic, social, and technical factors. As is well known, he sought to complement, not replace, other analyses that emphasized the causal importance of these latter factors. At the end of *The Protestant Ethic* Weber acknowledged the "one-sidedness" of that study, and he observed that for a more complete analysis of religious and economic change "it would also be necessary to investigate how Protestant asceticism was in turn influenced in its development and character by the totality of social conditions, especially economic."[10]

---

8. In view of the secondary literature that has called attention to major misinterpretations of the Weber thesis, it should not be necessary to do more than simply state (1) that Weber demonstrates a link between the ethical implications of religious tenets for the spirit of capitalism; (2) that this link is stronger in seventeenth-century Calvinism than in Calvin's own writings; (3) that this link was unanticipated by Calvinist clerics; and (4) that capitalism had other cultural and structural preconditions. See Julien Freund, *The Sociology of Max Weber* (New York, 1969), p. 208; Anthony Giddens, *Capitalism and Modern Social Theory* (Cambridge, 1971), pp. 119–32; Gordon Marshall, *Presbyteries and Profits: Calvinism and the Development of Capitalism in Scotland, 1560–1707* (Oxford, 1980), pp. 5, 14–27; Frank Parkin, *Max Weber* (London, 1982), p. 41.

9. *The Protestant Ethic* (New York, 1958), p. 91, and *The Religion of China* (Glencoe, Ill., 1951), pp. 247–48, and *Economy and Society* (Berkeley and Los Angeles, 1978), pp. 1199–1200.

10. *The Protestant Ethic*, p. 183. See also Parkin, *Max Weber*, pp. 53, 57.

My analysis of covenant theology shows that the ethical core of Puritan theology was indeed influenced by socioeconomic developments in early modern capitalism. Elements not only of asceticism but also of possessive individualism—found in a broad stratum of proprietors and small employers—provided Puritan clerics with pastoral exemplars of ascetic behavior and true faith in religious life. Beliefs about the utility of ascetic behavior for profit-seeking individuals in markets, and values that treated the possessions of such individuals as extensions or attributes of their persons, came from an early capitalist mentality, and they were used by Puritan clerics to create a doctrinal and pastoral literature that encouraged the laity to undertake the ascetic pursuit of their ultimate religious self-interest.

Evidence for this conclusion is, I think, more compelling than that adduced by Weber. His analysis of the link between religious asceticism and the spirit of capitalism rests on speculation about lay reception of Calvinism in terms of what he postulated to be the logical implications of Calvinist doctrine. Salvation anxiety among lay Calvinists, according to Weber, was resolved by a bastardization of orthodox Calvinism in which material success, along with ascetic conduct, became interpreted as a sign of God's grace. With regard to lay attitudes, my interpretation receives explicit support from clerical remarks and implicit support from my analysis of the organizational context in which covenant theology developed.

All this leads to the conclusion that the theological doctrine whose ethical content lent support to a capitalist mentality was not independent of that mentality and its social environment. Thus, the polemical point of an avowedly "one-sided" study like *The Protestant Ethic* loses its sharpness, as does the endless debate over that study. Even when it is correctly interpreted, Weber's study cannot be sustained on its essential contention: that ethical implications for economic life in English Calvinism represent an independent, theologically grounded source of the modern capitalist mentality.

Nonetheless, the more general aim of Weber's work remains intact. That is, my study does not undermine the larger argument of which Weber's thesis on Puritanism and capitalism is only a part. This larger argument concerns the uniqueness of Occidental society in terms of its formal rationality. Weber attributed this uniqueness to the simultaneous rationalization of the economic, juridical, religious, and technical spheres. He argued that, although rationalization was not entirely foreign to other civilizations, it was only in the West that it first occurred in all of the major spheres of social life. The combined effects of the rationalization of economic, legal, and religious institutions produced a unique historical configuration, which overcame obstacles, in the form of precedent and tradition, to the rise of a legal-rational society, organized bureaucratically and animated by instrumental forms of thought. This ultimately explains, for Weber, why a secular, capitalist civilization arose initially in the West and not elsewhere.

The analysis presented in my study is certainly not capable of assessing this larger thesis; cross-societal comparisons would be needed for that. The major conclusions of my study are, however, fully compatible with Weber's larger thesis, which leads one to expect an intimate relationship between the rationalization of economic and religious activities. For the larger thesis about the uniqueness of the West, it is irrelevant that the causal properties of this relationship, as they appear in my analysis, are the reverse of what Weber sought to demonstrate in *The Protestant Ethic and the Spirit of Capitalism*.

My study does, however, call into question a major theoretical premise that informs all of Weber's work on social change and rationalization: the premise that the rationalization of economic conduct, epitomized by the rise of acquisitive activity, must receive normative support from other institutions, specifically from religion. On this premise, the Protestant ethic created the normative structure that supplied a larger meaning, otherwise absent in the acquisitive behavior governed by a market rationality, *and* it was this normative structure alone that enabled the behavior dictated by a market rationality to break through the restrictions imposed by what Weber calls economic traditionalism.

This line of thought obviously has its roots in Weber's view of the fundamental types of legitimate order: the traditional, the charismatic, and the legal-rational. His conceptualization of these categories establishes the problematic nature of the rise of economic rationalism. The inherent lack of ultimate meaning in rational economic activity renders it unable to supply a motive for ignoring the appeal to traditional custom and precedent. Weber associates with traditionalism the ultimate values that produce magical world views, and these world views, since they are not dualistic, are incapable of supplying "leverage for influencing conduct through inner forces freed from tradition and convention." In his studies of the religions of China and India, Weber refers to the perception of the world as a "magical garden" which supports the "inviolability of tradition" and precludes the appearance of a "rational practical ethic and life methodology . . . which transformed all life."[11] Elsewhere he asserts flatly: "Only the methodical way of life of the ascetic sects could legitimate and put a halo around the economic 'individualist' impulses of the modern capitalist spirit."[12]

    11. *Religion of China*, pp. 227, 236, 240, and *The Religion of India* (Glencoe, Ill., 1958), p. 336; and see also Weber's *General Economic History* (New York, 1961), p. 265.
    12. H.H. Gerth and C.W. Mills, eds., *From Max Weber* (New York, 1958), p. 322.

The self-perpetuating nature of traditionalism can be broken only by something that formal-rational action lacks: a normative structure, shaped by what Weber calls ultimate values. He maintains that "wherever the direction of the whole way of life has been methodically rationalized, it has been profoundly determined by the ultimate values toward which this rationalization has been directed. These values and positions were thus religiously determined." [13] This reasoning implicitly invokes an assumption, later elaborated by Talcott Parsons, about an innate cultural tendency toward the hierarchical ordering of values. Cosmological values are the ultimate ground of other subordinate goals, and they thus make possible "an integrated system of ends." [14] Cultural universes are shaped not only by their constituent values but by the way in which goals are rank-ordered in terms of their normative significance. The unity of a culture emerges from an innate tendency toward a normative integration of goals, toward a single hierarchical organization of values. The point I am questioning, then, is not whether values are hierarchically organized but whether they exist, in any culture, in a single hierarchy dominated by cosmological values.

The implications of this question for Weber's analysis of change and rationalization are as follows. The rationalization of practical life could proceed only if the world view shaped by cosmological values—the "ultimate" values—supplied a motive for ignoring appeals to custom and precedent. Such appeals, which constituted traditionalism, were vulnerable to ethical religiosity, because religion possessed a higher, more purely cosmological significance than traditionalism, which was magical in nature. Ultimate values in the magical universe indiscriminately mingled practical and cosmological concerns, the worldly and the sacred. [15] The dualistic outlook of ethical religion received its legitimation from values that were higher, that transcended profane realities; thus it was able to legitimate a rationalization of practical conduct that went beyond traditionalism.

If we reject Weber's assumption about a uniform hierarchy of values, we are forced to reject also the way in which he poses the problem of tradi-

---

See also Weber's *General Economic History*, p. 261: "Traditional obstructions are not overcome by the economic impulse alone."

13. *From Max Weber*, p. 287.

14. Talcott Parsons, "The Place of Ultimate Values in Sociological Theory," *International Journal of Ethics* 45 (1935), p. 295 and passim. See also Parsons, *Societies: Evolutionary and Comparative Perspectives* (Englewood Cliffs, N.J., 1966), p. 11; *The Structure of Social Action* (New York, 1949), p. 717: "The ultimate value element came into Weber's work in the first instance with the systems of value attitudes associated with religious ideas."

15. See above, pp. 41–42.

tionalism and economic rationalism. The rationalization of economic life becomes far less of a historical puzzle when it is no longer assumed that a market rationality innately lacked a normative order which had to be supplied from other spheres of life. Indeed, my discussion about what led clerics to place contractarian discourse at the core of their theology empirically demonstrates what Weber precluded on theoretical grounds. Normative commitments associated with highly rationalized economic activities facilitated the rationalization of religious doctrine. The empirical problem established by Weber's theoretical presuppositions was to show how abstract ethical doctrines could influence everyday life. But it appears that practical ethics in profane activities can be no less influential for the formation of abstract doctrine, which supposedly expresses the ultimate values of a society.

This last conclusion should not be interpreted as evidence that rescues historical materialism from the criticisms Weber levelled against it.[16] I have not documented the conspicuously economic content of Puritan theology to prove the implausible thesis that Puritan doctrine was simply a by-product of the socioeconomic activities of the Puritan laity. Instead, I have shown that the relation between socioeconomic life and ideology, in the case of Puritan theology, was mediated by the organizational dynamics of a social movement. These dynamics concerned problems of control whose dimensions, with regard to clerical-lay relations, were fixed by religious issues. This conclusion leads away from all "one-sided" interpretations of ideologies, for it suggests that changes in beliefs cannot be linked to ideal or material interests without taking account of the specific organizational contexts which determine the salience of those interests for those who alter the beliefs, those who proclaim them, and those who receive them.

16. I have discussed this point in "From Weber to Parsons and Schutz," *American Journal of Sociology* 85 (1980).

Index

Adams, Thomas, 139
Agriculture, 12, 49–53
Ames, William, 23
Anabaptism, Anabaptists, 15, 57, 72, 97–99; and covenant theology, 130–32; 1535 revolt of, in Münster, 69, 79, 96
Anticlericalism: and dissent, 13, 26, 39–40, 43–46, 53; and Separatism, 110; sources of, 43
Antinomianism. *See* Family of Love; Heresy
Aristocracy: and Catholic recusancy, 75–77; and Erasmian reform, 39, 54; opposition of, to classis movement, 113; support of, for Puritan clergy, 13, 61–62, 78–89 passim, 111, 113
Artisans, 12, 47, 49, 164
Asceticism, economic and religious, 18, 163, 192–97, 205
Auricular confession, 42, 44, 70–71
Authority, political: and consent, 87–89; and enforcement of the early Reformation, 67–70; heretical attacks on, 79–80, 99, 102–3

Bacon, Francis, 114, 167
Baconian science, 25, 40
Ball, John, 152
Bancroft, Richard (archbishop of Canterbury), 113, 123

Barnes, Robert, 55
Barrow, Henry, 108, 138, 139, 140
Baynes, Paul, 145, 159
Becon, Thomas, 71
Beza, Theodore, 5, 37, 112, 148, 200
Bible, vernacular: aristocratic support for, 39; controversies about, in the early Reformation, 53–58; heresy as product of lay access to, 80, 98–99, 101–2; lay reading of, 27, 45–46, 56, 92, 98, 107–8, 116; in Lollard worship, 45–46; manuscript versions of, 35n, 45–46; printing of, 35, 57. *See also under* Covenant theology
Bigod, Sir Francis, 69
Bodin, Jean, 136
Bourgeois ideology, 173–74, 202. *See also* Contracts, and individualism; Contracts, principles of; Individualism
Bourgeoisie. *See* Entrepreneurial stratum
Bownde, Nicholas, 146, 148
Brinsley, John, 117–18
Browne, Robert, 108, 139
Brownists. *See* Separatism
Bucer, Martin, 130, 200
Bullinger, Henry, 5, 130, 132, 148, 200
Bunyan, John, 25
Burges, Cornelius, 94, 151
Burgess, John, 123